JIU-JITSU BRAVEHEARTS

Jiu-Jitsu Bravehearts

A Collection of Stories
from Ambassadors, Champions,
and Legends

Bobby Armijo

HOUNDSTOOTH
PRESS

COPYRIGHT © 2023 BOBBY ARMIJO
All rights reserved.

JIU-JITSU BRAVEHEARTS
A Collection of Stories from Ambassadors, Champions, and Legends
First Edition

ISBN	978-1-5445-3745-0	*Hardcover*
	978-1-5445-3743-6	*Paperback*
	978-1-5445-3744-3	*Ebook*
	978-1-5445-3746-7	*Audiobook*

Contents

Introduction **ix**

Marcelo Garcia **1**
Lucas Lepri **19**
Fábio Gurgel **33**
JT Torres **49**
Roger Gracie **63**
Romulo Barral **75**
Bia Mesquita **89**
Gordon Ryan **99**
Bernardo Faria **115**
Rodrigo Cavaca **129**
Michael Langhi **141**
Leticia Ribeiro **155**
Alex Atala **169**
Marcus "Buchecha" Almeida **177**
Aubrey Marcus **197**

Felipe Pena **209**
Alexandre "Xande" Ribeiro **219**
Rafael Lovato Jr. **237**
Kyra Gracie **253**
Braulio Estima **269**
Russell Brand **287**
Jocko Willink **297**
Rubens "Cobrinha" Charles Maciel **307**

A Reflection: What Jiu-Jitsu Means to Me **321**
Thank You, Thank You **329**
Call to Action **331**

Introduction

From the outside, jiu-jitsu may seem like two humans rolling around and squeezing each other while wearing pajamas. While this may be true on the surface level, the martial art is much deeper. A trained eye recognizes there are many more nuances to what's happening between those two people.

Jiu-jitsu is just like life: it's hard work, uphill battles, repetition, stoicism, and humility. It is forced problem-solving. You'll have bad days, have good days, experience confidence through achievement, experience the complete destruction of your self-esteem, and everything in between.

We all fail, and we all hurt. Sometimes, we lose faith in our own abilities. However, those who don't give up on their dreams come out on top. History favors the bold. Perseverance—this single characteristic of *not quitting*—is the common denominator I see in every admirable biography, and also the common denominator in every successful person I've ever met.

They didn't give up.

I've been fortunate enough to spend the last eight years around jiu-jitsu's best athletes. I quickly realized they have the same mentality as any mentor or person I look up to. They are resilient, prepared, shaken but unbroken, and mentally strong. They go through the same things we *all* do. There are times when they want to quit and times when they want to give up, but their mental fortitude has taken them to the pinnacle of the sport, and it's their discipline in the face of adversity that compels them to keep going.

I wrote this book both to capture a moment in history for all of us who train jiu-jitsu and to inspire those who may feel curious enough to give this sport a try. When we see successful people, we have a tendency to say things like, "It's easy for them because..." or "They are lucky because they had..." This book exists to show you *and* me that this type of assumptive, negative mentality not only limits our own personal growth, but it is also completely *false*.

My goal is to bring you closer to the martial artists many of us look up to. Sure, we all want to know about their training regimen, what they eat, or how they supplement, but you can already find plenty of resources for that. Instead, I want to give you a glimpse of their lives through a different lens.

I wanted to create something unique. An experience of sorts for the reader. I wanted to look behind the gold medals and see *why* the professionals in this sport are who they are. What is the mental makeup of a ten-time world champion? Do they struggle like me? Do they experience times in their life when they suffer from doubt? Is "imposter syndrome" a real

INTRODUCTION / XI

thing for all of us? (If you haven't heard of imposter syndrome, Google it!) Once I started digging and asking questions, I was shocked at the stories I heard, and I am beyond grateful that I get to share them in this book.

Like most people, I have been successful in some areas of my personal and professional life and failed miserably in others. (Next time we meet, ask me about my first jiu-jitsu tournament or first business venture.) More than once, I've wanted to quit a personal project or walk away from a half-finished business idea. What I've learned—in part because I practice jiu-jitsu—is this: repetition and consistency are key. The more I do something, the better I get at it and the more confident I feel.

I have long wanted to write a book about these life lessons, not because I think I'm special or have all the answers, but because I know I have experience in areas so many people can relate to. *Jiu-Jitsu Bravehearts* explores humiliation and perseverance, defeats and victories, pain, acceptance, and serenity. It shows what it means to be human through the eyes of nearly two dozen personalities who share one big love: jiu-jitsu.

I was first inspired to write this collection of stories about professional BJJ (Brazilian Jiu-Jitsu) athletes and other practitioners of the sport in October 2018. It was the second day of a two-day leadership conference I was attending in San Francisco—Jocko Willink's *Extreme Ownership Muster (MUSTER 002)*—and Willink was speaking. A retired United States Navy SEAL, Willink is best known in the public for his books, his courses, and his tenacity for discipline. As I listened to him, I realized that few people outside of his most avid followers likely knew he had trained jiu-jitsu for over two decades. More importantly, that meant few people understood *why* he loves and supports the sport and *how* his experience with jiu-jitsu has shaped his life.

That's when I saw *Jiu-Jitsu Bravehearts* before me. In my mind's eye, the project would contain many chapters on professional jiu-jitsu athletes who are well-known and admired in the community, along with other chapters about public figures from different backgrounds who also practice jiu-jitsu.

I wanted to show a crossover. Leading personalities like Willink, Aubrey Marcus, Alex Atala, and Russell Brand have used the sport to *excel* in their lives, regardless of when they started training. Further, champion jiu-jitsu professionals like Marcelo Garcia, who has long been known in the jiu-jitsu world as one of the greatest, demonstrate this crossover as well. By including both groups of different and exceptional leaders, I aim to share very different perspectives on this *one, shared passion*.

Most chapters in this book are based on face-to-face interviews with the very athletes and professionals I'm writing about. Whenever possible, I first paid for a private, one-on-one training session. Then, after each champion opponent taught me jiu-jitsu and ultimately destroyed me, we sat on the mat, where I conducted a one-hour interview give or take.

Choosing who to include in *Jiu-Jitsu Bravehearts* wasn't easy. There have been many great champions throughout the history of jiu-jitsu, and the idea that one is more deserving than another does a disservice to all those who have given so much to the sport. But obviously, I had to draw the line somewhere or this would have been a never-ending project.

Hence, it came down to my personal favorite jiu-jitsu stars, those with athletic accolades such as titles, those who have been ambassadors of the sport, and in some cases, their availability. You will probably notice some prominent names are missing from this book. Oftentimes, this is the case merely because they opted out. I hope they will reconsider for volume two! I am eager to share their stories and those of many others as soon as possible.

A common theme you may notice while reading is that *all these athletes still get nervous.*

If I'm being honest, I was surprised to discover this myself. At first, I thought, *These guys are professionals. Why would they get nervous?* I quickly realized we *all* have self-doubt. Our past failures lurk within our minds and tell us that we aren't good enough and we should run. The fight-or-flight response is strong, and it can overpower weeks of hard training the moment we step on the mat to compete and ultimately wreak mental havoc. We have to learn this response is a *normal* reaction. We are not flawed for thinking or noticing that we are nervous. We are not flawed because our opponent is looking particularly stoic. We are normal! It's okay to feel a sense of excitement and uncertainty when we put our egos on the line.

This life lesson can be used in many areas of our lives. Instead of feeding our anxious sensations, we can say, "Thanks for chiming in, Self-Doubt, but I've got it from here."

My journey writing this book has definitely been longer and more strenuous than I ever expected. Conducting interviews required a lot of travel: to New York City for Gordon Ryan and Marcelo Garcia; to Charlotte, North Carolina, to meet Lucas Lepri for the day; to Oklahoma City for the great Lovato Jr.; to São Paulo, Brazil, for more than half a dozen athletes; to London for Roger Gracie; to Birmingham, England, for Braulio Estima; to Belo Horizonte for Felipe Pena; and to Rio de Janeiro, Los Angeles, Miami, and more. The many trips also meant a lot of organizing: flights, hotels, rental cars, and Airbnbs needed to be lined up, and (until a few summers ago) visas for Brazil were required.

Of course, it was all totally worth it. Not only did I meet many inspiring people, I also learned more about the life lessons jiu-jitsu can teach us than I ever thought possible. I hope *Jiu-Jitsu Bravehearts* will do the same for you.

Speaking of meeting inspiring people, I must have been a white belt with only a stripe or two when the professor teaching my class matched me up with a petite, friendly, purple belt named Tracy. She was Asian American and probably no more than five feet tall and 110 pounds, while I'm six feet tall and 190 pounds.

What a mismatch! I thought.

My expectations going into the rolling session against Tracy were low, to say the least. Yes, jiu-jitsu was built on the premise that a smaller, weaker person can disarm a much bigger and stronger opponent. But if I'm honest, early on I doubted whether this could actually be true with respect to a female athlete. As for the one or two women who were in my class that day, all I could think was, *They aren't strong enough to be going against even some of the weaker guys in the class.* I certainly didn't believe for a second that it would be possible for a girl to make me tap and actually submit me.

Tracy and I slapped hands and fist-bumped the way every match starts in jiu-jitsu, and the next thing I knew, she was all over me, attacking and getting into position to apply submissions with leverage, technique, and to my surprise, a *lot* of strength. This memory reminds me of what MMA fighter Conor McGregor often tells his opponents and the media in the prefight buildup: "Precision beats power, and timing beats speed." This was ever so clear the day I rolled with Tracy. She was fast, decisive, and precise. Even though I resisted hard, she must have submitted me two or three times. It was an instant lesson. I need to respect the art, and I especially need to respect women who practice jiu-jitsu.

Fast-forward eight years, and I've had a chance to train with several world champion women. There is no question that they are just as dangerous and knowledgeable as their male counterparts. As the stories of Leticia Ribeiro, Kyra Gracie, and Beatriz Mesquita will show, these athletes are also no different from their male counterparts with respect to grit, mental sharpness, physical endurance, and the leadership qualities necessary for success.

Speaking of differences, I realize that the selection of athletes portrayed in *Jiu-Jitsu Bravehearts* skews overwhelmingly male. In a way, the imbalance reflects the current ratio of men to women in the sport overall. Our Alliance jiu-jitsu gym in San Diego has approximately sixty female students, and we are lucky to have a world champion female instructor, Jena Bishop, who teaches a women's class a few days a week.

I think sixty female members is a large number compared to most academies, so our ratios probably don't represent the norm. Even so, what inspires me most are the moms, sisters, aunts, and grandmothers who come to the academy to watch their young children train. They often see other women dressed in their gis while waiting for the kids' class to end and the adult class to begin. I hear these spectating ladies say things like, "Women do this? They're in their thirties, forties, and fifties and up, and training? Maybe I should try?"

When I see women start training jiu-jitsu, they are usually quick to embrace the benefits of practicing the martial art. Some may have already taken self-defense classes, but what they learned in those classes was often very theoretical. After all, remembering an instruction in other self-defense systems like "go for the groin" and then turning that thought into a targeted kick is difficult during a real-life attack. In jiu-jitsu, by contrast, students practice effective techniques in a safe environment until muscle memory can take over. Learning to feel comfortable in a close-combat situation better prepares and empowers us all to respond to an attacker with confidence. Both men and women in jiu-jitsu soon learn they can hold their own even against stronger, heavier athletes.

As you will see from Kyra Gracie's chapter (and you already know if you practice jiu-jitsu), the sport still hasn't given women equal recognition. While trainers and academies seem increasingly aware of attracting and retaining female athletes, we could all do better when it comes to showing women that they have a place in this traditionally male-dominated martial art.

Years ago, UFC President Dana White said he would never allow women to fight in the UFC. He claimed that if he did, it would make a circus of the MMA world. Then along came a woman MMA fighter by the name of Ronda Rousey. She single-handedly changed the game. She forced Dana to pay attention to her. Why? She was good, *really* good. People wanted to watch her, and they came out en masse just to get a glimpse of this superstar. She broke barriers and became the highest paid UFC star—male or female—in an incredibly short time. She remains an icon even after her unofficial retirement in 2018.

Women's MMA is now commonly the headline of any mixed martial arts card. And not because it's a "circus," but because it's the fight the fans *want* to see. Since 2018, it is no longer out of the ordinary to see a fight card with five fights total, four of them between men and *headlined* by a female MMA championship match.

Thanks to Ronda, the popularity of women's events in mixed martial arts has risen tremendously. In my opinion, this is because men see how good women really are. With increased exposure, so too comes an increased appreciation for their incredible talent. Male and female fans want to see women fight. Even casual female fans are starting to tune in more regularly because they no longer feel excluded from a gender perspective. MMA has started to evolve, transcending gender, and thus bringing more eyeballs to the screen. That means everybody wins financially, but more importantly, gender equality wins by being put in primetime TV spots.

Without a doubt, there's still work to do before we can say that women are an equal part of jiu-jitsu, but times are changing for the better. Women are here to stay, and jiu-jitsu is a sport for everyone. It belongs to *all* of us.

I designed this book to be read in many different ways. The choice is yours. You can read it from front to back like a traditional book, or you can skip to chapters featuring your favorite athletes or jiu-jitsu-practicing celebrities.

I myself am not the greatest reader, and my attention span can wander, so my intention was to make a book you could leaf through, reading parts or chapters in short bursts throughout your day. This gives you the flexibility to understand someone's story in less than fifteen minutes and still feel the satisfaction of completion. Who doesn't like a little dopamine hit, right? That said, I hope you will ultimately want to learn about everyone's journey, as each story has its own wisdom to share.

Each chapter starts with a brief bio, detailing the interviewee's jiu-jitsu credentials and some background information. You'll also notice I've included social media handles so you can follow your favorite people. Last, I included the academy addresses for those in this book who own their own gym, so be sure to stop in to say hi and train! If you live in their city, take a trial class and start your jiu-jitsu journey.

CHAPTER 1

Marcelo Garcia

marcelogarciajj.com
@marcelogarciajiujitsu
@marcelogarciajj
facebook.com/marcelo-garcia

Marcelo Garcia may just be the greatest competitor in Brazilian Jiu-Jitsu. Born in Formiga, Minas Gerais, Brazil, Garcia has won a World Championship at all belt levels: blue, purple, brown, and five times as a black belt. He is a four-time Abu Dhabi Combat Club (ADCC) Submission Wrestling World Champion (2003, 2005, 2007, 2011) who has also placed second and third in the Absolute Division (2007 and 2005, respectively).

His 2005 ADCC fight against Ricco Rodriguez—a competitor who outweighed him by one hundred pounds—is legendary.

Marcelo went against his giant opponent and, after being brutally fouled, still won by submission only moments later. This was absolutely must-see TV, a truly biblical David versus Goliath moment in time.

The public's reverence for Marcelo goes beyond just titles and accolades; he is also highly respected for his character as a human being. Marcelo is generous about sharing his passion for jiu-jitsu with others, and he is a pioneer in online training with a plethora of video tutorials in what now seems normal in the space (that is, video tutorials and online learning). In 2015, he appeared on a show called *The Tim Ferriss Experiment*. A *New York Times* bestselling author (*The 4-Hour Workweek* and *Tools of Titans*), Ferriss contacted Marcelo to attempt to learn how to prepare to fight Marcelo's student, world champion Jonathan Satava, in just five days. I'll leave it to you to ask Tim how that went.

When I first interviewed him, Marcelo struck me as patient, kind, and humble. I spoke with him at his academy in New York City located at 250 West 26th Street, Third Floor, New York, NY 10001.

- To see the match against Rodriguez, search YouTube for "Marcelo Garcia vs. Ricco Rodriguez."
- Episode #8 of *The Tim Ferriss Experiment* is available on iTunes for $1.99 and can also be found on YouTube.
- For a comprehensive library of Marcelo's online training videos, go to *MGinaction.com*.
- You can also purchase more of his recent online training through *BJJFanatics.com*.

EARLY LIFE
PROTECT YOURSELF LIKE THE KARATE KID

As a child, Marcelo Garcia loved to watch the 1989 TV series *The Karate Kid*. "The idea that you can protect yourself when you're being bullied and also come out on top after you win the trophy was fascinating to me. So, the whole martial arts thing came from *The Karate Kid*," Marcelo explained. "Martial arts, for me at that time, was all about learning how to protect yourself. You learn how to not let someone hurt you. Then, you can protect your family. You can protect your friends. You can protect anyone."

He took up karate as an eight-year-old because training opportunities were easy to find in Brazil, but he didn't really enjoy it. So, at age twelve, he started judo. A year and a half later, his judo instructor—who taught Brazilian Jiu-Jitsu every once in a while—introduced Marcelo to BJJ. The rest, as they say, is history.

Still, back when Marcelo started practicing jiu-jitsu, it wasn't nearly as popular as it is now. Today's academies can offer between five and twelve classes a day, but the small studio he trained at offered only two or three classes per *week*. The time in between training sessions felt like torture.

"Waiting even one day...you wouldn't believe how hard it was for me. Waking up and going to sleep, all I could think about was how much I wanted to do it again." For Marcelo, this was an early lesson in patience and passion.

ON PRESSURE AND ANXIETY
FREEZE OR FIGHT?

Marcelo admitted he had a lot of anxiety around competing when he was first training in and practicing martial arts. His karate fights never went well because he was, in his words, "bad at it. Really bad." He carried that sense of failure with him into judo as well as jiu-jitsu. The first time he won a martial arts competition wasn't until he competed in judo. He went into the tournament feeling deeply nervous. During one of his matches, Marcelo tells me he simply froze. He recalls going into a state of shock as his opponent paced back and forth, holding and shaking Marcelo by the kimono and violently trying to hip toss him with various techniques.

"The guy was shaking me hard, and I couldn't feel anything in my body. I wasn't there. I was not present, not in the moment," he said. "But then I thought, *Why am I freezing?*"

At that moment, a light came on for him. "I just held him and got him on the ground. No technique, no anything. And I won the tournament in my weight and belt category; it was only one or two matches total."

As Marcelo explained this story to me, I could visibly see he was reliving the moment in his mind. Not in a traumatic, stressful way, but rather he was almost in disbelief he could've felt that way. Not that he was above feeling worried or nervous, but it seemed as if he realized how far he has come, even if it was just a gentle reminder of his path to who he is today.

Despite where he is today, at the time, the anxiety and fear of competing stuck with Marcelo, even as he felt good about winning that first tournament. What if he couldn't win again? "I was just so upset," Marcelo said about the thought of competing again, shaking his head. "And I was being too dramatic about myself."

The cure for his paralytic fear was *training*. "I started training the next day, maybe the next week, and it was just so much fun," Marcelo told me. *The journey was more important than the destination.* As cliche as that phrase is, it's true. Very rarely does an achievement in and of itself result in lasting happiness. You see it over and over again, at every hall-of-fame speech of any athlete. They miss the camaraderie of the locker room and the physically grueling days of practice. They miss the conversations in the film room and times of learning to become better. Rarely do they ever say, "I was finally happy when we won," or "I miss that one day we won the championship." When those we look up to say it's about the journey, we should probably listen.

The fear of competing lasted another four or five years, and in a way, it is still there. But Marcelo never again felt so helpless that he couldn't move or breathe.

"I realized what's important for me is not just the win, but being able to go there, being healthy, and not getting hurt. And I also realized that if something really bad happens, my family is still going to be there. My coach is still going to be there. All my friends are still going to hang out with me. That made me feel good because a big part of my fear was about disappointing the people who are here for me. That's a *big* fear. But then, when you realize that you're surrounded by good people, people that you like, and people who like you no matter what, then that fear goes away."

Marcelo understood at a young age that a big part of his fear involved disappointing others. He also realized that those who love him don't care whether he wins or loses; they just want him to be happy. He saw that impressing other people wasn't important; in fact, it was a waste of mental energy. The lesson was clear: putting unnecessary pressure on yourself in terms of results only drains you. Removing this kind of pressure frees you to work harder.

I recently posted a quote on Instagram that really resonates with today's world and, in particular, with this part of Marcelo's journey and lesson learned: "Tension is who you think you should be, relaxation is who you are." (Buddhist saying)

BECOMING A CHAMPION

BODY IMAGE, BREATHING, AND BELIEF

When Marcelo started training, social media didn't yet exist; people weren't comparing themselves to models on Instagram. Even so, like many of us—including the biggest and the baddest in fitness, and those who are seemingly the most confident—he used to struggle with body image issues. Practicing martial arts helped him overcome his self-consciousness.

"As a teenager, I wasn't able to change clothes in the locker room," Marcelo admitted. "I never wanted to take my shirt off because I always felt fat. But I wasn't fat. I was probably chubby, but not enough to warrant feeling that bad. That's how crazy it is when you're a kid. But in jiu-jitsu, the changing room, the interaction of the kids—I began to see that we're all the same. Our bodies are different, but *everybody has that fear, that self-consciousness, whether they look good or not.*"

Obviously, Marcelo wasn't alone in this; many people find themselves in a rut and feeling isolated because of their body image, which is also often skewed. Although this can't be fixed in a book about jiu-jitsu, I would like to gently remind everyone who needs to hear it not to be so hard on yourself. We all have our physical self-doubts, regardless of how we may appear.

Marcelo started controlling his fear when he was a purple belt. He was looking forward to stepping out onto the mat when all at once he faced a new, critical challenge: breath. "I stopped breathing, and I started to hear my heart beating in my chest. I realized there was something wrong. In that moment, I was just feeling tired, feeling exhausted," he explained. "Nobody told me to breathe, but that's what I did. I started to pace my breathing, taking a full breath and then releasing it. I was just gonna try controlling it." Marcelo's story reminds me of one of my favorite Wim Hof quotes: "The breath knows how to go deeper than the mind."

Unbeknownst to Marcelo, perhaps to this day, he was teaching himself some of the techniques of the famous Dutch extreme athlete, Wim Hof. Wim Hof has a plethora of resources I highly suggest looking into, particularly when it comes to using breath to calm the mind. He's nicknamed "The Iceman" based on his accomplishments that involve extreme feats in extreme cold weather. These include climbing Mount Kilimanjaro in shorts, running a half marathon above the Arctic Circle barefoot, and standing in a container while covered in ice cubes for longer than 112 minutes. (For more on Wim Hof and his methods, you can visit *wimhofmethod.com*.)

Even though many people know Wim Hof for his breath classes and uncanny ability to withstand incredibly extreme conditions, what they might not know is that his wife jumped eight stories to her death when the couple had four young kids. On a podcast with Tom Bilyeu, Wim Hof explained, "My children made me survive, and nature healed me." Needless to say, his focus on his breath worked, and Marcelo also emphasizes its importance, constantly reminding himself and his students to breathe.

Further, Marcelo goes into fights confident about his game. He isn't fazed by last-minute warnings about an opponent's "really good triangle" or that the opponent " doesn't tap to a choke." He knows he will impose his game on the other fighter.

"'That guy doesn't tap in a choke' is something I've heard many times," Marcelo explains, growing more animated and throwing his hands up in the air. "But all I *do* is choke! How come I'm gonna fight someone that doesn't tap to a choke? And then, when I finally fight with the guy, sure enough, he taps on a choke. So that's one of those things that has made me stronger. Because you can't always think your way through a situation."

Marcelo's message is this: don't change your game because of what someone says before you step on the mat. You've been training for this! Trust in your ability and your skillset.

One of my favorite quote-and-image combinations of all time is of Olympic swimming medalist Michael Phelps racing to the finish line, head forward and laser focused on the end of the pool. His nearest opponent can be seen peeking his head above water, but his focus is different. Instead of looking at the finish line, this swimmer is looking to his left to determine how far ahead Michael is. The quote that accompanies the image says, "Winners focus on winning, losers focus on winners."

Like Michael Phelps, Marcelo was focused on winning—and win he did! Still, a winning mindset was something he had to develop, and it didn't happen overnight.

Marcelo came close to quitting jiu-jitsu not once but *twice*. The first time it happened he was sixteen and a blue belt. "I was going to regionals for my first really big tournament. I felt ready for this, but I lost in ten seconds. I was put to sleep. In a choke. It was the only time in my life that I was put to sleep in jiu-jitsu. I don't see it as a big deal now, but at that time, I had been doing this for two or three years. It was the biggest nightmare that could happen to me. I went back home, and I was like, okay, this means I should quit. That's a good reason to quit. That's like the perfect reason to quit jiu-jitsu."

"But then I started to think to myself, what was the most important thing? Was it winning the tournament or having the passion? What was I enjoying more?"

The second time, Marcelo was a purple belt. He was already living in the gym and training 24/7, but he just couldn't see himself getting any better in conditioning, strength, or technique, or against his training partner. Things seemed backward. Wasn't he supposed to feel like the greatest? And like he was getting better every day?

But then he realized, "That's okay. I'm still enjoying it, and it's still fun. I'm not learning one new move every day, but that's okay. So that worry passed, because I knew I would keep on doing this. And after a year, or a year and a half, I won... Worlds at brown belt—and then I realized, *Oh, so that's how it works!* You don't always see yourself getting better every day. You just have to believe. You just have to put in the effort."

Marcelo understood something important. "I don't need to submit everyone today. I don't need to feel great and invincible every day. I don't need to learn a move every day. As long as I'm being disciplined in what I'm willing to do, I'll get better."

After winning in Abu Dhabi and winning Mundials, Marcelo again felt he wasn't getting better. But this time he was ready. His response to those feelings was simply, "Get over it! You're having a bad day, so forget about it and go back to training tomorrow."

BEHIND THE SCENES

SUCCESS AND MISCONCEPTIONS

We see the successes of stars like Marcelo in any sport or profession. We see them on the podium, leaning over as a medal is placed around their neck. When they win one year and then the next, we expect them to keep winning. We think it's automatic, as if they *should* be winning. What we don't see are their struggles and the effort they put in. The trials and tribulations don't stop just because they win once or even twice. The hard work never stops on the road to the top, especially when you want to *stay* on top.

Marcelo made sacrifices to do what he loves doing, but he wouldn't have it any other way. "Jiu-jitsu is my big love, maybe my first love. So, why not be the best? Why not try everything? I never knew if I could actually be a world champ. There was no guarantee. Nobody ever knocked on my door and said, 'You're going to be a world champ one day.' But I put together something that was a big love of mine with a lot of time and hard work. I don't even know if I have the right to call it hard work because I love it so much."

To do the work, he distanced himself from everything else. "People would ask me to go out, and I couldn't go. When my girlfriend would say, 'It's raining outside, nobody's training. Let's just stay in bed,' and I was like, 'I can't,' that's what I call the hard work," Marcelo said softly, looking sad.

Mastering this martial art is hard work at every level. Marcelo told me people often don't see the ups and downs high-level athletes like him go through and how, to them, individual failures can often carry much more weight than any successes. "When you're down," he said, "you make that down seem so big. But no. It's just one day! It's just one tournament!"

Marcelo wants us to remember that anything that happens is just temporary. His attitude is reminiscent of a famous quote attributed to Roman emperor Marcus Aurelius: "The impediment to action advances action. What stands in the way becomes the way." Put differently, obstacles can become opportunities for growth if we know how to respond to a challenge. Do we follow the propaganda our minds generate when a situation seems catastrophic? Or do we try to stay calm, keep things in perspective, and focus on what we can control in any given situation?

The way someone conducts themselves in an interview—the way they interact—often says as much about them as their answers. Marcelo, who is ultra busy, always made time for me, and he is polite to a fault.

Toward the end of our interview, it became clear that Marcelo's next class was about to start. He had previously mentioned he wouldn't be available after that class because he had already made a commitment to be somewhere else. He and I were still sitting on the mat doing our Q&A when, thinking we might run out of time, I changed my final question.

"Marcelo," I said, "this is the last one. What impact do you want to make on the... Actually, I don't care about that one as much. I want to ask you instead: what is the most common misconception about you?"

Marcelo politely answered my question. He didn't rush, and he wasn't rude. Then, he asked my permission to *also* answer my initial, partial question about the impact he wanted to leave on the sport. Regardless of his time, regardless of his commitments, Marcelo wasn't going to let that question go unanswered.

That told me he wanted me to know that this idea of impact was also very important to him.

Part of being a champion is standing on a pedestal, both literally and figuratively. We look up to and idolize winners. When I interviewed him, Marcelo told me he wanted people to know he is just another human being. He has good days and bad days; he makes mistakes like everyone else; and sometimes he might find himself in a bad mood—just like the rest of us.

"I have done things that I regret, but just like everyone else, I try to get better every day. If I'm in a bad mood, I don't show it. I don't make people deal with my problems. I hope ten years from now, I'll be better than I am today and to be the best example possible. I didn't choose to be that example. But jiu-jitsu has helped me to be better, because people look up to me."

Marcelo understands that many people see him as a role model and try to watch his every move, even in the world beyond the mat. It was clear to me that Marcelo respected and accepted the responsibility that comes with his status. Yet, although I had met Marcelo only one time prior to our interview, I never got the impression that he felt I was watching him in any way. It felt like we were two old friends talking; it felt genuine. It felt very much like Marcelo was able to just be himself.

BEST ADVICE

"My parents always told me, 'Be safe, enjoy,' and just, 'Be happy.' They didn't really plan for me or expect me to go to school and graduate.

"And my coaches always tried to make me feel good. They showed me technique, but it wasn't the most important thing. They taught me that no matter if I was training, no matter if I was going to compete, they always told me, 'It's okay. You're going to be okay.' They never put pressure on me."

WORST ADVICE

When Marcelo was about sixteen, his former judo trainer tried to talk him out of jiu-jitsu.

"My judo coach—his dad was also a judo coach—was born on the mat. Born as a *judoka* (judo fighter)! He started training at five years old. Then, one day, I was at his dad's business where they sell and fix car batteries, and my coach was helping his dad. It's a very dirty, greasy scenario. Not bad work, but they really work hard there.

"My coach, who was already not teaching as much as he used to, said to me, 'Marcelo, you still training? You still doing jiu-jitsu in that place? You still going there?' I'm like, 'Yeah, I'm going there.' And he goes, 'Look at me, Marcelo. I was born on the mat, my dad was probably born on the mat, and look at me now, look at what I am doing now. Do you think you're gonna get where you wanna go?'

"Then he just stopped talking about it. But he tried to plant a seed. He was telling me that I wouldn't go that far and that I shouldn't put in that much time to jiu-jitsu. It was terrible advice. I was such a passionate teenager. But *I didn't listen to him that day.* I'm glad I didn't look at him and see myself."

FINAL THOUGHTS
ADVICE HAPPINESS AND IMPACT

"I feel fortunate to be doing something that was such a big passion from such a young age. So I have to just keep doing that, and I need to allow myself to enjoy it. But I don't put on the pressure anymore. Today, I know for sure that if you do something you really believe in and you really enjoy it, you'll be successful. *Happiness is a big deal. Happiness is a lot more important than your bank account.*"

When Marcelo talked about the impact he would like to leave on the sport, I expected something much different than what he actually said. I don't know why I expected that, but in retrospect it's probably because I was conditioned to accept jiu-jitsu fighters as they appear on the mat—brash, with their egos involved; anytime they show fear, it's seen as a weakness. Keeping in mind that I started jiu-jitsu much later in life, this perception makes sense since I didn't have the experience to know from a young age that jiu-jitsu is actually humbling. Marcelo educated me both about the sport itself and about the lessons the game teaches us to bring to the outside world.

When Marcelo started doing jiu-jitsu, there was a trend in the sport for fighters to look mean. He initially tried to appear that way himself, but eventually realized it wasn't necessary. "As a black belt and as a brown belt, I realized you don't have to look like a badass to win the tournament. So I started changing. I decided to be smiling and happy, to express myself. When

I step on the mat, I'll be serious about that. But I don't think I need to act tough all the time."

Marcelo changed jiu-jitsu. Fighters began talking more to each other right before competitions and sometimes even afterward. Today, the tide seems to be turning again and Marcelo worries for the sport; he implores other athletes to drop the trash talk and stop intimidating each other.

"Today, I see the sport going in a bad direction, and I'm still working very hard to not let it go there. People want to see you win the match. You don't need to be a bad guy; you don't need to look bad or mean or tough or put the other person down to become the best. You can do all this with kindness and still be serious when it's time to fight."

Marcelo looked serious and concerned as we spoke about this. He seemed to almost hurt a little for the athletes who posture and make the sport ugly as a result. I could feel him pleading for a change, and my hope is that his message comes through to all the athletes competing. We could all be a little more like Marcelo.

He relates jiu-jitsu to life outside the academy and hopes people will take what they learn from the sport into the real world.

"Jiu-jitsu puts you in touch with the world we live in because in jiu-jitsu, you're dealing with people. People are sweating on your face, trying to get you down, to choke you out. They're trying to beat you at your game. I hope people can learn from that and use it in the outside world to be better and to see other people as human beings and see when a decision might hurt someone or screw someone. Because it's real people out there."

I think back to Marcelo when I need a reminder about patience, which sometimes seems to be a lost art. These days, I think we're all too quick to explode on each other. This is compounded by the fact that mental health is at an all-time low, and not everyone has access to mental-health solutions like therapy, or is educated about the various ways to relieve stress, outside of self-medicating. When I find myself feeling short on patience, I try to think back to what Marcelo said to me that day: it's real people out there. And as the old quote goes, "Be kind, you never know what someone else could be going through."

CHAPTER 2

Lucas Lepri

lepribjj.com
 @lucaslepri
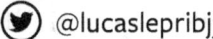 @lucaslepribjj
 facebook.com/lucaslepribjj

L ucas Lepri is a nine-time black belt world champion and one of few athletes to have won every major jiu-jitsu tournament (The World Jiu-Jitsu Championship, The Pan American Championship, The European Championship, and The Brazilian National Jiu-Jitsu Championship). His black-belt competition record began when he won a gold medal in the 2007 World Championships.

Born in 1984 in Uberlândia, Minas Gerais, Brazil, Lucas received his black belt under Elan Santiago. He moved to New York City in 2009 to teach at Alliance, and now he lives in

Charlotte, North Carolina. He is the founder, CEO, and head instructor of Lucas Lepri Brazilian Jiu-Jitsu & Fitness located at 1636 Sardis Road North, Suite A-170, Charlotte, NC 28270.

- To watch a great thirty-minute interview Lucas did with the IBJJF, go to YouTube and search "Lucas Lepri on Achieving Greatness and Making History."
- To see a comprehensive library of his jiu-jitsu positions and the techniques that won him multiple world titles and championships, go to his online library at *lepribjjonline.com*.
- Go to YouTube to watch several of his best fights. If you want to watch him go against giants who outweighed him by over a hundred pounds, run a search for "Absolute Division IBJJF Europeans 2019 Lucas Lepri."

EARLY LIFE

DISCIPLINE AND SACRIFICE

Lucas's fascination with jiu-jitsu began when he was fifteen years old. His curiosity was sparked after he watched Fernando "Margarida" Pontes prepare for the Pan-American Championship on TV. What impressed him just as much as the sport itself was Fernando's discipline: wake up, eat, work out, train jiu-jitsu, and sleep. Lucas really liked the routine and thought, *Man, that sport is so awesome. I need to find this in my city.*

At the time, only two places in Uberlândia offered jiu-jitsu classes, and the martial art had a bad reputation in Brazil. For the most part, the general public associated it with street gangs. Lucas shared his desire to try jiu-jitsu with one friend who had already started taking lessons. Lucas decided to join his friend for a class.

He was immediately hooked.

Even though it meant making sacrifices, Lucas embraced the same discipline as Margarida from day one. "I didn't go out and party with my friends because usually I was resting for a tournament or resting to train the next day. I didn't want to go to bed late, otherwise I'd wake up late. I'd wake up tired, but then I have to train. So, then I'm going to be tired, and then my performance will drop."

His willingness to make sacrifices in this way was something he learned from his mother when he asked her for permission to start training. "At the time, the kimono (gi) was pretty expensive. And my mom didn't have money to buy it. But she said, 'Okay, let me get my salary in two weeks. I'll buy you a kimono, and then you can start.'"

For two weeks, he went to the gym almost every day after school. He didn't have his gi yet, so he was forced to simply watch the training. "As soon as my mom received the money for the kimono, I started," he said. "And then, after that, I never stopped."

Lucas's finances were tight for many years. He took the bus instead of flying to tournaments and slept on the mat rather than booking a hotel. At the beginning of his career, Lucas had a daily budget of just twenty Brazilian reais, which today is about $4 USD, to cover his breakfast, lunch, and dinner. Needless to say, he had to find a way to survive—and he did.

"We sacrifice a lot of things to win," Lucas told me, "and people don't always see it. But I'm not saying the sacrifices are bad. I had to make them to become who I am today. Sacrifices helped me get where I am today."

ON PRESSURE AND ANXIETY
FIGHT FOR WHAT YOU WANT

Jiu-jitsu taught Lucas that there will be tough times again and again, *and* those tough times will pass. That goes for life as much as for the sport. As Lucas said, "When someone gets a good position on you, you might be stuck for a while, but if you persist, you can get out."

Enduring tough times taught Lucas an important lesson: adversity can help us grow, and we must *fight* for what we want. The experience of a struggle is not enough to build strength. Rather, it is the reaction we have to our struggles and experiences that can be life defining. "The tough times made me fight hard for what I want to be," Lucas explained. "And that is what I think everyone needs to remember: fight for what you want because *nobody* is going to fight for you."

Part of Lucas's discipline—and that of any other champion—includes training and competing, no matter what obstacles exist. Fatigue and injuries (unless they are major) are no excuse for not showing up. The desire to win is not enough.

There needs to be commitment, discipline, and a promise that you must keep to yourself.

"Everyone says they want to be a world champion, and then they don't want to train when they're tired. If they get a little hurt, they don't want to train. I think every champion needs to learn how to train tired and a little injured, and to train with a little pain."

Lucas competed many times while injured. He knows how hard it can be—and it's not just about the pain. It's a mental thing too. "It messes with your head," he explained. "There's an inner voice that tells you, *Man, I don't know if I can do this. I'm injured.* It messes with your confidence."

Being physically vulnerable has a way of depleting your mental strength. The most dangerous thing I have personally experienced and also observed in many athletes when it comes to injuries is this: they provide a way out. The thought can seep into your brain and snatch your previous motivation if you're not proactive about blocking this negative inkling. This poisonous thought process can be the single biggest thief of your best future self if you allow it to be. It provides you the path to say, "It's okay, I don't *need* to win. I'm hurt." Similarly, this line of thinking is not helpful during a fight. "I can quit in this difficult situation because I am hurt." If we know in our heart we quit something too early, we still have to answer to ourselves at night. We may be able to fool others, but the easiest person to fool is ourselves.

Lucas's next comment really struck me: "Not having the confidence that you're at 100 percent is actually good. That way you're not overconfident."

Lucas walks a fine line between not enough and too much confidence. "It's two mentalities," he explained. Deep inside, he knows and believes he will be able to win. Still, as the tournament draws closer, doubts and questions surface, like, *Am I training enough? Am I resting enough? Is my technique sharp enough?*

When Lucas competes, he's also working out a mental game in his head. "It's like you're having a conversation with ten people," he told me with a serious look, "and you're fighting against your own thoughts." The things he tells himself during a fight can go from *I'm going to take this guy down* to *This guy's balance is too good,* and then back to *I'm good enough, I'm going to submit this guy!* The internal dialogue is intense, especially in moments when things are not going as planned.

When asked for advice on the topic, Lucas emphasized the importance of immediately stopping any negative self-talk. "If you start thinking, *My opponent is so strong; he's too tough,* you're going to be in trouble. But human beings are like machines. You can reprogram negative thinking right away—and you actually *must* do just that. If you don't, your opponent is going to take over."

For me, Lucas's words echoed something I had once read in Ryan Holiday's book *The Obstacle Is the Way*. On the topic of negative thinking, Ryan writes: "Don't let the negativity in, don't let those emotions even get started. Just say, 'No, thank you. I can't afford to panic.'"

Many of Lucas's stressors and issues used to revolve around money. When he began looking for sponsors as a brown belt, he received so many rejections that he almost gave up. Unable to afford traveling to tournaments, he began to doubt his passion for jiu-jitsu would ever provide him with a stable living. Lucas admitted he sometimes told himself, *This doesn't make money. I do what I love, but I don't have any money.*

Thankfully, Lucas's pessimistic inner voice was quieted by another, more powerful, encouraging voice. The latter voice said, *Keep going. One day, you're going to be able to walk with your own money.* In other words, be proud that you can support yourself doing something you love, a career that can pay a good living.

Right after being promoted to black belt, Lucas started winning prize money for paid matches. From that moment on, he began to see glimpses of the proverbial "light." Lucas's dedication and passion had the power to promote him to living the life of a professional athlete. To this day, he has never looked back.

Similarly, when Lucas decided to try to open his academy, some people told him, "Now is not the time." Conversely, others said, "Go ahead and do it; you're going to be very successful."

Lucas often asked himself when it would ever be the right time. The answer, as he discovered, came from a place of stoicism.

"If you think it's the right time, just do it."

"If you regret it later on, at least you tried."

"If you fail—everybody fails. It's normal."

"If you get submitted, start over."

"If you fail in business, start over."

"If you fail in a relationship, start over."

"Just start over."

The year Lucas won his first World Championship, 2007, was especially challenging. It began with a breakup with his girlfriend of five years. Lucas chose to use his emotional pain to his advantage. He pushed his emotions onto the mat and started training six hours a day or more. "I was more motivated than ever," he explained.

I find this interesting because, on the other end of the spectrum, we can become almost *too* still when something hurts emotionally. The common advice that seems to work for those who have rough patches in their life is to keep moving. Be active. Keep busy. Don't sit there and feel sorry for yourself, but instead look forward. Don't look in a rearview mirror because you aren't going that way!

What I've personally learned about emotions is this: we need to face them. Being busy is great, but for most of us, ignoring the hurt, the pain, and the trauma is a recipe for disaster. At the same time, sitting and doing nothing for eternity is equally debilitating. If you are going through a rough time in your life, the message here is to focus on putting one foot in front of the other. Keep moving. Keep moving toward repairing your energy; keep moving to feel your emotions; and keep moving as you look for another way to live your life.

BECOMING A CHAMPION

GOALS, ROUTINES, AND A HUNGER TO WIN

When Lucas first started doing jiu-jitsu, his goal was to learn the martial art, not necessarily to compete. However, after just two months of training, he and thirty other guys were on a bus, traveling from his hometown to Rio de Janeiro to participate in his first tournament. As a white belt, he took second place behind a blue belt and soon became hungry for more challenges. Next up were much larger tournaments, like the Brazilian Nationals and the World Championships. Lucas became hungry to win.

"You have to have a goal," he told me. "Otherwise, you're going to start losing your motivation. When you have a goal, you start pushing yourself all the time."

Many years and titles later, Lucas admitted he may retire soon. Still, he has goals. "By giving them an example they can follow, I have already been pushing my students to help them conquer their dreams," he told me. "I know I can help them even more when I stop competing because I can put everything that I have into them."

Lucas's mindset throughout his career has been to always believe he can win. "I always held that in my mind, even after losing previous matches: *I'm going to win.*"

His confidence came from how he trained and dedicated himself and from how disciplined he was. He would tell himself, *Nobody is training harder than me. Nobody is more dedicated than I am.* When he lost in the semifinal or final round of a major tournament, he would think, *I want to train even harder, because the next time I want to get gold.* As big as the wins were, his losses provided him with the driving force to improve.

"This mindset helped with my motivation. It helped me get big results and made me who I am today," Lucas said with a grin.

Lucas is also big on precision, hence his tagline "BE PRE-CISE." Rather than typical drilling like most BJJ practitioners, he likes to work on techniques live during rolling, which I find fascinating for the following reason:

He is *that* good.

It takes an enormous amount of skill to be able to "drill" during a live sparring session. The ability to get yourself into a situation that you're planning to practice on a live opponent is rare and shows just how dominant Lucas really is. He can literally take you two or three positions ahead to then get to the spot he wants to drill.

"I try the techniques live over and over so that the other guy is reacting. I get that action-reaction. When I'm just traditionally drilling, I don't feel that I'm getting the technique correctly."

BEHIND THE SCENES

DAILY ROUTINES, MENTORS, AND FAMILY

Lucas and I met for our interview on a weekend in late 2018 at his academy in Charlotte, North Carolina. I flew into Charlotte solely for the interview, and when our appointment kept getting rescheduled for later and later in the day, I half expected I'd be leaving empty-handed.

Lucas did what true professionals do: he followed through on his commitment. We finally sat down for the interview around 10:00 p.m., after a late training session where he and I sparred a few rounds and discussed technique. Even though he had a young infant at home and a strength-training session scheduled right after our meeting, he didn't rush me at any point.

I asked the champion about his off-season habits, though I could tell just by looking at him what his answer would probably be. Lucas stays in shape off-season. Like the uber successful Hall of Fame former boxer Floyd Mayweather, Lucas is always on weight and only needs to lose six or seven pounds for a competition. Oftentimes, combat athletes need to lose twenty to forty pounds before their competition. The idea here is usually that they will be a large opponent for their division. Some see this as an irresponsible way to be when not in preparation for a match. Why gain so much weight only to be forced into focusing more on cutting it back during camp?

Alternatively, someone like Lucas is able to spend eight weeks focusing on his technique and actual jiu-jitsu versus battling the scale. Twenty-four hours a day, seven days a week, three hundred and sixty-five days a year, Lucas is the consummate professional. Between tournaments, he sleeps until 9:30 or 10:00 a.m. and starts teaching at noon. He trains from 7:30 to 9:00 p.m., goes to the gym, and then takes a sauna or goes swimming. At midnight, he's done for the day and heads home.

For all the time and effort Lucas dedicates to jiu-jitsu, he is also well aware that mentors were a critical part of his success. Elan Santiago and Fernando "Tererê" Augusto were two of the people who helped him through the toughest spots. When he felt demoralized because he wasn't making money, Santiago would reassure him. "Look, every athlete goes through this kind of stuff." Augusto, whom Lucas looked up to as his hero, used to call and encourage him. "How's the training going? Don't give up. Keep it up!"

And while his mother supported him from day one and sacrificed her paycheck to buy him his first kimono, he knows that such backing is not always a given. On the topic, Lucas told me, "Sometimes the closest people are the ones who discourage us the most. And sometimes the people who don't know us are the ones who encourage us the most."

BEST ADVICE

When asked about the best advice he ever received, Lucas answered in Portuguese. *"Eu não menosprezo ninguém."* This translates to, "Don't disrespect anyone, don't discount anyone." Focus on each opponent and don't think of them as less than anyone else.

"He has a 50 percent chance of winning, and I have 50 percent," Lucas explains. "If you don't believe that your opponent can beat you, you won't pay attention. If you're not paying attention, he can beat you. So, respect your opponent."

WORST ADVICE

Before Lucas started winning tournaments, people told him to get "a real job." It's a good thing he didn't listen. Instead, Lucas asked in return, "What is a 'real' job? Is it a place where you go for eight hours a day and you get a check at the end of the month?"

Even so, he admitted that the comments sometimes brought him down. At one point, Lucas doubted his path so strongly that he seriously considered whether he should make a huge life change, and started looking for more secure jobs in the banking industry. The pay was decent, and having a consistent paycheck seemed much more refreshing than wondering where the next payday for a jiu-jitsu match would come from. After all, this was during the rough times of his early earning career in jiu-jitsu, and the best was yet to come.

Thankfully for all of us fans, Lucas stuck with jiu-jitsu. The more energy and effort he poured into his passion, the more he persevered.

FINAL THOUGHTS
BELIEVE IT'S POSSIBLE

Lucas named *Psychology of Champions—How to Win at Sports and Life with the Focus Edge of Super-Athletes* by James J. Barrell as his favorite book. The main message he took from it was, "It's possible." When you think something is possible, it changes your mindset. In other words, when we believe it's possible, we actually try!

At the end of our time together, Lucas told me his experiences had taught him a valuable, overarching lesson about life. "You are your own destiny," he said. "You write your own story. You have to follow what's right for you."

CHAPTER 3

Fábio Gurgel

fabiogurgel.com.br
 @fabiogurgel
 facebook.com/fabiogurgeljj

Born in 1970 in Rio de Janeiro, Fábio Gurgel began his jiu-jitsu training at thirteen years old. Six years later, Romero "Jacaré" Cavalcanti promoted him to black belt. In 1993, Fábio co-founded the Alliance team with Alexandre Paiva and Jacaré. A prime school in Brazil almost from the get-go, Alliance opened its first US affiliate in New York in 1998. Today, Alliance has well over 250 affiliates in different countries around the world. With thirteen World Championship titles, Alliance is the most successful academy association in jiu-jitsu.

In the few years I've had the opportunity to train with Fábio at the Alliance headquarters in São Paulo, this particular martial artist has taught me many lessons about life through jiu-jitsu, and I am extremely grateful to him for that. Though his nickname is "The General," he treats his students with respect. In return, their admiration for him is evident as soon as he walks through the academy door.

He has a booming voice, natural charisma, and a signature smile—one that gives the false feeling he's incapable of hurting a soul. Make no mistake, Fábio earned multiple World titles in one of the more brutal eras of jiu-jitsu. I've seen him roll multiple rounds with his students five days a week, submit and punish them, and give many of the current world champions a run for their money. I've felt The General's infamous shoulder pressure during sparring one too many times! At fifty years young, he's an inspiration to us all.

Fábio and I spoke at Alliance Jiu-Jitsu HQ in São Paulo, Brazil, located in Rua Nova Cidade, n° 182—Vila Olímpia São Paulo—SP—CEP: 04547-070.

- For a video of Fábio's fight against Mark Kerr—which you'll read more about in this chapter—search YouTube for "Gurgel vs. Kerr."
- For a comprehensive library of Fábio's techniques, go to BJJFanatics.com.
- To learn more about Alliance and be a part of their team, visit allianceofficial.com.

EARLY LIFE
FROM BRUCE LEE TO JACARÉ CAVALCANTI

Fábio began training in martial arts as a young teen, once he began to venture away from home and into the streets of Rio de Janeiro. Life felt unsafe there, and he wanted to learn how to protect himself. In the early 1980s, jiu-jitsu was somewhat popular in Brazil among the older generation, but young people looked up to Bruce Lee. As a result, Fábio initially took up karate. After three or four months of training, he'd had enough.

"I felt bored," he said, shrugging his shoulders. "My older brother destroyed me in every household fight. My karate didn't work at all."

When his sister's boyfriend showed him some jiu-jitsu moves in the living room, Fábio instantly quit karate and switched martial arts. He loved jiu-jitsu immediately. Even though he wasn't notably strong and only trained twice a week, he was soon beating his brother in their inevitable sibling fights.

Then, suddenly, the academy closed. It was a huge blow of course, but it was probably also the best thing that could ever happen to Fábio. One thing led to another, and eventually he began training at a new school where the now infamous Romero "Jacaré" Cavalcanti had just started teaching. Early life lesson #1: *timing is everything!*

Jacaré, who later founded the Alliance Jiu-Jitsu Team, has now graduated what must be more than three hundred black belts, but Fábio was his very first. When Jacaré eventually bought the academy, sixteen-year-old Fábio became a teacher there. With the academy located halfway between home and the school where he took English classes, Fábio stopped by to help out whenever he could.

Fábio told me that, looking back, he appreciates how things fell into place for him. He was young, and teaching allowed him to pay for first-class instruction. Jacaré was also young and in the process of building his first academy, so he had tons of energy to invest not only in his business but in teaching Fábio about the academy. Eventually, the two became partners in the school and, later, co-founders of a much larger Alliance Team.

"I was there at the right time," Fábio told me.

Although Fábio's humility is admirable, I have to point out that he was at the right place at the right time *because of his instinct to follow his passion.* I heard a quote once, I don't know from where, but I think it applies here: diligence is the mother of good luck.

ON PRESSURE AND ANXIETY

THERE'S ALWAYS ROOM FOR GREATNESS

Many jiu-jitsu pros I've talked with shared similar stories of resistance coming from family or close friends when they decided to make jiu-jitsu their life. People often tried to discourage them: "Go get a regular job!" Go do this! Go do that!

Not so for Fábio, who remembers a life-plan family conversation that took place years ago at his family's kitchen table. Fábio's dad first spoke with Fábio's older, college-bound brother, who wanted to go into engineering. Then his father turned to Fábio and asked, "Hey, what about you? What are you going to do when you grow up?"

Fábio was already helping out in Jacaré's studio and answered, "Jiu-jitsu. I'm gonna teach jiu-jitsu."

"That's nice," his dad said. "Do you know the size of the jiu-jitsu market? It's pretty small, but do you think you can be *really* good? Because if you *believe* that you can be *really* good, there's always a spot."

From then on, Fábio wanted to prove to himself that jiu-jitsu was the right choice. He considered his work in Jacaré's studio from a business perspective. How could he run the business better? How could he help Jacaré grow the school?

Fábio said, "I used to take care of the attendance cards, paint the academy, change the mats, and go to the bank to make deposits. Everything. I was trying to understand the business because I had these words on my mind: *You need to be good. You need to be the best. If you cannot reach that level, you won't make a good living.*"

Fábio's story struck a chord in me. I once attended a seminar for sixty entrepreneurs in Boulder, Colorado, where American entrepreneur and podcaster Tim Ferriss was taking questions from the stage. A concerned, fledgling business owner asked about the stiff competition in their respective fields. Tim paused for a moment before responding, "There is *always* room for greatness." That advice is true now as much as it was back when Fábio was just starting out. If you're *great*—not good, but *great*—there will always be a spot for you. Even so, *you have to truly work your craft to be one of the best.*

Competition is a good thing. Oftentimes, we want to entertain as little competition as possible, especially when it comes to business or work. But competition has an upside. We can't control competitors sprouting up around us, but in response to them, we can elevate our service, our offering, or our message. By doing that, we show the public the value we have to offer, and that value creates space. In other words: strive to be the best, and there will always be room for you.

BECOMING A CHAMPION
LESSONS LEARNED FROM FIGHTING BIG GUYS

The story of Fábio's 1997 fight against wrestler Mark Kerr is legendary. Though you may already know the outcome, it is worth repeating yet again. Fábio was in São Paulo and scheduled to go against Jerry Bohlander, an American-born mixed-martial-arts fighter. At the last minute, Jerry dropped out of the fight. This frustrated Fábio, as he had prepared for the fight for three months. So, Fábio signed up for a three-fight tournament that had neither time limits nor weight classes—the Vale Tudo Championship 3. All three fights were to take place on the same night, and several big guys were competing, like Paul "Polar Bear" Varelans and Mark Kerr.

After winning his first two matches, Fábio went up against Mark Kerr. Mark outweighed him by more than seventy pounds. The match was scheduled to go into ten minutes of overtime if neither competitor had won after thirty minutes. However, from the very beginning, the win-lose dichotomy didn't mean much to Fábio. His mindset was always the same in every fight: "If the guy doesn't kill me, he doesn't win."

At some point in the fight, Fábio took a hit to the eye that resulted in so much swelling that the referee urged him to stop. Fábio was fierce about continuing in spite of his injury. He also felt frustrated because the referee was talking to him in the middle of such a brutal battle.

"Man, come on," Fábio yelled at the ref. *"Fuck you, I'm fighting!"*

At the same time, he was beginning to feel exhausted. "Kerr was on top, grinding and pounding on me," Fábio told me as he threw short air punches. "He weighed 275 pounds, and I was barely even trying to hit back because I was so tired. I was pushing him away from my body, it seemed like forever."

Fábio almost quit, but twelve minutes before the end of the first thirty-minute round, his fighting spirit returned. How? Fábio shifted his head and looked at me as if he was about to tell me something I should never forget.

You know what? he told himself, *I won't quit. I'm tired, but I cannot allow myself to quit because I know I will never forgive myself the next day. Let's see if the guy can kill me because that's the only way he can win.*

Instantly, Fábio began to relax. As he relaxed, Mark Kerr slowed down and it was evident he was tiring himself out.

Fábio eventually lost the fight. After the first thirty-minute round was over, the doctors on staff wouldn't let him continue into overtime. Nevertheless, Fábio had just learned the biggest lesson of his career. At that crucial intersection of either giving up or persevering, he realized that the mind fatigues long before the body does. "When you get really tired, you must know that it's not your body that's resisting. It's your *mind* blocking you."

Fábio's advice reminds me of author and Navy SEAL David Goggins in *Can't Hurt Me: Master Your Mind and Defy the Odds*. He describes how we tend to give up when we have exhausted only *40 percent* of our maximum capacity. "Even when we feel like we've reached our absolute limit, we still have 60 percent more to give," writes Goggins. "Once you know that to be true, it's simply a matter of stretching your pain tolerance…"

Fábio learned another valuable lesson during a long training session against Rickson Gracie. All things considered, Fábio felt good and technically proficient during this particular training session—that is to say, until the moment when a dead-tired Fábio caught the expression on Rickson's face.

It was blank and totally relaxed. Stoic.

Fábio realized that even if he could find the right position, he would lack the energy and physical strength to finish a submission on Rickson. Although jiu-jitsu is known as the "gentle art," there are several moments when applied strength is necessary. This is especially true against a world-class fighter. This short, final burst of energy to finish a submission can be a death sentence if you don't actually *finish* your opponent. Imagine squeezing something with your arms and hands as hard as you can for several seconds, and then letting go. Now, imagine your opponent escapes, and you have to defend yourself! The blood rushing to your arms and hands makes them feel like they are being weighed down by cement blocks. Lifting them up to so much as scratch your face seems like an impossible task. Hell, closing your hands into a ball after losing a submission grip is a victory in itself!

All Fábio could think was, *This guy is so relaxed and not even tired. How can I beat him? It's Rickson! He's the best guy in the game. He has the best defense. He's the best fighter I've ever rolled with.*

Rickson swept Fábio and reversed positions for top and bottom, and though Fábio was going to defend himself, he knew the proverbial blood was already in the water, and the shark would come for him. Rickson went for the submission and successfully finished Fábio. After Fábio tapped, Rickson flopped onto his back, now clearly physically exhausted. After a few extra deep breaths, Rickson said, "Man, I was as tired as you."

As flattering as that might have been, it was what Rickson told Fábio next that permanently seared itself into his mind. Rickson told him, "In a fight, there's a moment that's about acting. You cannot show your emotions. You cannot show what you think. You cannot show what you're feeling. Because if you show your weakness to your opponent, of course they're gonna use it against you."

Rickson's point was that the mind will put up barriers and try to resist. Jiu-jitsu is about the mind. It's about how we deal with our thoughts and fears. The mind is designed to protect us and our ego. It is meant to help us best protect our bodies, and this includes the sensation of fatigue. These attributes are ancient in their purpose, so we have to redirect our minds to focus on more situationally helpful thoughts and reactions.

Again, I am reminded of David Goggins and his comments about his Navy SEAL training. "We didn't care about muscle fatigue or breakdown because after a certain point, we were training our minds, not our bodies."

BEHIND THE SCENES

THE GENERAL LEADS THE YOUNG

Fábio received his nickname, "The General," from one of his students years ago. The young guy had just started training with Fábio and was living with other BJJ students. They were all serious enough about their training, but they were often up until 2:00 a.m. exploring the fun side of San Pablo. At seven o'clock in the morning, Fábio would invariably knock on his students' door and summon them for a run or sprint on the stairs.

"I don't care what you do when you're not training," he would tell them. "But get up now, and let's work!" He issued these orders like a general, and the name stuck.

Looking back, Fábio says he may have been more demanding than was necessary. While he still believes the way to success is through discipline and consistency, he has adapted his leadership style.

"I have the same strong hand," he said as he smiled ear to ear, "but now I lead with a soft heart."

Fábio knows exactly what an impact he, as an instructor and role model, can have on the lives of the young people he trains. Fábio never shies away from this responsibility. One of his world champions, Isaque Bahiense, is a testament to this.

Isaque came from a very poor neighborhood in Rio. He tried to finance his first tournament trip by organizing a raffle and hitting up rich people. Fábio immediately called him into his office.

"Look! There are two ways to go," he said to Isaque. "You must choose. You can be the guy that's always begging for help from other people, or you can be a champion and people will beg for *your* help. It's up to you."

He assured Isaque that his talent and drive could carry him all the way to the top, but he also made it clear there would be no fundraising raffles in his academy. Fábio also reminded Isaque to show respect for people with money.

"Don't think that the guy with a hundred million dollars has an easy life!" Fábio insisted. "He has the same problems as you, sometimes even bigger."

Isaque listened. In that single interaction, Fábio had taught a simple lesson to Isaque about the principles of money, respect for others, and how to carry himself.

"It's the type of thing that I think is important to teach the students—even more than jiu-jitsu."

BEST ADVICE

"Don't talk bad about people," Fábio told me matter-of-factly. "If you do talk bad about others," he warned, "you're showing a negative side of yourself. You're showing that you have a weakness."

The idea that sharing negativity is also broadcasting weakness was powerful and rang true for me. It's easy to get caught in gossip or wanting to talk poorly about people, but in the end, it lets those who you're talking to know that you like to point out the negative in others. It also shows them you are willing to speak negatively about someone when they are not present to defend themselves.

To that end, Fábio also mentioned he wanted us all to listen more and talk less.

"We have only one mouth and two ears for a reason," he said, laughing as he referenced the old adage.

During our interview, Fábio brought up a bestselling self-help book first published thirty years ago, Stephen Covey's *7 Habits of Highly Effective People*. According to Covey, the fifth habit is, "Seek first to understand, then to be understood." Covey writes that people usually don't listen well because they are either truly talking to themselves or they are preparing their response while the other person is speaking. In essence, we're usually completely ignoring what the other person is saying, pretending to listen without really being present, listening selectively and hearing only parts of what is being said, or listening attentively without genuinely wanting to understand.

Covey recommends we approach conversations with the intent to understand. That means being empathetic listeners and trying to see the world the way our counterpart sees it.

Fábio explained that listening in this way demonstrates *respect* for the other person because it shows how interested we are in their story. It also creates an opening for learning. As I've heard it said before, we already know everything about ourselves, so why not listen and learn about someone else instead?

WORST ADVICE

Fábio's wise and kindhearted nature was apparent throughout our interview, but when I asked him about the worst advice he'd ever received, those elements of his personality took center stage.

Fábio laughed and said, "Hmmm, I probably forgot!"

FINAL THOUGHTS
JIU-JITSU'S IMPACT

For many athletes, jiu-jitsu becomes a form of self-discovery. We learn a lot about ourselves on the mat. For example, we learn to practice patience when we can't breathe because someone is trying to choke us. It takes drive and determination to try to survive and escape before passing out. We learn to check our ego by tapping and starting over. We also learn to respect our opponent's skills by being humbled over and over in defeat. When I asked what jiu-jitsu taught Fábio in terms of self-discovery, he shared three key lessons:

1. Jiu-Jitsu Will Show You Who You Are

"Jiu-jitsu will show you, your friends, and other people who you are," Fábio stated. "You're always hiding who you are from other people, and in jiu-jitsu, there is no chance you are going to hide who you are. If you're not a good person, and if you have a chance in the middle of a sparring match to hurt someone, you will do it. People will see whether you're a fair guy or not."

2. Jiu-Jitsu Teaches You How to Live

For Fábio, jiu-jitsu has become more than a sport—it is a way of life. The discipline he has in his thinking and in everything he does came from training jiu-jitsu. "I was raised with jiu-jitsu, and the way that I think is *through* jiu-jitsu," he explained.

From watching others, he also learned that all successful people have two things in common: perseverance and confidence. "To be successful in jiu-jitsu, I needed to have both," he said. He has also applied this knowledge to his life beyond the mat.

3. Connection Matters on the Mat and in Business

Fábio understands better than anyone why some students excel on the mat and in life while others don't. He has taught many world champions in his academy and graduated over 150 black belts. By watching people like Marcelo Garcia, Lucas Lepri, Michael Langhi, and Bruno Malfacine, he realized they have something in common. They have an intuitive perception of connection that is, as he put it, "between the lines but makes them incredibly effective."

This connection mindset guides Fábio through life. "I don't make my next move without thinking what could happen next. Anticipating what might happen—that's how I make the connections in my life."

He conducts himself the same way in business that he conducts himself in jiu-jitsu: by trying to predict the consequences any of his moves might have.

"The further I can make the connections of what might happen, the safer I am," Fábio concluded.

Fábio has big dreams for jiu-jitsu, not only for his academy but also for the sport in general. He wants to bring it to the masses. Fábio made it clear he would like the pros in this business to understand that competitions—while important for the evolution of technique—are just a small part of a larger picture.

"We should deliver jiu-jitsu to everybody," he said. "Jiu-jitsu is the most effective form of self-defense. If we lose sight of that, one day we will lose everything. Jiu-jitsu has the potential to be one hundred times bigger than it is."

He told me he thinks it is important for instructors to approach teaching jiu-jitsu in a caring, authentic manner that seeks to provide the best classes possible. In his view, people should feel good when they finish a lesson. As I listened to him, I was reminded of a favorite quote by legendary American poet Maya Angelou: "I've learned that people will forget what you said, people will forget what you did, but people will never forget how you made them feel."

Fábio's role model for good teaching is Jacaré. Jacaré taught with his students in mind, not his bank account. In doing so, he outlasted every competing instructor.

"Where are those guys who were teaching at the same time as Jacaré?" Fábio asked rhetorically with his hands in the air. "They're all gone because maybe, perhaps, they were just there to get the money." He pointed his finger to the ground and continued, "Being an instructor means you have to *love* the evolution of the other person."

What he said made sense to me. When we become more interested in another person's goals than just our own goal, it elevates us all. "Rising tides lift all boats," as they say. A scarcity mindset often leads to selfishness and lack of growth. Happiness is not a zero sum game; in other words, happiness is not scarce by nature. Just because you are happy or succeeding, it has no bearing on if I can also achieve the same. Shifting our paradigm and realizing happiness is not scarce shifts us out of jealousy and, instead, allows us to truly experience happiness for other people's successes. What a relief that we don't always have to be the person winning. And with this new mindset, we can become better leaders, teachers, parents, partners, and spouses.

In short, we can become better human beings.

CHAPTER 4

JT Torres

essentialbjj.com
@jtorresbjj, @essentialbjj
@jtorresbjj
facebook.com/jttorresbjj

JT Torres is one of the best-known American jiu-jitsu fighters. He grew up in the State of New York and earned his black belt under Lloyd Irvin in 2009. In 2013, he moved to San Diego and joined Team Atos, under the great André Galvão. Since then, JT has started his own academy, Essential BJJ, back in New York.

He won gold at ADCC in 2017, a feat he repeated in 2019 as the ADCC champion. Although he has medaled in many classic tournaments in IBJJF, JT's ADCC titles are the world-class achievements he is most proud of.

Here's a fun fact: JT received his black belt in *just over four years!* Mind blowing. For the sake of comparison, I was a blue belt alone for four years.

JT welcomed me into his gym in Hartsdale (since relocated to White Plains), New York, in November 2018. His gym's new location in White Plains is at 10 County Center Rd G1, White Plains, NY 10607.

As the reigning ADCC champion, JT was obviously the best in the world in NoGi, so I wasn't exactly sure what to expect from the training session we had scheduled prior to the interview. What impressed me most on the mat was his attention to detail. I was actually somewhat shocked by his level of heartfelt authenticity. For example, he made absolutely sure I understood a position before we moved on to the next technique. On a personal note, he instinctively understood something about me that most other instructors miss: when I nod my head, what looks like "Yes, I get it" really means "I'm lost. Can we do it again?" In our interview that followed, it became evident through JT's approach to teaching why he is so sharp. He is a true student of the game, and he makes sure to give his all in anything he does.

Two years later, during the pandemic and when everything was locked down, JT was the only instructor I reached out to for Zoom video training sessions. He really is that good at teaching! Big thank you to his wife, Jolanda, for being the dummy training partner (and his sweet French bulldog, Oliver, walking in and out of the Zoom screen).

- For videos of JT competing at ADCC in both 2017 and 2019, go to YouTube and search "JT Torres ADCC."
- Visit *BJJFanatics.com* for a comprehensive library of JT's techniques.
- JT also has his own platform for instructional videos, which he is constantly updating, at *essentialbjjonline.com*.

EARLY LIFE
FROM KARATE TO JIU-JITSU

JT began training in karate at the age of eleven. He earned his karate black belt before he even turned fifteen. JT recalled trying to switch to basketball once he started high school because, at the time, practicing martial arts just seemed too nerdy for a kid his age. Unfortunately—or fortunately, as it turns out—basketball was not for him. Though he tried, he never made the team. At five feet seven, JT realized he was simply not tall enough for the sport.

His dad, a lifelong athlete, tried bringing him back to karate. JT refused.

"What about jiu-jitsu?" his father suggested.

JT was initially a little hesitant, but finally agreed to give it a shot and see if he liked it. He and his dad began watching the UFC. There, they saw Royce Gracie choke people out in a no-rules fighting setting. JT found himself thinking, *This jiu-jitsu stuff really works.*

Similar to the way Marcelo Garcia was introduced to the martial art, JT took a few jiu-jitsu lessons with his former karate teacher. Instantly, he was hooked.

"The cool thing was, I had a natural thing for it," he told me with a proud smirk. "I just fell in love with it. A few months into training, I told myself, 'I'm going to marry jiu-jitsu.'"

Soon, JT was soaking up as much information as he could possibly find on the subject of jiu-jitsu.

ON PRESSURE AND ANXIETY
LEARNING FROM PREDATORS

One decade into his career as a full-time jiu-jitsu practitioner, JT now goes into every fight and tournament knowing he can win.

"I don't ever doubt my ability to be the best, or to defend my title, or win another major title," he explained. "I don't doubt myself."

But for all the confidence, before every fight there's still that last-second thought, a moment where he thinks, *This guy is really good, and he looks jacked. He's in shape. He could beat me today.*

JT says that he learned to control his nerves by studying the behavior of animal predators, like lions and tigers. In videos, he would see the hair on the back of their necks stick up when they were about to attack their prey. After doing some research, he understood that raised hair is a reaction similar to his own anxiety.

From then on, he told himself, *Even lions and tigers get a feeling of alertness right before they go take down that gazelle over there, and they are one-thousand-pound killing machines. If they can feel nervous, it's okay for me to feel nervous.* He now uses his nervousness in a positive way, by reminding himself that the feeling is there for a good reason.

"My nervousness keeps me alert," he concluded. "The nerves keep me focused."

As is true for many fighters, jiu-jitsu taught JT lessons that went way beyond the mat. The two big ones were staying focused in difficult life situations and problem-solving.

When he first started doing jiu-jitsu, JT's parents were going through a difficult divorce. Their separation was hard on him.

"It messed with me," he admitted. But jiu-jitsu was there for him; as he put it, "It really helped me stay on a path—stay focused on what I had to do."

The other thing he learned was the benefit of methodical problem-solving. Even as a young adult, he understood that he couldn't run from practical problems like paying car or cell phone bills or making money to buy food. He knew those issues needed to be addressed. Jiu-jitsu taught him to avoid seeking out a quick fix. Instead, he learned to come up with a game plan for solving long-term problems.

"I don't rush to anything," he told me. "If the boiler breaks at the gym or something happens in the gym, I don't panic and run to the first possible solution. I'll sit in silence for ten minutes, and I'll think."

In a nutshell, JT says, "Jiu-jitsu taught me how to feel comfortable being uncomfortable." This one statement seems to embody one of the pillars of jiu-jitsu throughout the community. Panic leads to poor decisions and being uncomfortable can lead to a type of panic. When the mind is stressed, it can focus only on what it can lose, not what it can gain. If we can harness and internalize this single thought, we have the ability to creatively address our challenges, which will usually result in a better outcome.

BECOMING A CHAMPION

JT WAS SELF-TAUGHT

JT was an almost entirely self-taught jiu-jitsu athlete during his first two years of training. He started hanging out at the local Barnes & Noble bookstore, leafing through books and reading magazines like *Grappling*. He was desperately hungry for information. Back then, YouTube wasn't nearly the learning tool it is today, so JT did the next best thing available: he ordered DVDs. The DVDs featured big IBJJF tournament matches: Worlds and PanAms. At the time, there was also an old website he visited, bjj.org, which featured lots of photos demonstrating and teaching techniques. Step one, Step two, Step three. It was the old-school way of learning with words and static pictures. For those more modern readers who currently study and practice the martial art: could you imagine your jiu-jitsu life without YouTube?

Though JT physically trained no more than once or twice a week (and with a somewhat inexperienced blue belt instructor), he still considered himself a full-time practitioner of the sport. Mentally, he trained all day long. He was either studying jiu-jitsu material or running through drills in his mind.

"I would order the DVDs and sit on my couch and watch the high-level black belts," he said as he leaned back on an imaginary couch. "I did that for hours. Whatever I would see them do, in my next training, I would try it myself."

JT's passion is never more evident than in a story he tells about a certain jacket he would wear to school during winter.

JT sat Indian style across from me on his school's jiu-jitsu mat, leaning forward and hunching his body over as if he was putting himself back in the classroom chair, head down, in deep thought about jiu-jitsu.

"In the classroom at school, I would put my jacket on my little desk around my chair and constantly grab the sleeve because it was wrapped around my back. I would go over the top of the arm and practice kimuras. One day, one of my teachers asked, 'Mr. Torres, what are you doing? Stop playing with your jacket!' All I was doing is just sitting there, kimura-ing my jacket over and over, and people in class were wondering, 'What the hell is he doing?'"

In essence, JT had become the martial arts nerd he never knew he wanted to be. He was infatuated with the sport; he wanted to practice always and everywhere; and he used his creativity to come up with a new type of practice dummy: his jacket and a school desk. This is an example of using time wisely at its finest!

At age seventeen, JT graduated from high school. He was a purple belt, and on the first of September that same year, just one day before his eighteenth birthday, he received his brown belt. JT's eyes lit up as he told me how much he enjoyed competing. At the time, he attempted to hit all the local tournaments in the New York area where he lived.

His biggest desire back then was to "take a shot at Worlds." But Worlds, like PanAms, took place on the West Coast. Since he was only training a couple of days a week and generally lacked funds and access to sponsorships, these big competitions seemed almost out of reach.

At the time, JT didn't see how he could get himself to a competitive level where he could fly to California. So, he agreed to his parents' dream for him: a college degree. He enrolled in community college, sat through the first semester, and failed all his classes. Not exactly the start his parents were hoping for in JT's educational career.

"I wasn't focused," he said. "My mind was on jiu-jitsu. I was trying to figure out how to get to the next level, how to make my dream come true."

His chance came when he was given the opportunity to train in Maryland. Needless to say, he took it. *Screw it!* he told himself. *I'm going to go against what my parents say and go against what everyone else thinks. I'm going to chase this dream because I know I love this thing.* Making this decision was hard, and his parents were clearly upset when he told them he had dropped out of college. This was, in part, because they felt uncertain he'd make it.

JT wasn't sure he'd succeed either. A doubtful chatter played out in his head, telling him, *I don't know if this is going to work out because I haven't tested myself against the high-level guys.* Then a much more confident voice spoke up. *I know I'm good, and I think I'm good enough to beat them. I want to at least give it a shot.*

Needless to say, JT never regretted his decision. Things improved for him immediately. He got more exposure, fought in bigger tournaments, and continued to build confidence until, one day, he knew for sure, *I can do this. I can be a world champion.*

Today, when JT looks back on his struggles as an eighteen-year-old, he commends his younger self for taking the leap.

"I pulled the trigger," he told me. "I was a young brown belt, dropped out of college, moved down to Maryland, and started training full time down there. It's been an amazing journey."

Does he sometimes wonder where he would be if he hadn't had the courage to follow his dream? Yes. The way JT sees things, he might still be doing jiu-jitsu, but as a hobby and just to stay in shape. He thinks maybe he would've been working a corporate job. Who knows? In the end, his story proves that sometimes in life *not taking a risk is the biggest risk you can take.*

As for his parents? "They couldn't be prouder," said JT, beaming with pride.

BEST ADVICE

"Probably the best thing I've ever heard—and it's so true—is: 'Fuck what everyone else thinks!'"

WORST ADVICE

"The worst advice I ever received was: 'Why don't you relax?' My response to this is, 'It's not time to relax, man! I've got to work.'"

FINAL THOUGHTS
LOSING AND MAINTAINING POSITIVE ENERGY

When JT loses a fight, he withdraws for a few minutes afterward. He uses the space to put himself back together. "I disappear from my dad, girlfriend [now wife], whoever's with me at the venue. I go sit somewhere, and I think. I think for a good ten minutes by myself in silence. After a while, I think, *Okay, back on track! Now I know what I've gotta do. I have 364 days until my next go-round at this tournament. Let's go!*"

Whether it's at a tournament, in training, or in the business of jiu-jitsu, JT has learned to use setbacks as motivators. Faced with a bad day of business, he asks, "What can I do to strike back harder tomorrow? How can we market to customers better? Where can I advertise more? How do I break up the classes in a better way?" If he has a bad day during training camps, he tells himself, *I can't wait to train again tomorrow. Now I know what I need to work on.*

JT admits that only a few years ago, bad days in training would throw him off. He'd think, *Man, I suck. I'm not ready for this tournament.* But things have changed. He has learned to appreciate setbacks.

"Now, bad days fire me up. They make me feel alive."

If anyone is driven, it's JT. When he received the invite for ADCC in 2017—this was his third time participating—he had just moved back East from San Diego to open a gym in New York. Preparing for the launch of his business was hard enough, but with the relocation he had also lost access to top competitors who trained at Atos in San Diego. His initial response to the ADCC invitation was, "I can't do it. I don't even have a gym yet."

JT is not one to make excuses, and he once again answered the call. *I'm going to make it. I will do the best I can*, he told himself. In the beginning of camp, he rented a small mat space at a fitness studio where he trained with just a few students. In June, three months before ADCC, he was finally able to open his gym, Essential Jiu-Jitsu. That's when the grind began.

His daily routine followed a strict schedule and included training for ADCC while teaching every single class at his studio. He outlined an average day for me: wake up at 5:00 a.m. and be at the gym by 6:00 a.m.; open up and teach from 6:30 a.m. to 7:30 a.m.; shower and eat some breakfast; rest from 8:30 a.m. to 11:00 a.m.; train from 11:00 a.m. to 1:00 p.m.; eat lunch and rest again until 4:00 p.m.; lift weights until 5:00 p.m.; teach the kids, then the white belts, and finally the adults from 5:00 p.m. until 8:30 p.m.; clean the gym; be home by 11:00 p.m. Wake up at 5:00 a.m. and repeat.

In between classes, JT would sometimes lie on a couch at the back of his gym, look up, and pray, "God, please let this be worth it, because I'm killing myself right now. I'm killing myself." He reenacted this, putting his hands together and looking up at the ceiling. It felt like he was saying the words to me, and also reliving the moment as if he were pleading with God all over again.

To get ready for ADCC, JT remotely followed the program André Galvão was using in California.

"I followed it to a T," he recalled. "Everything was right. I didn't skip a beat."

Except, of course, that JT's general circumstances were less than optimal. While most gyms may have dozens of top-level guys, his only three training partners were purple belts. And JT was far from being able to focus solely on prepping for ADCC—he had a brand-new business to run.

If all of this wasn't enough, JT's gym initially lacked air conditioning. If you aren't familiar with New York summers, the humidity is sweltering. By 8:30 a.m., the gym was so hot that it felt almost unbearable. To stay cool while resting between training sessions, JT laid on a mat in front of a fan with his French bulldog, Oliver.

At the time, he was also feeling very nervous about the gym. He didn't know if it would succeed or fail. He had no more than thirty or forty students enrolled at a time and some days only a few would actually show up for class, which was not enough to cover his expenses. New York is very expensive; the rent for the gym was high, and he often wondered whether he'd even make it to the next month financially.

In the end, JT pulled through in every way. He won ADCC, and his studio also added practitioners. It was all worth it.

"I kept marching forward," he said. "I was pouring my heart out like I still do every day. Even though I was dead tired, I would still teach every class 100 percent. I had great energy, and I would teach great techniques. The students started seeing that. From that, more students came."

The way I see it, this story offers a valuable lesson about energy. Good energy brings more good energy, and people *want* to follow others who are positive. JT could easily have told himself, *Let me focus on my business. I've done enough in my career. I've won plenty of titles.* Instead, he kept following the same strict routine every day for months. He was wiped out, and yet he kept going. He kept doing double duty as he trained for ADCC while also getting his business off the ground. His positive attitude saved his business. It flourished precisely because of his dedication to his students and the inspiration his positivity gave them.

JT told me that looking back, his life leading up to ADCC in 2017 was a grind. Then he paused, looked to the side, and added, "I'm still living the grind."

How did he do it? How does he *still* do it?

"I've never been someone who's satisfied. I always want more. And not in a bad way; I just always want to accomplish more."

CHAPTER 5

Roger Gracie

rogergracie.com
@rogergracie
@rogergraciehq
facebook.com/rogergraciepage

Considered by many to be the best jiu-jitsu competitor of all time, Roger Gracie is a ten-time world champion. The grandson of Carlos Gracie, one of the creators of BJJ, Roger has won every big title in the sport and is known as a *submission hunter*.

Roger unquestionably has a remarkable résumé. I have always considered his ADCC run in 2005 to be one of the most impressive things about him. However, Roger himself corrected me on this. He agreed that ADCC was great, for sure, but what really makes him feel proud about ADCC specifically was his mentality.

In 2005, Roger was a second-year black belt. He wasn't favored to win anything at ADCC that year. Physically, ADCC was much harder for him than Gi competitions. The NoGi wrestling style in ADCC was slippery, faster, and more intense. Many of his matches went into overtime.

Roger Gracie won all eight fights by submission—four in his weight class and four in the Absolute Division. This amazing feat had never been accomplished prior to 2005, and it has not happened at any ADCC event since.

So, if not this incredible achievement, then what makes Roger the most proud overall? The answer is IBJJF Worlds 2009, where he submitted all nine opponents—this time, four in his weight class and five in the Absolute Division—using the *exact same submission*: a cross choke from the mount. Roger explained that a dominant finish in the same position in each fight meant his technique was at a super-high level. It's one thing to finish your sparring partners in the gym, and it's a whole different story when you submit nine opponents over two days using the exact same position. Incredible.

Roger is an extremely warm person, and he was generous with his time. He and I spoke at the academy he founded and owns in London, where he has lived since age twenty. The opportunity to train with him one-on-one before the interview was definitely a dream come true.

- To see him in *Men's Health* magazine, search "Roger Gracie Men's Health."

- For a comprehensive library of his teachings, go to *rogergracietv.com*. (Note: I would rate the online library of his website as one of the easiest to navigate and the most user-friendly. Finding positions you're looking to practice isn't cumbersome like it can be on other sites I've tried. As a bonus, the videos are ultra-high quality and come with excellent explanations of the moves and techniques they demonstrate.)

EARLY LIFE
A CHAMPION IS BORN

Roger Gracie Gomes—better known as simply Roger Gracie—inherited the BJJ gene from both sides of his family. His mother, Reila, was a second-generation Gracie, and his father, Mauricio Motta Gomes, earned his black belt under famed Rolls Gracie in 1981, the same year Roger was born.

Roger told me he has very early memories of wearing a gi and interrupting classes at his uncle's academy in Rio. He recalled running around the mats with a bunch of his cousins. It would be years until Roger made a conscious decision to practice the martial art.

"When you're born as a Gracie, you're in a situation where you just find yourself on the mat with the gi on," he said, smiling. "But I wasn't serious about it and didn't dream of being a teacher or a fighter."

After his parents split, Roger lived with his mom for several years and then moved in with his dad. For a while, he practiced judo, but it wasn't until he moved back in with his mom at age fifteen that he began taking jiu-jitsu more seriously. He started training with his uncle Carlos at Gracie Barra, but even then, he was only on the mat once or twice a week. Basically, he was practicing jiu-jitsu because it was simply what his family did.

Things changed during a holiday visit when Roger went to see two of his uncles living in the south of Brazil. While staying at their house, he had the opportunity to truly see what it meant to live the jiu-jitsu lifestyle and train at an academy every day. *Their life is great*, he reflected during his trip back home. He had finally fallen in love with the sport and made a commitment to himself to train every day, lose weight, and get in shape.

Roger shared that, looking back, his decision had a lot to do with his age. As a teenager, he had begun to catch enough glimpses of adulthood to realize it confronts us with an important question: what will I do with my life?

Roger Gracie's answer was, *I want to be a champion.*

ON PRESSURE AND ANXIETY
THE FAMILY NAME

Being a Gracie can sometimes make things harder. During our interview, I brought up Roger's infamous 2004 fight against Jacaré Souza, who is, as of this writing, a top-ranked UFC MMA fighter. During their match, Roger broke Jacaré's arm but ultimately still lost in the match by points.

On occasion, Roger has clearly experienced his last name as a hindrance. While he admitted to feeling angry with himself after losing to Jacaré, he also told me that he half-expects the referees to be against him before a match even starts, thanks to his family name. If it ever comes down to a referee's decision, Roger can't be sure the ruling doesn't have something to do with his fame.

"That's sort of been my life ever since I was a blue belt," he admitted with a bit of an irritable shrug. He recalled how an entire stadium would often *boo* when referees decided in his favor. "When you start winning, a lot of people bet against you, saying, 'He's a Gracie! He doesn't need any help! Let's help the other guy!'"

The achievements of people born into families who excel at a particular sport or business are often dismissed with sentiments like, "Well, that can't have been hard for them! They basically *grew up* doing it." The same thing happens in jiu-jitsu if your last name is Gracie.

When Roger talks about the biggest challenge he has faced, it becomes evident that such dismissiveness misses the point: the journey to the top is long and hard for *everyone,* and Roger's ambition is never-ending. This was the true differentiator between Roger and his opponents. His success had nothing to do with his name.

A name doesn't put in the work.

BECOMING A CHAMPION
SET YOUR OWN EXPECTATIONS

Roger remembers the Gracie clan getting together for big reunions while his grandfather, Carlos, was still alive. On

Sundays, the family would hang out at his uncle's house to talk and train jiu-jitsu. After the BJJ founder's death in 1995, family members began to disperse. Everyone was living in a different city or country, and the reunions grew smaller and smaller.

"I think where we got together the most was on the mat," he explained.

Being born a Gracie quite obviously means being born into a highly competitive family, but no one ever seemed to have high expectations for Roger.

"I was a chubby kid and I used to get beat up all the time," he said, laughing. "No one in my family ever looked at me and said, 'Oh, he has potential.' I never heard that. There were no expectations of me."

On visits with his cousins in the south of Brazil, Roger overheard the pep talks his uncle Rolls barked at his son, Rolles. "You train because you're going to be the heavyweight champion!" Rolls would say. Then, he would turn to Roger and tell him, "Rolles is a heavyweight, but don't worry, you can be the middleweight champion."

Roger understood he was being looked at as secondary, but he refused to let that assessment define him.

Looking directly at me, he said sternly, "I remember saying to myself, *NO! I can be the best.*"

Proving to his family that they shouldn't discount him became part of Roger's motivation and fueled his ambition. "People thought less of me, but I said, 'I'm going to prove them all wrong. I'm going to train to be the best.' And I did," Roger said matter-of-factly. "I think the main challenge is developing yourself. How far can you develop yourself, your jiu-jitsu, your own technique? I believe there is no limit."

As I listened intently, I was reminded of an Oscar Wilde quote: "Be yourself, everybody else is already taken." Roger comes from the premier lineage of jiu-jitsu athletes, but he wanted to create a name for himself and become a champion in his own right. He knew testing himself with the loftiest of goals would push him toward the heights of the game that he desired.

The biggest challenge for Roger has nothing to do with tournaments and wins. Instead, Roger considers his greatest challenge the constant need to stretch and grow in his own development.

"There's no bigger challenge than that," he said, "because somebody who's not really good can still win something [in jiu-jitsu]. They can even win a world title." Roger paused for a moment, and then continued, "I mean, okay, they have to be good to win a world title, but they don't have to be amazing. They don't have to be *special*."

I think it's clear that Roger always wanted to be special, and he set the benchmark for many others to know what that actually, truly means: *dominate* your opponent, don't just win. And winning a world title one time isn't special in his eyes. Athletes and human beings should strive for more than the mass recognition of a benchmark, such a single world title.

Before Roger and I met for our interview in London, I watched a video where he explained why a win on advantages or points would mean little to him. (To watch this video, go to *graciemag.com* and search for "Roger Gracie on winning by advantages.") When I approached the topic, he reminded me of his lifelong goal in jiu-jitsu: to be the *best* fighter.

"The only way for me to be the best fighter is by dominating a fight, by being superior in a fight. And there's no way of being more superior than by submitting someone," he explained.

Roger says beating someone by a few points or an advantage just shows someone's lead at that moment in time; he doesn't feel it indicates overall superiority. If he wins by points, he interprets the victory as lacking.

"If I beat you by two points, it doesn't mean that I'm much better than you," he said. "If I was much better than you, I wouldn't just beat you by two points; I would have dominated you during the whole fight, and submitted you for the victory."

Roger says he doesn't care much whether he actually wins or loses a tournament.

"Of course it brings a lot of joy to win and be a world champion," he concedes. "But winning medals was never my goal. If I don't win, what makes me sad is that I lost to my *opponent*. It's about losing to another person." To give me an example, he referenced another Jacaré Souza fight and said, "I was mad that I lost...I was mad, of course, for losing, but I was really mad at myself for letting it be that close to begin with."

I was shocked when Roger told me it took years to bring his jiu-jitsu game up to a truly competitive level. Getting better as a fighter, he explained, is a journey. As a yellow belt, he would be, as he put it, "smashed around the mat like there's no tomorrow" and defeated "hundreds of times." These defeats taught him the value of developing a good defense.

"When I'm in a bad position, I know how to defend myself and get out."

Roger received his blue belt at age sixteen and stayed at that level for three years. In his final year at blue belt, he was beating people who used to beat him, even tapping some black belts in training. Once he had his purple belt, there was no doubting how good he was. *I'm a really good purple belt,* he told himself. *I'm on the right path, and I just need to carry on and do what I'm doing.*

Like everyone, Roger experienced bad days and setbacks. Right before his first World Championship as a juvenile, he got submitted and footlocked (a straight ankle lock) in a fight that he was otherwise winning by six points. After the fight, Roger had to use crutches for a week. Those who have experienced a footlock know it is painful as hell, but Roger's response was simple: "I just have to train harder."

He never accepted defeat, never doubted himself, and in his own words, "never had an inch of quit" in him. His mode of operating is, "If you have a bad fight, you dedicate yourself even more, spend more time on the mat, or change the way you train. You become better and make sure it won't happen again."

Behind all these responses are conviction and resolve, and a philosophy that goes even deeper. "You choose a path and you just stay faithful to your choice. It doesn't matter what happens," Roger told me.

When I asked Roger what jiu-jitsu has taught him about himself, he shared the same insight with me as Fábio Gurgel: there's no hiding who you are when you're on the mat. Perhaps you are too aggressive or passive or have no patience. Whatever it is, your time on the mat will bring you to discover these things about yourself and more.

He added that this kind of awareness will develop sooner or later, simply because of the repetitive nature of the training.

"It's the daily repetition that makes things happen," he said. "Like in chess, you repeat the same move over and over again, and the answer might not come straightaway, but eventually it will. In jiu-jitsu, you might not see how you are at first, but others will see it. And ten or twenty years of training will show you too, how you treat others, how you react when you're in a bad position, or if you're in the advantageous position, or simply angry. Suddenly, there's no more hiding."

That inspired me to ask Roger another question: what do people believe about you that's not true? As he responded to me, the corners of his mouth slowly lifted into a subtle grin. "People think my success has to do with my size. But it's not like that. It's actually my technique. They just can't do it."

BEST ADVICE

Advice comes in many different shapes and forms. Roger found it in books. His takeaway from reading stories about highly accomplished historical figures like Alexander the Great and Genghis Khan is that *nothing is impossible.* He operates with a conviction that there are no barriers in life, that what we see as a problem is often self-created. From the day he decided to dedicate his life to jiu-jitsu, Roger set a goal for himself that was far in the distance.

"I was a chubby kid, and my jiu-jitsu at that time was in the range of average to bad, but I was saying, 'I'm going to be the best fighter in the world.'" Roger's friends in the academy just looked at him and laughed when he shared his aspirations. Still, his conviction never wavered. "I never doubted myself. I don't create barriers against the goals I set for myself. It's what has led me to where I am today."

To me, Roger is living proof that how, where, or with whom we train does not determine how far we get. In London all those years ago, he didn't have access to the high level of training offered in other parts of the world, such as Rio de Janeiro in Brazil, and yet he achieved what he did and became what he is—the best jiu-jitsu fighter in the world.

"The secret to success," he explained, "lies within us. If it were only about training with the best, then all my training partners would also be world champions." The lesson? You need to *really* want it. Then and only then will the "impossible" become possible.

WORST ADVICE

When the time came to write this book, I realized I hadn't asked Roger about the worst advice he'd ever received. I followed up with this question, and Roger couldn't think of any. As I told him, "Must be nice!" But the truth is that based on what I've come to understand about Roger, I expect he wouldn't be deterred by bad advice, anyway.

FINAL THOUGHTS
FOCUS AND CONNECTION

As a true leader, Roger understands that he is working not so much for himself but for the people he serves through jiu-jitsu. Living in London, he can clearly see how stressful people's lives have become. He knows what jiu-jitsu offers in terms of relaxation and resetting our minds. Roger's words about jiu-jitsu being an outlet for stress will ring true for many athletes. Russell Brand, whose chapter appears later in this book, talked about how jiu-jitsu can be a sort of forced meditation. You must be focused on the moment. You can't grab your phone to read a text or social media notification while sparring. Jiu-jitsu requires you to be present. Through this presence, you can develop a deeper connection with others and with yourself.

Roger knows how much jiu-jitsu has helped him in his life, and he wants to pay it forward by reaching out to and helping as many people as he can.

"This is not about business for money," he said. "Yes, there are bills to pay, but there's a personal link with people. That I can do something to help other people in their lives is something really amazing."

CHAPTER 6

Romulo Barral

gbnorthridge.com
 @romulobarral
 facebook.com/romulobarral

One of the top BJJ competitors and coaches of all time, Romulo Barral was born in Diamantina, Minas Gerais, Brazil, in 1982. He became passionate about taekwondo at a young age, then moved on to MMA, and ultimately found his way to jiu-jitsu.

A black belt under Vinicius "Draculino" Magalhães, Romulo is a ten-time world champion, including five black belt World Championships in the medium-heavy division. He is a 2013 ADCC champion and a NoGi world champion. After moving to the US, he opened a Gracie Barra academy in Northridge, California, in 2011. He is especially known for his spider guard and knee-cut pass. He used both to toss me around and dominate during our training session before the interview.

Romulo didn't charge me for our private lesson, nor did he ask for any other form of payment. In the end, his generous habit of paying it forward inspired me to donate to his non-profit organization, Everyday Porrada. I don't say this to brag about my contribution to charity. Rather, I hope to show the power and influence of kindness. In this case, the butterfly effect started with Romulo's giving spirit and will continue on to positively impact people I've never met. It's the small things like this that the world needs more of.

Romulo and I spoke at his academy in 2019 at 19520 Nordhoff St., Unit 10, Northridge, CA 91324. He has an undeniably magnetic energy and a disarming smile. On the day we were scheduled to train and interview, we ended up talking about life and business for a few hours before we even got started. It was one of many conversations with him I won't soon forget.

- To see several of his matches, go to YouTube and search "Romulo Barral."
- For training videos, visit *BJJFanatics.com* for his "Everyday Porrada Spider Guard" and *jiujitsux.com* for his most recent high-quality instructionals.

EARLY LIFE

HARD WORK LEADS TO CONFIDENCE

Romulo was fifteen years old and already practicing mixed martial arts when he left his hometown to chase his dream.

Romulo wanted to become a great MMA fighter, and to do that he decided he wanted to get really good at jiu-jitsu.

"I always liked doing my own thing," he said as he described packing up as a teenager to start training BJJ with the best. The two-hundred-mile move to Belo Horizonte was indicative of his attitude toward anything he's passionate about—Romulo goes all in.

His talent was soon obvious to people around him, and Romulo began hearing the same advice over and over: "You're good at this," and "Focus on BJJ." Reviewing his accomplishments now, you might think his confidence was innate, but this is not the case. Romulo told me it was other people's faith in him that cemented his own, personal belief. By the time he was a brown belt, he was finally truly believing he could be one of the best black belts in the world.

Of course, faith alone isn't enough. What helped Romulo build confidence more than anything else was his unquestionably hard work ethic. He recalled looking at different gyms, noticing that no one worked as hard as he did. That's when he knew he could get further than anyone else.

"I'm the type of person to put my heart into it," he told me earnestly. "I work very hard. And then I start to believe not only the good things others say about me, but I start to believe in myself and my work ethic." He went on to say that he quickly realized his willingness to work so hard was going to make all the difference. He told himself, *This is going to take me to a different place than them, because I'm working three or four times harder.*

For a stretch of seven years, a typical day included multiple jiu-jitsu training sessions, MMA training, conditioning, cardio, and teaching. He was at the gym at 8:00 a.m. and finished his final session at midnight.

"I trained once a day, but *all day*," he said seriously. "Even my professor once told me, 'Romulo, you should fight ADCC, but no pressure, no crazy training.' I said to him, 'Then I shouldn't fight, because that's not who I am.' If I decide to do something, I do it 100 percent. I dedicate myself the way nobody does. What defines me is my work ethic. If you ask anyone, they will say the same thing. And from my work ethic comes the confidence."

ON PRESSURE AND ANXIETY
DREAMERS, SUPPORTERS, AND NAYSAYERS

If there was ever a time when Romulo wanted to quit jiu-jitsu and go back home, it was immediately after leaving Diamantina. Like many mothers, Romulo's mom didn't want him to leave home. However, his dad, who Romulo didn't often speak with, looked him dead in the eye and said, "Let him go! He'll be back in two weeks when he runs out of money and food. When his clothes are dirty." To this day, Romulo believes his dad probably did this to motivate him in some way, but that intense stare never left his memory.

The first two weeks were very hard, so hard that Romulo felt maybe his dad was right. "I was dying to come back home," he told me, laughing. Remembering his father's words both broke him down and fueled his desire to stay.

Fortunately, he had a very supportive friend in his life, Adaltinho. Adaltinho supported Romulo for many years by giving him work. During Romulo's wavering moment of weakness in Belo Horizonte, Adaltinho told him, "The only thing that walks backward is a crab. Are you a crab?" Then and there, Romulo made the tough decision to "suck it up" and stay.

Only one other person thoroughly believed in Romulo from the very beginning, and that was his sister, Deise. Romulo lit up with pride when he talked about her. It was clear to me that he appreciated his sister's early support and that it was a big force of reassurance he needed early on. Deise had always told Romulo she'd see his picture in a magazine someday.

"You're going to be in this magazine one day. I know it," he recalled her saying. "You're going to be the best!"

I'd like to put his sister's comments in perspective. While there are several podcasts, magazines, websites, and YouTube channels dedicated to the sport today, at the time Deise offered her words of encouragement, this wasn't remotely the case. Back then, for a jiu-jitsu fighter to have their name mentioned on even the back of a magazine required doing something as noteworthy as being labeled a champion at the purple belt level. Exposure wasn't what it is today, and having a picture published in print media would have been an *incredible* achievement. Nonetheless, from the outset, Romulo's sister had about as lofty hopes for him as anyone could have.

Fast-forward to today, and Romulo has made it in every way. He has a very successful academy. In fact, by my estimation, his facility is in the top 3 percent of academies for retained monthly students. He also has a flourishing brand, Everyday Porrada, which he is equally proud of. Considering his financial, business, and personal successes, coupled with the fact that Romulo came to the United States later in life and had to start everything from scratch, it is not a stretch to say Romulo Barral is literally living the American dream.

Romulo and I didn't discuss the extent of his success during our interview, nor did he boast about it. His life experience proves just how impressively things can grow when we put our mind to something the way Romulo has. His intensity is unmatched, and it shows in his results. Oftentimes, when we think of our own goals, we may see them as just too far away, or we believe it will take forever to attain them. The challenge is to be realistic about what's possible. One of my favorite Bill Gates quotes rings true when reflecting on all Romulo has achieved: "Most people overestimate what they can do in one year and underestimate what they can do in ten years." Needless to say, I can't wait to see what Romulo does in twenty!

Romulo has also come to understand what separates the naysayers from dreamers is *a willingness to walk a different path*. "Ninety percent of the population, or 95 percent, take the same path," he explained. "I just chose a different path and nobody believed and that's okay. People who aren't visionaries will never believe in another person's vision."

In fact, Romulo remembers people saying to him, "You don't own a house. You don't have a car. Who are you? Are you a loser? Are you a bum?" He kept believing in his own journey, regardless of their words, and continued following his path. "And now," he said, with one eyebrow raised, "everybody who didn't believe in my path is my fan."

His experience mirrored something a mentor once told me. They said, "Everyone is going to tell you that you can't do it until, of course, you do it. Then they're going to say, 'I always knew you could.'"

Romulo embodies the idea that if you really put your heart into something, somehow it's going to work out, regardless of what other people say.

BECOMING A CHAMPION
THE STRUGGLE IS THE WAY

When I asked Romulo what he learned about himself on the mat, it once again became clear that practicing jiu-jitsu can teach us so much more than can be witnessed on the surface. For this champion, jiu-jitsu has been his only tool for growth, in all areas of his life.

"Everything I know is from jiu-jitsu," he said with conviction. "I built my character; I built my personality; I built *who I am* through jiu-jitsu. Jiu-jitsu was my school. People tell themselves, *I'm street smart*, but for me, I'm jiu-jitsu smart. It defines who I am. There is not one area in my life where I don't think the way I do in jiu-jitsu."

Romulo learned to deal with everything that happens in business and in life through his daily grind on the mat. His life lessons came from the continuous struggle to assess, practice, and improve. When his students enter tournaments, he asks them about their expectations. "Do you expect to win or to struggle?" he asks. "If you expect only to win, you might not win, because in order to win you must expect to struggle." He reminds them why they train for months and months just to go into a ten-minute match. The daily struggle gives them all the tools they will need in the short fight. We must expect resistance, turmoil, chaos, and things not going to plan. Because when it happens—and trust me, it *will* during competition—it's better to be mentally prepared to push past the roadblock instead of being surprised things aren't going in textbook fashion.

As we spoke, Romulo revealed he knows that his career as a fighter has been exemplary. "Sixteen finals in a black belt World Championship—who can do that? People fight their whole life to make it just once," he said to me, raising his finger in the air. "Just once." If this sounds like arrogance, I assure you it's not. Both humble and confident, Romulo went on to explain that it is *because* he knows pulling off such a feat is rare that he developed the confidence to believe anything is possible—and not just on the mat.

He said, "If I could learn how to get there sixteen times, by struggling every single day and never thinking about quitting, what can I do off the mat? Outside of jiu-jitsu? My academy, Everyday Porrada, and everything else that I have accomplished besides jiu-jitsu was possible because of my struggles in jiu-jitsu. Jiu-jitsu *built me*. I use jiu-jitsu as a tool for everything. Some people who train jiu-jitsu say, 'It changed my life.' Jiu-jitsu didn't change my life. It *is* my life. It's a different perspective."

Speaking of perspective, Romulo admitted he is sometimes surprised to see how much the sport has grown in terms of prestige, leverage, and how famous individual fighters have become. For him, fighting was always about beating his own demons.

"I never fought for fame. I fought for pride," he said.

Though Romulo is arguably one of the top fighters in history in the medium-heavyweight class, he explained that his wins mean little to him because he was just doing his job. He had promised himself he would be the best, and so that's what he worked toward.

As a competitor, he didn't accomplish everything he thought he would. Even on the days he won, Romulo felt dissatisfied because he didn't fight the way he wanted or the way he had prepared. In the World Championships, he won nine silver medals to his five golds and remembers leaving those big tournaments where he won sad more often than happy. If you look at the photos of him, hand raised by the referee after a victory, Romulo's not smiling. This is because he felt he didn't fight his best, and ultimately, he wasn't satisfied.

Additionally, I couldn't help but notice another quiet example of the champion's humility. There were no medals on the walls of Romulo's academy, and no World Championship or IBJJF trophies on display. When I pointed this out to him, he kindly admitted, "To be honest, I'm not really proud of any title that I have in jiu-jitsu." Instead, his biggest wins—the ones that "count" and make him feel proud—were earned *off* the mat. He feels proud for having become the person, father, husband, and son that he is today. He is also currently one of the most respected coaches in BJJ, and he has trained champions like Felipe "Preguiça" Pena, Edwin Najmi, Gabriel Arges, and other top fighters.

"The most memorable times of my life have been when I impacted someone's life," he concluded.

It gave me chills when he told me about the moment he understood how important it was to him to be a part of someone else's success. "When Felipe (Pena) won Worlds, I never felt so happy in my life. If I personally win a tournament—for me, it doesn't mean much. It doesn't make me feel happy because I'm supposed to win. But the first time that I pushed someone, just a little push, to make them accomplish their goals—that's when I thought, *Okay, this is my purpose.* My purpose in life isn't to win for me. It is to push someone else, to help them accomplish their goals."

BEHIND THE SCENES
A PUSH TO THE LIMITS

Romulo has always stretched himself to the limit by challenging himself in new and sometimes absurd-sounding ways. He craves the kind of intense pressure that would make other people flee, freeze, or maybe even break. For instance, Romulo spent seven years in Brazil where he trained every day—and he literally trained all day. A coin that someone made for him later in his career speaks to this. It is engraved with the words, "All day, every day. No excuse," and he keeps that coin in his pocket as a reminder.

"People might see this as BS," he said, "but I did train all day." His daily schedule at the time looked like this:

- 8:00 a.m.—training class
- 9:00 a.m.—MMA training
- 11:00 a.m.—conditioning
- 12:00 p.m.—jiu-jitsu training
- 3:00 p.m.—nap on the mats
- 5:00 p.m.—another class
- 6:30 p.m.—break for food
- 7:00 p.m.—cardio
- 7:30 p.m.—train
- 9:00 p.m.—go to a different gym to teach a class until midnight
- 12:00 a.m.—take two buses to arrive at home at 2:00 a.m.

The next morning, he started over again. Romulo admitted that he doesn't like being comfortable. "It is something that bores me," he told me, leaning back in his office, with a tone that indicated he was almost disgusted at the thought of being comfortable in life.

It seems Romulo has adopted a militant attitude with himself. It reminded me of one of my favorite passages from Jocko

Willink's book *Discipline Equals Freedom: Field Manual.* In it, Jocko writes, "Emotion and logic will both reach their limitations. And when one fails, you need to rely on the other. When it just doesn't make any logical sense to go on, that's when you use your emotion, your anger, your frustration, your fear, to push further, to push you to say one thing: I don't stop."

To Romulo, the concept of training jiu-jitsu and counting training rounds or alternating training and recovery is nothing short of foreign. He told me, "Again, people might think it's BS or something, but all I have to do is train jiu-jitsu. So, what do people expect? That I'll go home, sit on the couch, and play video games? I've never had a video game, never even had a TV in my house. All I do is train."

The way he used to train, all day and every day, is just one example of how he goes to extremes. In another instance, he recently challenged himself to teach ten seminars in ten cities in ten days. Some of these were out of the country, and all the while he had a gym to run back home in Los Angeles, not to mention his wife and two daughters. What Romulo did in that ten-day period must be a record of sorts and definitely sounds near impossible to pull off, but this is his mentality. This is who he is. Every single day, he pushes himself one step further.

FINAL THOUGHTS
#EVERYDAYPORRADA

In May 2018, Romulo used a phrase in an interview that sparked a new movement in jiu-jitsu: Everyday Porrada.

Porrada is a Portuguese word that means "brawl" or "fight." In the context of BJJ, Everyday Porrada stands for giving your best and more of yourself in every fight and every training. It means doing BJJ the way Romulo does everything. At one point during our interview, Romulo told me, "You know, we all have heard of Nike's 'Just do it,' so why not create something more powerful than 'Just do it'?"

The hashtag #EverydayPorrada has gone viral on social media in the last two years. When Romulo saw the variety of people using the tag to connect their stories—soccer players, singers, moms and dads working three or more different jobs, a kid with cancer, and a man in a wheelchair—he recognized the power the concept had to change people's lives well beyond jiu-jitsu. For him, it has become a tool for making the world a better place.

Romulo learned the value of supporting others, of trying to lift them up, after he moved to the United States in 2010. "Here (in the US), you are encouraged to be a good citizen. And even though it's a lot of work, I try to touch people's lives and do the right thing. It's little by little, but when it happens, it is such an amazing feeling."

The core message Romulo wants to spread through Everyday Porrada is, "The world is not all sunshine. But once you learn to deal with the struggle, you can accomplish anything you want."

The logo he and his team recently designed consists of three diamonds. This is a direct reference to his hometown, Diamantina, but it also stands for something more. Just like the precious stone, which first needs to be polished before it can shine, we must work hard if we want to become the best version of ourselves.

I think Socrates described it best when he said, "It is a shame for a man to grow old without seeing the beauty and strength of which his body is capable."

There is so much potential simmering within each of us. Don't let it go to waste!

CHAPTER 7

Bia Mesquita

@biamesquitajj
facebook.com/biamesquitabjj
Bia Mesquita BJJ

Born in 1991, Beatriz "Bia" Mesquita received her black belt in 2011 from Leticia Ribeiro. As of late 2019, Bia has earned nine gold medals, and she has won more IBJJF World Championships at a black belt level than any other competitor. Her impressive twenty-three titles at black belt across all four major championships make her more successful than any other fighter in Gi and NoGi. She is a five-time Abu Dhabi World Professional Champion, a 2017 ADCC Champion, and an EBI Bantamweight Champion.

Bia started training as a five-year-old in Rio de Janeiro, Brazil. Once she moved to San Diego, California, in 2018, she began training and teaching at Gracie Humaita South Bay. She and I met there in the summer of 2019 for the following interview. She taught me some techniques during our training together, and then we sparred a few rounds. Once again, I was reminded that women are a force in this sport.

- To watch several of her matches, search "Bia Mesquita" on YouTube.
- To see her twenty-minute interview with Choke_lab, search for the Choke_lab YouTube channel.

EARLY LIFE
FALLING IN LOVE WITH BJJ

When Bia was five and saw her ten-year-old brother do jiu-jitsu, she immediately wanted to train as well. He quit the sport after a year, but Bia was hooked. She started fighting in national tournaments at just six years old. Competitive by nature, she continued to pursue jiu-jitsu even after her family moved from Rio de Janeiro to the small town of Saquarema, two hours north along the coast. In Saquarema, the high-caliber training found in Brazil's bigger cities did not exist, and Bia had to make do with a tiny, one-mat academy.

Bia's success is proof that you don't need fancy equipment to make it to the pinnacle of jiu-jitsu. What Bia had was a dream, and she followed that dream with a relentless willingness to work hard. Her passion for the sport not only attracted mentors like Leticia Ribeiro, but also earned Bia support from her school and an early sponsor. Thanks to financial help from a family friend and to teachers who were understanding, Bia was able to travel to tournaments and train hard all through high school and college. On some weekends, she even participated in two different events.

As a teenager, she also competed successfully in wrestling, judo, and swimming, but BJJ remained her main focus. "I really fell in love with jiu-jitsu," she admitted, "and I just wanted to do it more and more."

ON PRESSURE AND ANXIETY
PRIORITIZE POSITIVITY

Like any top athlete, Bia knows how performance pressure feels, but she has learned to conquer the fear of disappointing herself and others by prioritizing positive feelings and her desire to win.

"I focus on how much I want to be at this tournament, on what I want for myself and on how I can inspire other young women or girls," she explained.

Her biggest takeaway from all setbacks and from being on the mat for so many years has been that she can always stretch herself further. "Sometimes you think you've reached the end of the line, but then you try a little harder and you realize you can go even further. It really matters how much you want something. With dedication, you can stretch yourself beyond your limits."

BECOMING A CHAMPION
OVERCOMING GENDER BIAS

In big jiu-jitsu tournaments, women still constitute a small minority, though their numbers have been growing at a steady pace. When Bia was fourteen or fifteen years old and competing as a blue belt in Worlds, there weren't even ten girls in her bracket. Today, there are almost ten times as many girls competing in blue belt categories. The same goes for the adults, especially at the black belt level. Two decades ago, maybe half a dozen women, including Letitia Ribeiro and Kyra Gracie, competed professionally. Now, there could be twenty or thirty in a single division.

Bia told me that though she never experienced any bullying or sexual harassment, she certainly faced gender-based discrimination as soon as she went pro. Potential sponsors used to constantly question her commitment. They would defend their reluctance to support her with arguments like, "Nah, she's a girl! She could change her mind tomorrow. It's hard to invest because you don't know what might happen."

People have often asked Bia how she feels about being a woman in the male-dominated world of jiu-jitsu. She tells them it's not an issue because she grew up doing the sport. She also feels proud for showing everyone that women can do jiu-jitsu.

"It is proof that girls aren't fragile," she says.

In the end, the resistance she faced only strengthened her resolve. She told me she hopes her accomplishments will show others what is possible. "I proved to everyone that I can do jiu-jitsu professionally. I hope this will inspire others and younger girls, especially. If you want it, you can do it."

Gender bias wasn't the only challenge Bia faced over the course of her career. With sponsors on the fence about supporting her, money was often an issue. Like other fighters who start at a young age, Bia found herself making sacrifices as a teenager. While her thirteen- and fourteen-year-old friends were hanging out together on the weekends, she was at tournaments, missing out on the fun.

Many times she doubted whether she really wanted to pursue jiu-jitsu as a profession and toyed with becoming a lawyer or doctor instead. Even so, she never thought of quitting altogether. "I just love jiu-jitsu too much," she said with a smile. Bia told me she has never regretted making jiu-jitsu her profession, but she has found herself explaining to people that it is a career like any other, and that athletes get paid to train.

Arguably, an injury she sustained at Worlds 2013 may have been Bia's biggest challenge to overcome. Just after winning her division, she entered the Absolute finals against Gabi Garcia and tore a hamstring. The injury required surgery, and Bia had to cancel her participation in ADCC the same year.

Bia had already experienced a miraculous comeback from an accident once before. At age twelve, she sustained a broken leg when a car hit the motorcycle she and her mom were riding on. At the time, doctors told her that she'd never do jiu-jitsu again. But incredibly, she was back on the mat again after a few short months.

By the time she tore her hamstring, Bia was a two-time world champion and her career as an athlete was in full swing. Her first thought when it happened was, *Oh, my God, what am I going to do now?* The recovery was, indeed, hard. She had to abstain from training for six months. She gained weight from a lack of mobility, and she fought her own thoughts much more than she had after the motorcycle accident. With her surgeon reluctant to guarantee a full recovery, Bia almost obsessed about eventually returning to the mat, thinking, *I want to come back at a hundred percent. I just want to go back.* Bia told me, "The hamstring accident really affected my mind because I was at the height of my career as a black belt." She found herself doubting whether she could return to her pre-injury championship form.

Bia is a champion through and through. Once again, she overcame the odds. *Only one year* after the hamstring tear, surgery, and rehabilitation, she won the PanAms and the World Championship in 2014, both in her weight category and in the open class, black belt level.

BEHIND THE SCENES
A STRONG SUPPORT SYSTEM

Unlike many other jiu-jitsu athletes, Bia has very supportive parents. She recalled how, when she was younger, her dad tried to find sponsors for her trips to the PanAms or Worlds. At the same time, her mom took care of administrative business, such as registering her for competitions. When she was in college and wondering whether she should pick a profession that would guarantee a solid income, her parents reminded her, "You love jiu-jitsu, right? Then you will make it."

Bia decided to leave Brazil for the United States at the beginning of 2018. Moving away from home and putting six thousand miles between herself and her family was hard, but she likes her new hometown of San Diego. The Southern California city reminds her of Saquarema.

"It is calm. There's jiu-jitsu. Everybody is friendly, and I just love going to the beach."

The person she relies on in San Diego is her trainer, Leticia Ribeiro, who instills confidence in her by saying, "You can do it. Look how many times you've been training and competing! You've always done really well, and you will do it again."

When athletes like Bia are successful year after year, outside observers often deny them credit for the effort it took to reach the top. After she had won a couple of times, Bia noticed people often said, "Oh, yeah, of course you won again! I knew you would." She has never appreciated this kind of nonchalance. She thinks, *They knew it? What the heck? Not even I knew I would win!*

What she does know is how hard she prepares during the four to eight weeks leading up to each tournament. In training camp, a typical day includes one hour of physical training in the morning, a jiu-jitsu session at noon, and another one in the evening to go over technique, tips, and positions. She applies the same routine Monday through Friday and trains a little less hard on Saturdays. On Sundays, she does yoga, cardio, or another form of workout—but no jiu-jitsu. "This gets my mind fresh for Monday," she explained.

BEST ADVICE

When I asked this question, Bia had an immediate answer. In fact, the champion sees this particular advice from parents and coaches as crucial: *believe in yourself!* For Bia, this means feeling confident about her training and knowing how much she wants to be successful. "When I go into a tournament," she said, "I think how hard I worked to be there and that I'm really going to make the ten-minute match worth the training effort. I remind myself how much I want to be there and that I want this title more than anyone else."

WORST ADVICE

While she didn't give me any specific worst advice moments in her life, it's a good thing Bia didn't listen to her doctors' timelines. She carved her own path, and because of that she is the Lady GOAT (greatest of all time) that we all know today.

FINAL THOUGHTS
BRINGING JIU-JITSU TO MMA

A misconception people seem to have about Bia is that she might not be friendly. This seems a bit odd to me because I found her to be extremely warm and personable. She was polite, welcoming, and super generous with her time. People see her before fights in her Gi or NoGi uniform with her eyes closed, headphones on, and a straight but intimidating face. Later, they say, "I was scared to talk to you. I didn't know that you're actually nice." Bia laughs in response. "I was competing," she tells them. "I can't be smiling for my opponent if I want to kill her on the mat." Point well taken.

At the time of our interview, Bia was thinking about possibly transitioning to mixed martial arts, where she would primarily be using her jiu-jitsu to win matches. Her goal would be to introduce BJJ to a much bigger MMA audience.

"I want to show the world how amazing jiu-jitsu is in real fighting."

CHAPTER 8

Gordon Ryan

@gordonlovesjiujitsu
@kingryanbjj
facebook.com/gordon.ryan.754

Gordon Ryan is to jiu-jitsu what Floyd Mayweather is to boxing—the bad boy of his sport. On social media, he is a brash trash-talker, and often gets into intense verbal sparring with nearly all other athletes and trolling fans alike.

That said, there's no denying his accomplishments, particularly his rapid ascent to the top. Born in New Jersey in 1995, his breakout moment was winning the 2016 Eddie Bravo International Championship. En route to the title, he submitted every single opponent, including World Champion Yuri Simões and grappler Rustam Chsiev. This victory was especially notable because Gordon had started training jiu-jitsu only five years earlier, and was a relatively new black belt. Prior to his graduation by Garry Tonon, Gordon had been a brown belt for only six months.

In 2017, Gordon defeated Dillon Danis, Romulo Barral, Xande Ribeiro, and Keenan Cornelius to win ADCC in the under-88-kilogram (approximately under-194-pound) division. In the Absolute Division, he submitted all of his opponents except for Felipe Pena, who he lost to in the final. Gordon also successfully defended his EBI title. In 2018, he won his weight class and the Absolute Division at the IBJJF Pan NoGi. At the IBJJF NoGi Worlds in California, he took gold in both divisions.

In 2019, Gordon faced a series of injuries but still won big. While competing at the KASAI Super Series in January, he hurt his knee several times during a superfight against João Gabriel Rocha. Gordon won the match, but ultimately discovered he had torn his LCL, which required surgery. In September of the same year, only days before ADCC, he came down with the stomach flu. Even worse, at almost the exact same time, Gordon fractured his hand in a freak electric bike accident. One of his tires had gone flat, so the champion hoisted the bike onto his shoulders to carry it. Gordon didn't realize that the e-motor was still running. When he accidentally hit the throttle, his hand was pulled into the gap between the fender and the tire, resulting in a fracture, cuts, and swelling.

I already find it incredible that Gordon could overcome such a severe knee injury in just eight months, but to know he then went on to win double gold at ADCC with a heavily bandaged hand while recovering from the flu is astonishing.

Gordon and I met for our interview in October 2018 at the Renzo Gracie Academy in New York City, where he trains and teaches. It is located at 224 W. 30th St., New York, NY 10001. Our interview was spread over the course of two separate days, and both conversations took place in the famous "blue basement" of the academy. Given Gordon's ominous reputation and the colorful history of the room with its blue mats and blue walls, it felt fitting that we met for the first time on Halloween Day.

Our first interview was cut short when Gordon received and agreed to a last-minute request to fill in for another instructor. I was struck by his professionalism. The self-proclaimed "King" obviously didn't believe that teaching a class was beneath him. Moreover, Gordon immediately offered to make himself available to me the following day in order to complete our interview.

In the thirty minutes I sat with him, Gordon came across as a well-spoken, approachable athlete who is undoubtedly obsessively dedicated to the sport. Toward the end of our interview, I asked if he sometimes feels misunderstood because of the type of trash-talking posts he does online. Gordon made no excuses, but did offer an interesting explanation for why people dislike him. In Gordon's opinion, people mistake his presentation online for who he actually is, rather than an act. Without the opportunity to get to know him face-to-face, others see the persona rather than the person. He was insistent and didn't hold back as he told me, "On the internet, I'm loud, and I attack everybody, but when people meet me in person, they go, 'Oh, you're cool! You're soft-spoken.' They don't really understand the difference between a persona and the actual personality."

- For several videos of his fights, go to YouTube and search "Gordon Ryan."
- To see an extensive list of his accomplishments, go to *Wikipedia.com*.
- For a comprehensive library of his instructional videos, go to *BJJFanatics.com*.

EARLY LIFE
A LESSON IN HUMILITY

Gordon's path to jiu-jitsu began in after-school daycare when his teacher suggested he watch a 1994 UFC video. On it was footage of a famous fight in which Royce Gracie defeated Keith Hackney within the first five-and-a-half minutes of the first round. Gordon told me he watched that entire fight with his jaw dropped. After watching it, he knew. *This is what I'm going to do when I grow up. I'm going to be a professional fighter.*

The daycare teacher had no jiu-jitsu training but kept bringing in martial arts videos for the kids to watch. This teacher also had them drilling kimuras, armbars, and other submissions. Gordon recalled how they would "gather up in a circle, wrestle around, and just beat each other up."

This went on for years until 2011, when Gordon came across Ricardo Almeida's Brunswick BJJ school while running errands with his mom. He began training with Miguel Benitez, who was still a blue belt, and stayed with him until switching to Garry Tonon a few years later.

As he described his first six months in jiu-jitsu, Gordon admitted that he must have been a horrible training partner. He was, as he put it, "a teenager trying to kill forty-year-old men after watching a few UFC fights." He laughed and I could tell he was a bit embarrassed, maybe even regretful. Perhaps because I was approaching forty years old and he remembered as he told his story I would've been the exact age of one of his victims? "I would just go in and go as hard as I possibly could."

In the beginning, things seemed easy for him. People treated him gently, and while he may have lacked technique, Gordon made up for it with confidence. He grinned and shook his head as he told me, "I literally thought, *There's no one on the planet who's better than me at jiu-jitsu*. And that was without ever having trained!"

A lesson in humility awaited him. Once Gordon's game improved, his partners started treating him like less of a beginner. The increase in difficulty was noticeable, and he began to doubt whether he was actually as good as he had initially thought. The final reckoning came as he was reviewing videos of his matches from one of his first tournaments. Gordon had been under the impression that he was executing everything beautifully. The footage offered him a reality check.

"I thought, *Wow, I suck at this. My movements are all over the place*," Gordon admitted.

ON PRESSURE AND ANXIETY
IT'S ABOUT CONTROL

For all of his seemingly limitless confidence, Gordon still feels nervous before tournaments. He told me, "Until I get on the mat, I'm nervous for a little bit. There's nothing you can do to really get rid of those nerves, but you can control them." Gordon tells himself the audience has come to see *him* fight, that his opponent is basically screwed, and that he's prepared. "Once I'm on the mat," he explained, "I'm ready to go. I'm like, this is just what we do every day. Just in a different setting. So, I'm kind of relaxed."

While he has rarely lost a fight, Gordon knows defeat can happen to him any day.

"You always have to remember that, at the highest levels, anybody can win on any given day. It's just a matter of who's more on point. And, unless you're Mayweather, you have to accept the fact that you're gonna lose. How you handle that loss is what's going to define you as a champion. Whether you win or lose, you should be doing the same things."

Gordon shows up for training and teaching no matter what happens the weekend of competition. On the rare occasion when he's lost a tournament on Saturday, he'll wake up at 5:45 a.m. to start his day the Monday right after. It's no different if he wins. He doesn't take a month or two off to feel good and celebrate; it's hard work as usual. On this topic, Gordon told me, "For me it's just—if I lose, I'm pissed and want to get better. If I win, I'm pissed I didn't submit everybody or that I didn't have a perfect performance. Either way, I still want to go back to the gym on Monday morning...to get better."

BECOMING A CHAMPION
MONEY AND FIGHTING ADVERSITY

Gordon has faced his share of adversity. After graduating from high school with no money and not much of a plan, he took a job as a garbage man. He described the work as "just throwing trash bags into the back of a truck for a year." His goal was to save up enough money to lease a car to drive into New York City for daily BJJ training. Until then, Gordon had to rely on his coach and mentor, Garry Tonon, to drive him into the city and to pay for tolls, parking, and gas—a monthly bill of about $2,000.

Gordon certainly knows how much of his success he owes to Garry, who is only four years older than him. Gordon feels grateful for his support. He told me, "I literally had no money saved after high school. Garry, at the time, was just starting his professional career. He was in college and doing sixteen or eighteen credits a semester. He had rented his own apartment, and he was basically paying his rent by winning $1,000 Absolute tournaments. Still, he was taking the time to drive me into the city whenever I was free. He was a huge part of my development."

As a purple belt, Gordon eventually started winning small amounts of prize money here and there. It wasn't until he received a check for $25,000 at EBI that he felt he could make grappling his career.

Money aside, Gordon's greatest challenge has been his health. Late in his career, he was diagnosed with MRSA, a virulent skin infection, twice in as many months. The medication he was prescribed helped the infection, but caused severe acid reflux. He felt nauseous for months.

"From the time I woke up to the time I went to sleep, I was just nauseous," Gordon said, making a face at the memory. "I couldn't eat. I lost twenty-five pounds. Every time I would go to do jiu-jitsu or go to lift, I would get nauseous. I couldn't train."

Taking a prescription anti-nausea drug made things more manageable, but even six months after the MRSA infection had cleared, the nausea still flared up sometimes. As I listened to Gordon tell this story, I found myself admiring how he didn't use bad experiences or injuries as an excuse. He could have quit or skipped training and dropped out of tournaments because he wasn't feeling well. Instead, he did what every single winner in any field does: Gordon showed up and did the work.

A dedicated student of the sport, he frequently watches recordings of other people fighting. The athlete he studied most during his first years of training was Keenan Cornelius. At the time, Keenan was his favorite grappler. "He was the person I watched coming up as a blue and purple belt because he was a tall, lanky American dude just like me. He was also pretty flexible, and I saw that we have the same game."

When I asked Gordon about his toughest opponent, he named none other than Felipe Pena. Felipe impresses Gordon because he is well-rounded and has particular strengths others lack. When he talked about Felipe, Gordon's respect for the

Brazilian's game shone through his every word: "He's probably the physically strongest person I've competed against. He's not very explosive. He just has a weird isometric strength that you feel and where you go, *This guy's strong*. He's a big guy, and for a big guy he has a very good guard. He has a hard guard to pass. He's very good at passing. He has a good submission defense and offense. He actually goes out and finishes people. But the thing he does better than almost anybody in the world is he has a true gift for getting to the most dominant position in the sport, which is taking people's backs."

Gordon told me he appreciates that Felipe can get out of any bad position and is willing to risk injury. "I saw a match with him and Erberth Santos once. Erberth almost broke Felipe's arm in half. Felipe falls to the mat, and he still doesn't tap. You have a guy who's good at *everything*—really good at taking the back—and on top of that, he's willing to take breaks to get a win."

BEHIND THE SCENES

HARD WORK, NERVES, NO EXCUSES

Everyone sees the accomplishments of successful athletes like Gordon, but few look at what it takes to make it happen. His fast ascent to being the best NoGi grappler is, if anything, a testament to the value of hard work. He has a no-excuses mentality, he studies the game relentlessly, and he is willing to practice movements over and over to get them right. *He sleeps on the mat with a hoodie over his head and uses his lunchbox for a pillow.* I saw it with my own eyes the day I interviewed him.

The man literally lives in the gym. Some say they want to be the best, and some do the things that are required to be the best. As they say, the secret is: there is no secret.

On the first day of our interview—and this was a typical day for him—he got up at 5:45 a.m., ate breakfast, and took the subway from his apartment to the academy for a 7:45 a.m. class with John Danaher. They did about forty-five minutes of drilling and forty minutes of rolling. After taking a fifteen-minute break, he did one hour of MMA drills with John, taught an hour-long private lesson at 10:30 a.m., then showered and ate. He rested for fifteen minutes before taking another class with John at 12:30 p.m. They drilled for an additional forty-five minutes and trained for another forty minutes until about 3:00 p.m.

After that, he watched Garry Tonon (who now has a budding MMA career) do MMA sparring until about 4:00 p.m., ate again, and napped until 5:00 p.m. He taught a second private lesson from 5:00 p.m. to 6:00 p.m., talked to me until 7:00 p.m., taught a class from 7:30 p.m. to 9:00 p.m., and then went to train some more afterward. "There are definitely no easy days," he says. "But *people who are successful are people who get shit done.* If you just sit around and feel sorry for yourself all day, no one's going to care. You're just going to be another regular guy."

Earlier, I mentioned that his haters like to portray Gordon as an almost insufferable person. Online, Gordon may be a trash-talker and denigrator, but on the mat, he shows respect for opponents in ways other athletes don't. He is willing to fight under nearly any set of rules. If he's challenging someone and they don't want to allow heel hooks, he'll respond, "Fine. You know I'm good at heel hooks, but let's take it out." On the mat, he is a gracious winner as well. After beating an opponent by submission, they raise Gordon's hand and that's it. He will be face-to-face with his opponent, and there's no screaming, no hand waving, no jumping up and down.

However, when I asked him what he believes is the public's most common misconception about him, Gordon went in an entirely different direction. He said people don't realize that he wins not simply because of strength but because he is *jiu-jitsu smart*.

"Most people just think I'm some big, tall dude who's strong. But I think as far as understanding the concepts of jiu-jitsu, I'm one of the most intelligent people in NoGi grappling."

Gordon explained that only people who have watched him train, taken private sessions with him, or attended his seminars see his intelligence. To make his qualities as a fighter known to a wider audience, he has begun posting clips of instructional videos online. Aside from John Danaher, Gordon is probably the bestselling grappler on *BJJFanatics.com*. This is not only because of the price point he can command but also his frequent posts to social media about his sales.

Gordon's rise to the top has been incredibly fast, and he knows he could simply retire from competing, open a school, teach seminars around the world, and make more money than most people. "I don't really have anything left to prove," he said. "I had the most successful ADCC debut in history, and people have made a lot more than me off a lot less."

But he has bigger dreams and aspirations. He says he "got roped into grappling" when he first started fighting, but his goal was never to be just the greatest of all time in any single discipline. "My goal was always to be the best *fighter* of all time," he emphasized.

BEST ADVICE

The best advice Gordon ever received came from coach John Danaher: work just as hard or even harder mentally than you do physically. Gordon went on to describe a well-known martial arts fallacy, one where some people believe that if you're the toughest guy, you'll win—you just have to be physically strong and train hard. He compared combat martial arts to college: "You actually have to *study it*, and the person with the most technique and the most knowledge wins."

Gordon suggests training mentally by studying videos, reflecting after each training session, and being creative during rolls. He described the time he blew out his knee against Gabriel Rocha. During recovery, his movement was extremely limited. The injury not only required reconstructive surgery, it also kept him in a wheelchair (and then on crutches) for a long time. How is it that he got *better* at his game while not being able to train? The answer is through study. Despite being sidelined, Gordon relentlessly leaned into his studying, harder than he had before the injury. Gordon knew that was what it would take if he wanted to return from his injury as if he'd never stopped training. He studied film at home and at the academy. He continued teaching and sold out seminars from his wheelchair.

Gordon's ability to explain a position without simultaneously being physically involved in the movements is a sign of his true understanding of the martial art's mechanics. This, in turn, makes his transfer of information even more effective. He is certainly one of the best instructors I have ever worked with.

Gordon told me he urges athletes to stay on top of developments in the sport. To illustrate the pace of change in jiu-jitsu, he used the military as an example. "You take jiu-jitsu in 1994 and compare it to now, and people have gotten better—not because everyone got tougher, but because they know more. It's just like the US military of 1965. If you compare it to the 2018 US military, it will get crushed. They just have better technology now, just like we have better technology in our sport."

He warned that athletes who "get comfortable beating people and then kind of coast on that" will fall behind. "Literally every week," he explained, "we're changing and getting better. I do a seminar tour somewhere for two weeks, and when I return to the academy here in NYC, there's a whole bunch of new shit that people are doing, where I go, 'What is this?'"

Staying on top of new developments is mental work too, and it takes dedication. Gordon told me, "Mental work is the hardest to do. That's why people try to avoid it as much as they can."

WORST ADVICE

When I asked Gordon about the worst advice he's ever received, he answered without hesitation, "Just believe in yourself." He once again used a military analogy as he explained how sending soldiers into a war with the instruction to "believe in themselves" without superior equipment would just get everyone killed. Gordon cited historical battles where one side claimed victory in a very short time thanks to the use of more advanced tools. He shared a story John Danaher once told him about the British attacking members of the Matabele tribe with Maxim machine guns. At the time, the weapon was a recent invention, and the Matabele warriors had only spears and rifles to fight back. Only four British soldiers were killed, but sixteen hundred tribesmen lost their lives.

Gordon went on to say, "You need to believe in yourself, yes. But unless you have an actual game plan and the knowledge and skills necessary to execute your plan, self-belief isn't going to be nearly enough to get you where you want."

FINAL THOUGHTS
GOALS FOR THE SPORT

Gordon wants jiu-jitsu to receive more recognition. His ultimate goal is to ensure that jiu-jitsu athletes get paid to compete at the highest level rather than just receiving a medal. "We're going in and fighting four fights to win $1,000," he explained, shaking his head. "That's less than desirable. I think jiu-jitsu athletes should start to get paid as real athletes."

One reason they aren't getting paid is that jiu-jitsu doesn't have the lucrative spectator sport status of football or basketball. "No one's going to pay you $50,000 for grappling if they're only going to sell five tickets for people to watch you," Gordon said. His plan for reaching bigger audiences begins with making wins in jiu-jitsu about submissions rather than advantage. He told me, "As an amateur athlete, all you have to worry about is winning. As a professional athlete, you have to worry about not only winning, but being exciting for a crowd to watch so that people actually want to pay you. One way to be exciting is to go and get submissions. At the end of the day, a submission in our sport is like a knockout in boxing."

He wants people to realize how hard it is to submit top fighters and how comparatively easy it is to win by an advantage or to win a tactical match. "People go into jiu-jitsu matches, and they take submissions when they're available," he said. "When someone gives you something, you take it. Great. But guys like Marcelo, guys like Roger, they *take* submissions from people. They expose your limbs, they expose necks, they expose arms, and they finish people. That's what we should be pushing our students to do."

Gordon told me all of this in October 2018. Since then, many things have happened. On August 7, 2022, on Tezos' WNO show, Gordon and Felipe Pena fought for a third time in a hotly anticipated match. The night before, one of Felipe Pena's best friends, jiu-jitsu legend Leandro Lo, was shot in the head and killed while at a concert in Brazil. It shook the entire jiu-jitsu community on the eve of one of the most anticipated rematches of all time. There are rumors about what was said on each side prior to the match, and of course there was controversy and finger-pointing on both ends. But the event went on and, sadly, there was a lot of bad blood afterward. Ultimately, Gordon forced Felipe to quit in less than forty-five minutes of a no-time-limit match.

In the end, Gordon has grown into the most dominant NoGi grappler of all time. He has made strides in the sport by getting athletes in jiu-jitsu paid like they never have before, and opening up opportunities for others to get sponsorship deals and more. This summer, the ADCC will be in Las Vegas again, and Gordon has the richest endorsement ever signed by a BJJ athlete—a $100,000 deal to wear the Bitcoin Cash logo on his rash guard during the event.

Say what you want about him, but Gordon is doing what he said he would do, and he's doing it in record fashion.

CHAPTER 9
Bernardo Faría

bernardofariaacademy.com, bjjfanatics.com
◎ @bernardofariabjj
🐦 @bernardofariajj
ⓕ facebook.com/bernardofariabjj

One of the greatest super heavyweights to ever compete, Bernardo Faria is a five-time black belt IBJJF World Champion and is an IBJJF European, Pan-American, and Brazilian National Champion.

Born in 1987 in Juiz de Fora, Minas Gerais, Brazil, Bernardo received all belts in his hometown and from the same professor, Ricardo Marques. After receiving his black belt in 2009, he relocated to the Alliance Jiu-Jitsu headquarters in São Paulo to train with Fábio Gurgel. Only one year later, he won the coveted IBJJF World Championship for the first time.

In 2013, Bernardo moved to New York City to train and teach at Marcelo Garcia's Academy. A passionate teacher, Bernardo opened his own academy when he moved to the Boston area in 2017. He subsequently retired from competition and co-founded *BJJFanatics.com, the* premier website for jiu-jitsu instructional content, videos, and DVDs. Bernardo posts free instructional material on his YouTube channel and has been followed by more than 249,000 subscribers.

Our interview took place over the phone in 2019, but it felt relaxed from the start. While most of the interviews included in this book were set up via social media or email, Bernardo was different. I randomly sat next to him at the 2019 World Championships, and was able to introduce myself. He was nice enough to agree to be in the book. Bernardo is approachable, thoughtful, and a great storyteller. I got some good laughs out of our one-hour conversation.

The Bernardo Faria Academy is located in Bedford, Massachusetts, at 131A Great Road, Bedford, MA 01730.

- To watch him compete, go to YouTube and search "Bernardo Faria."
- For a comprehensive library of his instructional videos, go to *BJJFanatics.com.*
- To learn more about his academy, go to *bernardofariaacademy.com.*

EARLY LIFE
IF YOU BUILD IT, THEY WILL COME

One of Bernardo's older brothers liked to grapple with friends at the Faria family home. As Bernardo watched, he noticed the smallest one of his brother's friends tended to win these fights time and time again.

That guy was a jiu-jitsu blue belt.

The day after a quarrel between his brother and this friend, Bernardo went to inquire about lessons. Only fourteen years old at the time, and completely unaware that the quality of instruction would differ from school to school, he tried his luck at the gym where he already trained weightlifting. Why would he train weights at one facility only to have to pack up and visit another to train BJJ?

So, there he was at the weightlifting gym. He approached the front desk with a big smile and even bigger eyes. "How can I sign up for jiu-jitsu?" he asked.

The response he received was less than helpful. The employee handed him a class schedule and gave no further advice. Bernardo felt brushed off and a bit deflated.

But the future champion didn't give up. As fate would have it, the lukewarm dismissal Bernardo had experienced at that gym put him on a much better path, where, as it turned out, a whole new set of opportunities awaited him.

Together with a friend, Bernardo approached another school. When the two boys asked about lessons for fourteen-year-olds, the instructor, Ricardo Marques, told them he'd create a new class just for them. "It's going to be Mondays, Wednesdays, and Fridays at 5:00 p.m.," Ricardo said.

The story reminded me of the motto, "If you build it, they will come." Ricardo's customer-friendly business attitude certainly went a long way, and it paid off many times over. This turned out to be the start of Ricardo's youth program, and classes for children soon followed.

For Bernardo, it was the start of his training to become a world champion.

Bernardo has been on a jiu-jitsu journey ever since he first started training in 2001. He told me, "You're only going to make progress in anything if you keep on learning, right? Even in jiu-jitsu, if you're winning a tournament, it's probably because you've been learning new techniques or how to be more confident."

As a teenager, he sacrificed everything to improve his game, but he was happy because he was making progress. "Some people might feel very bored if they train for ten years and they can't do any dating or partying. It's a very strict life," he admitted. "But I got obsessive about jiu-jitsu because the feeling that I am learning and getting better at something makes me happy."

That resonated with something I learned from brain performance expert Jim Kwik. On a recent podcast, Kwik described how, in psychology, there's something called a *competence-confidence loop*. He explains, "The more competent and skilled you get at something, the more confident you feel doing it. And because you're more confident, you're more likely to do it, which, in turn, makes you get better at it and so on."

ON PRESSURE AND ANXIETY
TWO INNER VOICES

Until he was a brown belt, Bernardo pursued his passion for BJJ with little interest from home. His dad initially advised against a career in jiu-jitsu because he worried it wouldn't be possible to make a good living—and understandably so. Bernardo has two brothers, and the assumption in his family was always that all three boys would find work as lawyers, doctors, or engineers. In fact, one brother did become an engineer and another became a doctor, but neither brother was Bernardo.

Instead, he held onto his jiu-jitsu dream. After his battle with appendicitis in 2007, he finally saw his father's attitude change.

"When my dad visited me in the hospital and saw how upset I was about maybe missing Worlds, he understood how much I wanted to do jiu-jitsu. He has supported me since then, and now he's my biggest fan. He's my best friend."

When I asked Bernardo about his time as a competitor, he told me that he prepared hard for every tournament. That meant there was always a lot on the line. "I didn't just want to throw that in the trash," he recalled.

He told me he remembers feeling nervous before every single match, though his anxiety was much higher when he participated in his first few tournaments. The way he sees it, nervousness is essential. "If you're completely relaxed, it's because you don't care if you win or lose."

Bernardo described going into tournaments and matches with two competing voices in his head. There was a loser's voice and a winner's voice. One would tell him that he was in trouble. The other would say, "This is my day. I'm going to win, no matter what." The challenge was always to feed the winner's voice and silence the loser.

That said, Bernardo thought about quitting more than once. His triggers included health issues and other factors. "Everybody gets to that point," he told me with a sense of acceptance. "But that's the loser's voice talking."

That first health crisis of appendicitis left Bernardo unable to train for twelve weeks afterward. When it seemed like he might have to miss Worlds he thought, *If I don't go to Worlds this year, it's one year lost in my career.* He did compete in the championship, but the next year, things got even harder.

In 2008, he had to skip Worlds because of a torn meniscus and elbow surgery. At the same time, he was finishing college and facing a choice about his future. Should he stay in his hometown, Juiz de Fora? Should he move to São Paulo? Or should he move to the United States and pursue a career in jiu-jitsu?

His relocation to São Paulo in 2009 didn't necessarily make things easier. During the first six months, he was living in a very poor neighborhood far from Fabio Gurgel's school. Bernardo had to take three buses each way to get there and back.

Plus, he lost in every single tournament.

"I didn't win anything," he explained, "and so I questioned myself. *This is a hard life! What am I doing here?*" But even then, his winner's voice spoke up to steer him true. It told him, *Don't quit now! Just go a little bit further!*

When Bernardo finally did start to think about retiring from competing, he didn't simply follow an impulse; he transitioned into the next phase of his career. "I continued to compete at the highest level, even after I started doing the online stuff, and I had my most successful year in 2015. Then, little by little, I spent more time and motivation on the internet than on training. And eventually I said, 'One more Worlds, and then I'll quit.'"

Bernardo is glad that he never gave up in an ill-advised spur of the moment. His advice for dealing with thoughts about quitting is, "Sometimes in life we have to quit, yes. But do think it through first. Wait one more month. Wait six months. Just don't get stuck doing nothing waiting for the next move."

BECOMING A CHAMPION
THE ORIGIN OF BJJ FANATICS

Bernardo's transition from successful athlete to successful business owner is not unheard of. In fact, owning your own BJJ academy is common among top fighters and, in that respect, Bernardo is no different. However, *BJJFanatics.com* is a game changer. There, Bernardo provides a free clip of an instructional video for Instagram every day. He also partners with the industry's top athletes to help promote their best moves online for a fee. Naturally, I was interested to hear about the origins of this project, because like most challenges, they can reveal amazing new journeys.

Of all things, this great story of success started with an injury. Late in 2013, Bernardo was living in New York City and feeling somewhat frustrated with his life. He was training up to three hours a day and teaching for at least as long. Because there was some inconsistency to his schedule, he occasionally experienced long stretches of downtime with nothing to do. "I was pretty much spending my free time just checking people's Instagram and seeing their lives," he said in a dejected tone.

After his meniscus surgery in December and reinjuring himself at the 2014 Pan-Ams, Bernardo found things were only getting worse. "I wanted to find something I could do in my free time, where I could be productive when I wasn't training or teaching," he explained.

Enter Michael Zenga. A big fan of Bernardo's half guard, Michael invited Bernardo to do a training session with him in Boston and create a jiu-jitsu DVD. Bernardo left Massachusetts much wiser. Michael had shared with him his secrets for doing business online and encouraged him to promote himself via a YouTube channel and social media. The idea was that an online presence would result in more invitations to seminars and tournaments. Such visibility could potentially drive students toward his school if he were to open one.

Grateful for something to do in his free time, Bernardo jumped into learning about Facebook ads and internet traffic. He read the books Michael recommended, including one by Tim Ferriss that has also played a huge role in my life, *The 4-Hour Workweek*. He and Michael began trading knowledge about BJJ and marketing strategies. Before long, they partnered to create a website for the sale of instructional DVDs: *BJJFanatics.com*.

Bernardo told me it is no coincidence that the next year, 2015, was the best year of his career as a fighter. He earned double gold at the Pan-Ams and double gold at Worlds. Prior to running the website, he had always felt immense pressure going into competitions. He would tell himself, *I cannot lose because jiu-jitsu is the only thing I have. It is my only way to make a living.*

While the website was small in the beginning, having this side project changed Bernardo's thinking. He said, "I fought better because I didn't feel the pressure that jiu-jitsu was the only thing that I had anymore. And I had less free time to worry about how good my opponents were."

I found the whole story really inspiring. After his injury, Bernardo thought, *Man, this sucks.* He experienced self-doubt and worries about the potential loss of his competitive edge—and even his career—but then he found another way to be productive. From the challenge grew a new opportunity.

A thousand lessons could be derived from Bernardo's experience, but a common thread woven through the journey of every amazing person I interviewed for this book is this: *keep moving.*

BEHIND THE SCENES
LESSONS LEARNED FROM JIU-JITSU

When I asked him how the lessons he learned from practicing jiu-jitsu have translated to other parts of his life, Bernardo answered without a moment's hesitation. He said, "Everything I do in my life right now is based on the experience I have through jiu-jitsu. All theories I have about life come from jiu-jitsu." Beyond this very general and heartfelt response, he also gave me examples of more specific lessons.

1. Everything Is Temporary

One major lesson he learned is that nothing lasts forever. All things are temporary. On any given day, if he's not feeling motivated, he reminds himself how showing up for training will bring back excitement for the sport. He said, "I think about the days where I didn't want to go train, but then I'd train anyway. Two days later, I was always excited to go and win the tournament on the weekend." After a pause, Bernardo added, "There will be bad days, but just keep doing what you're doing."

There were times when he'd be training really poorly before a tournament but win every single fight on the weekend. Then, there were times where the opposite was true. "Sometimes the training would be amazing," he insisted. "I was the lion of the gym. Nobody could beat me. Then I would compete in the tournament and lose in the first match. So now, when things are going very well, I tell myself, *Don't get too excited because it doesn't mean anything.* And if things are going badly, I'm like, *Don't get too upset because this also doesn't mean anything.*"

Yes, it's important to care about the outcome of a tournament or a match, but it is also important to stay sane and grounded if things change. The lesson is to not get attached to feeling good or bad about something because everything can and *will* change over time. Resting on our results is a dangerous trap that breeds long-term unhappiness because we then attach our results to our process, and the process is actually the most important part. Emotions are fleeting. They come and go like the seasons, and getting attached to an emotion, whether that emotion is tied to an outcome or not, can lead us to mistakenly think we need to control and maintain that emotion forever. Detaching from the idea that it's critical to remain happy will free you from expectations, which can lead to disappointment and feelings of failure. In other words, control what you can, and let the rest go!

2. Don't Settle for Less

Competing at the highest level taught Bernardo to bring confidence to everything else he does or wants to pursue. "Anything you do at the highest level," he told me, "is going to change you. It's going to mold you in different ways. It's going to make you think in different ways."

He recalled competing as a blue, purple, and brown belt, and how he saw people with black belts as superheroes. *How do they do it?* he used to ask himself. Looking toward Worlds, he thought merely making it to the semifinals and taking third place would be amazing.

When he received his black belt, his instructor convinced him to leave his hometown to train at Fábio Gurgel's school in São Paulo. Bernardo did, and he gained immediate access to athletes like Michael Langhi, Sergio Moraes, and Tarsis Humphreys. He eventually learned that they weren't that different from him, after all.

"I started seeing that I was on that level as well," he said excitedly. "That raised my confidence through the roof."

Yet even after the move to São Paulo, Bernardo still had an important lesson to learn: don't settle for less. When he reached the semifinals during Worlds 2009, he fought Roger Gracie. Before their match, Bernardo was already mentally celebrating—*I'm going to get at least third place!* Of course, those limiting thoughts transformed into a self-fulfilling prophecy. Gracie beat Bernardo and, as a result, Bernardo placed third.

By 2010, he was done settling for less. *I don't want to get third place again*, he told himself. *If I get third place I'm going to go out of here crying and completely frustrated.*

That year, Bernardo won the title: Black Belt World Champion.

Training near so many athletes who were actually winning completely changed Bernardo's mentality. In the span of a year, he went from a willingness to settle for third place to believing he could win the top spot. This shift in attitude led to better results in major tournaments.

It also presented Bernardo with another valuable lesson, and that is to surround ourselves with the people we want to be like. We are the average of the five people we spend the most time with. Of course, good company alone will not create success—the work still needs to be done! I would venture to say it's not that the top people elevate you to be great. Rather, they allow you to see *they are also human*, which means you can accomplish greatness too. Again, your success is not promised, but it does give you permission to step into your own profound capabilities.

BEST ADVICE

When he won his first world title in 2010, Bernardo expected his financial life to change drastically. He thought he'd move and open a school or receive offers from sponsors and people who wanted him to teach seminars.

But nothing happened.

His phone didn't ring once and doubt began to creep in. *I need to make money*, he thought. *What am I going to do with my life?*

At the time, Fábio Gurgel stepped in with wise words. "Be patient," he advised Bernardo. "Success is at the very end of the road. You still have a very long road until you're making real money or until you're really successful."

Bernardo understood then that his only job was to focus on training, and he held onto Fábio's advice. Even today, whenever he feels anxious about getting something done fast, he tells himself, *Wait a second! If I don't die, I have all my life to get this done. So, let's just keep going.*

WORST ADVICE

The worst advice came from people that he loved—both his family and friends back home in Brazil. They told him to work nine to five and go to college, which he did. But he also decided to follow his dream of jiu-jitsu. The traditional path is fine, and he has no ill feelings toward anyone who chooses that path, but he definitely prefers his current choice. Bernardo said, "They say life is short, but I think life is also long, right? So if you're going to do something for forty to fifty years, you should really love it!"

FINAL THOUGHTS
A REGULAR GUY

Closing the performance gap between himself and the jiu-jitsu athletes Bernardo used to see as superheroes taught the champion a valuable lesson. In fact, it is one he now takes into his business life: *highly successful people aren't different from anyone else.*

"I see a huge company and the guy who formed it, and it may seem that he is like Superman and much smarter than I am," Bernardo explained. "But I know now that if I ever meet him, he's going to be a regular guy with two arms and two legs." Bernardo says this not to discredit anyone, but rather to instill the belief in himself and others that we are also capable of being our own Superman (or Superwoman, for that matter).

Despite his celebrated status in BJJ, Bernardo wants others to see him as a regular, hard-working guy who wants to succeed. Throughout his life, he's seen how others can be left out because they weren't "cool" or considered "winners" by society's standards. For his part, Bernardo has always tried to be mindful, conscientiously treating *everyone* equally, regardless of socioeconomic status.

"I'm not better than anybody," the champion concluded. "I'm just a regular person determined to reach my goals. Maybe I'll succeed, maybe I won't, but I don't see a reason to look down on others."

CHAPTER 10

Rodrigo Cavaca

@rodrigocavaca
facebook.com/rodrigo.cavaca

Born in Santos, São Paulo, Brazil, in 1981, Rodrigo Cavaca was a top fighter in the super heavyweight division. He won the Worlds in 2010 and 2013 when he closed the division with Buchecha, his black belt World Champion student at the time.

Cavaca, as most people call him, is a two-time European and Brazilian National Champion and has become famous for making the painful footlock position popular. He has an impressive figure, with large hands and feet that made me fearful of getting onto the mat with him. But what's even more impressive is his flexibility. He is as flexible as a rooster-weight competitor but brings a hundred more pounds to the scale. Remarkably, this fighter received his black belt from Elcio Figueiredo in 2005, only five years after first trying jiu-jitsu.

Cavaca was initially with an Alliance satellite and then with Integração. Both were in his hometown. After receiving his black belt in 2005, he taught and trained at Brasa in São Paolo. When the team split in 2007, he soon followed instructor Leonardo Vieira to Checkmat, an organization Leonardo founded in 2008. In 2013, Cavaca left Checkmat to lead a team of his own, Zenith, with Robert Drysdale.

Our interview took place in 2019 at the Zenith headquarters in Santos, Brazil. Cavaca and I were friends long before our meeting, but this was a particularly special interview because I learned much more about his story and, ultimately, how hard he worked to earn the coveted world title.

- For a video of Cavaca finishing a match in less than eleven seconds by his infamous footlock, search YouTube for "Rodrigo Cavaca leglock."
- To download a comprehensive library of his techniques, go to *BJJFanatics.com*.

EARLY LIFE
LATE START, FAST PROGRESS

When I think about Cavaca's start in jiu-jitsu, I'm reminded of George Eliot. She once said, "It is never too late to be what you might have been." Being late to a game doesn't mean you can't win. Cavaca was nineteen years old when three of his blue belt friends introduced him to BJJ. He participated in other sports before, especially soccer, but jiu-jitsu had an immediate appeal. "From the moment I put on my gi and started training, things felt different. I knew this is what I wanted for my life," he told me.

Even as a white belt, Cavaca wanted nothing more than to be a champion. He soon started competing, and with every tournament, his hunger to succeed only grew. In 2001, he placed third in Worlds, which motivated him to train harder. When he lost in his 2002 Worlds' semifinal round, he decided to step it up even more.

"I was sure I would win in 2002, but then I didn't. Back home in Santos, I trained twice as hard," Cavaca told me, sitting straight up in his chair and sounding motivated, even as he looked back on that time nearly twenty years later. He trained at the gym all day and did four jiu-jitsu sessions plus conditioning. The next year at purple belt, he submitted everybody by triangle—five matches, five triangles.

As for the blue belt friends who had introduced him to the sport, Cavaca soon bypassed them in jiu-jitsu. And to make the story even more compelling, Cavaca was the one who gave them their black belts as *their* professor.

ON PRESSURE AND ANXIETY
A GRUELING SCHEDULE AND LITTLE MONEY

Cavaca started teaching at Integração in Santos as soon as he was a black belt and continued to train at Brasa in São Paolo. It was a ninety-minute drive from Santos to São Paolo, but Brasa was one of the top teams in the area. That gave him access to athletes like Robert Drysdale, André Galvão, and Lucas Leite. Cavaca's mindset was to win at all costs, and he did what he had to do. After all, the goal was to be a world champion.

His schedule was grueling. For four years, he woke up at 7:00 a.m. to arrive at Integração in Santos by 8:00 a.m. First up was conditioning for ninety minutes. Once finished, he would jump in the car for the ninety-minute commute in heavy traffic to São Paolo, where he trained from noon until 3:00 p.m. Every day, he trained for ninety minutes in gi, and then for ninety minutes in NoGi. After taking a shower and eating lunch, he headed back to Santos to teach three consecutive classes. Finally, at 10:30 p.m., he headed home for the day.

This routine was not only hard to follow, it was also financially draining. Still, he told me he believes it was all worth it. Cavaca found a few sponsors willing to finance his training and transportation. It was just enough for food, gas, and shelter, but it allowed him to deeply immerse himself in the training, "At Brasa, I trained with the best every day, and my level went up," he recalled.

I can't help but scream from the rafters the importance of this lesson. I don't know who first said it, but I'm sure I've heard Tim Ferriss tell me before—and I'm paraphrasing, but it goes something like this: you are the average of the five people you spend the most time with. This doesn't apply only to those people you physically see or speak to; it also goes for people you don't even know. For example, if you consistently read self-improvement books by a single author and spend a majority of your time learning that author's habits, secrets, and techniques, then guess what? He or she is probably in your top five. So, the moral of the story is to ensure your top five people align with who and what you want to be.

Cavaca was used to submitting everyone in Santos during practice rounds, so he was in for a shock when he first started training at Brasa. Cavaca made Robert Drysdale his personal barometer for how much he was learning and how fast he was improving. In fact, during our interview, Cavaca described the man as "a beast" with a tone of total admiration. He went on to say, "In Santos, I never tapped. But when I arrived in São Paolo, Robert submitted me five times within seven minutes in practice. He broke my mind."

Measuring himself against the best helped Cavaca gain confidence. Once he eventually started to beat Robert in training, he knew he had made it. "It gave me power for all the competitions between 2009 and 2013," he said as he looked up at me and his posture straightened a bit. "When I stepped on the mat, I was *ready*. I knew that nobody could beat me. I was nervous, and I put a lot of pressure on myself, but my mind was strong. If somebody scored a point against me, I would get upset and think, *You scored a point? I will kill you.*"

Though he trained hard with Robert, one particular opponent still gave Cavaca a tough time: ultra heavyweight fighter Luiz Felipe Theodoro, also known as Big Mac. Big Mac had a reputation for being nearly invincible. Cavaca recalled how, after he received his black belt in 2005, Professor Elcio told him, "I'm giving this black belt to you, and you're going to beat Big Mac."

Cavaca readily accepted the challenge, but it was harder than he expected. In the two years that followed, Cavaca lost to Big Mac *six times*. Finally, in 2010, Cavaca secured victory. This was their last fight, and Cavaca now laughs when he tells his students, "The last time counts. The others don't."

BECOMING A CHAMPION
FOOTLOCKS CHANGED THE GAME

In 2010, a decade after his introduction to jiu-jitsu, Cavaca won his first black belt world title. The story of his success is also the story of a technique he popularized: the straight footlock.

Cavaca first saw the potential of this position in 2009, while rolling with grappling coach Rolando "Roli" Delgado in Arkansas. After practicing the technique with both Roli and Roli's trainer, Max Bishop, Cavaca creatively adapted their footlock game to the gi. Then, Cavaca trained hard to master the position himself. In one private session, he and Max spent over five hours working on the technique, recording it over and over.

Once he was back in Brazil, Cavaca studied the videos again and again. Once he felt that he really understood the position, he took the technique to his academy, Checkmat BJJ—but didn't tell any of his students about it. When he submitted them one by one with this newfound technique, they were blown away, and asked, "What the *fuck* is this, Cavaca?"

From that point on, the champion became obsessed with teaching straight footlocks. For three months, he and his students practiced nothing else for every single class, five classes a day, six days a week. If you were a brand-new white belt and just paid for a membership that day or that month, guess what? You were learning footlocks—not open guard, not armbars, not fundamentals. Nothing but footlocks.

His students went home limping because of the strain practice put on their Achilles tendons. Even their wrists and forearms were sore, bruised, and beat up from the amount of pressure and repetition required to apply and master the move. But the aches were worth it. "I could see right away how my level and the level of my team improved," he said excitedly. "They started to submit everyone."

When he arrived at Worlds in 2010, Cavaca's opponents still thought he was all about triangles, guard playing, and shoulder locks. Instead, he won the title in his division by submitting three of his opponents via straight footlock. Though he lost the final round in the open division to Roger Gracie, he submitted three other opponents using the same technique. His creativity and relentless focus paid off.

I think Bruce Lee put it best when he said, "I fear not the man who has practiced ten thousand kicks once, but I fear the man who has practiced one kick ten thousand times."

Of course, like any competitive athlete, Cavaca experienced challenges and setbacks throughout his career. Some were health-related and others were financial.

From the very beginning, Cavaca had to scramble for money. Finding sponsors in Santos wasn't easy because many people didn't believe it would be possible to make a living doing jiu-jitsu. To stack the odds further against acquiring sponsorships, no one before him had ever done it *specifically* from Santos, Brazil. He recounted for me a conversation about sponsorships he once had as a purple belt with a local business owner. The guy first asked him, "What do you do?"

"I'm a jiu-jitsu fighter," Cavaca answered.

"What do you need?"

"I need support to continue my training."

"I can give you work in my company," the business owner offered.

"I have work. Jiu-jitsu is my work."

It was one of many times Cavaca left empty-handed, but he never gave up. Eventually, sponsorships came his way.

Cavaca had to face his biggest challenge after winning Worlds in 2010. His knees had been giving him problems since 2007, and after enduring his fifth surgery in 2011, Cavaca couldn't fully train for two years. He seriously considered quitting, but his students, one of whom was Marcus "Buchecha" Almeida's father, Clayton, wouldn't have it. His students urged him to start training again. "You can do it. Everyone believes in you," they insisted.

Once again, he set his eyes on Worlds in 2013. After earning second place in Europeans, Cavaca planned to skip the Abu Dhabi Pro tournament because he didn't have enough money to enter both it and Worlds. However, his students insisted that he not give up. "Cavaca," they told him, "we need to do Abu Dhabi together. We'll help you."

And they did. His support network came through, resulting in a sponsorship lucrative enough to cover the cost of plane tickets. Abu Dhabi was on.

Cavaca ended up closing the bracket with Buchecha in both Abu Dhabi and Worlds, making 2013 a high point in his career. "What I felt then was different from everything I felt before," he said proudly. "Buchecha started with me when he was fourteen years old and a white belt. All of a sudden, we were in the same division and had the same belt. That I could help him get there and still train at a high level myself—it was a crazy feeling. Maybe God gave me this opportunity."

Sadly, the teacher-student duo parted ways shortly after the 2013 tournaments concluded. Cavaca started a new team, Zenith, together with Robert Drysdale, and Buchecha didn't come with him. "We didn't have the power at Zenith to support Buchecha, and I had no right to get in the way of Buchecha's dreams. It was better for him to work on his objectives and stay where he was, with Checkmat," Cavaca explained.

BEHIND THE SCENES

PRIORITIES MATTER (OTHER PEOPLE'S TOO)

Cavaca has been very successful as a fighter and a trainer, and he made it to the top quickly. *He did this by pursuing his passion with laser-sharp focus,* and sacrificed many other things in the process. When he started out at nineteen years old, he said goodbye to parties, alcohol, and friends. Shortly before receiving his black belt, he ended a relationship with a woman he loved. She was older than he was and wanted to start a family. He understood there was a huge conflict in this situation. His dream for a career in jiu-jitsu was at odds with her dream of having a child and starting a family.

"I could see that she was the best girl to be a mother, to have a family," he said sincerely. He paused, shook his head, and then continued, "But it wasn't the right moment for me. When you're married and have a baby, you change the focus. You put it 100 percent on the kid. I had to focus 100 percent on jiu-jitsu."

As I listened to the champion open up about this relationship and why it ended, I could feel the emotion behind Cavaca's words. I can't be sure if it was regret, but his respect for this woman was clear. Cavaca knew if he stayed, pursuing his passion would place him directly in the way of her dreams. Even though she was amazing, Cavaca had to let her go. My respect for him swelled. Cavaca made a selfless choice and refused to let his dream overshadow someone else's.

BEST ADVICE

Cavaca's advice for anyone facing adversity is to stay focused and be disciplined. When his students go to a place of negativity, he reminds them that they need to work hard.

"Stop crying and work! *If you put the bad story in front, you're blocking the way. It stops the dream. Put the bad story behind you and keep going!*"

Cavaca wasn't saying that it is easy to become successful. Anything of value and anything that can make you great will take time. However, experience has also taught him that we have a choice in how we think about *any* situation. "You won't reach your goal until your heart is strong enough to push you there," he explained. "When my students say, 'It is difficult,' I tell them, 'Things aren't difficult. It's your *mind* that makes them difficult.'"

As I listened, I couldn't help but once again be reminded of the stoicism these professionals share. Stoics see obstacles as an opportunity for growth. I'm also reminded of a quote from author and rapper/musician Kanwer Singh, better known as Humble the Poet. In Humble's book *Unlearn* he says, "If you know what you want from life, don't let anyone tell you that it can't be obtained, especially if the one telling you is yourself."

WORST ADVICE

Although Cavaca didn't give me any of his worst advice during our interview, I can tell you he was never a fan of excuses. One of the biggest reasons he was so successful in such a short period of time was his laser focus on moving forward on what he could control. I suspect he would tell me the worst advice would've been something to the effect of, "It's okay, just do it tomorrow!"

FINAL THOUGHTS
YOU DON'T HAVE TO REINVENT THE WHEEL

Cavaca told me something he tries to impress upon his students is the idea that they *don't need to reinvent jiu-jitsu to be successful*. Athletes who have come before can show them the way. Cavaca pointed to his own story as an example. As an athlete, he followed Robert Drysdale's lead to become a world champion. As a gym and association owner, Cavaca traveled a path Fábio Gurgel had first explored. Cavaca explained, "Eighty percent of what they do, I can use for myself. They left a blueprint for us to use, so let's use it."

In other words, as an old mentor of mine used to say, "*Success leaves clues.*"

CHAPTER 11

Michael Langhi

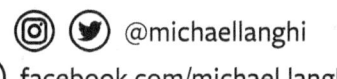
@michaellanghi
facebook.com/michael.langhi

Michael Langhi is one of the most celebrated lightweight champions in jiu-jitsu history. He is considered by many to be the greatest of all time in the lightweight category. He is also one of the select few athletes to have won every major BJJ championship at least twice. He holds four world champion titles, three of them in Gi (2009, 2010, 2015) and one in NoGi (2015). Michael has earned five Pan-American Champion titles (2009, 2010, 2011, 2013, and 2014) and seven European titles (2009, 2010, 2011, 2013, 2014, 2015, and 2018). He is also a five-time Brazilian national champion (2008, 2009, 2013, 2016, and 2017).

Born in São Carlos, São Paulo, Brazil, in 1985, Michael started out as a student under Rubens "Cobrinha" Charles

Maciel (a champion also profiled in this book). Michael was successful in jiu-jitsu competitions from the get-go. He received his black belt in 2007 and became especially known for his mastery of spider and open guard.

Michael retired from competing in 2019. Today, he focuses on his work as a trainer and as head instructor and owner of Alliance's São Paulo HQ, located at Rua Nova Cidade, n° 182—Vila Olímpia São Paulo—SP—CEP: 04547-070.

After a private training session at Michael's Alliance Academy, we moved across the street to my rented apartment in São Paulo for our interview. We sat on my balcony overlooking the massive concrete city with our gis still on from training. While we spoke, we could hear large, commercial planes flying overhead as they sped toward GRU, São Paulo's main airport. It was a unique setting for an interview, for sure. I guess I highlight this to point out that not all conditions need to be perfect for us to learn and grow.

- For a short biography on Michael, go to *bjjheroes.com*.
- To see many of his best matches, go to YouTube and search "Michael Langhi."

EARLY LIFE

FROM COBRINHA CAPOEIRA TO COBRINHA BJJ

Michael Langhi discovered jiu-jitsu via Capoeira, a martial art that was popular in Brazil long before BJJ. His Capoeira trainer,

Rubens "Cobrinha" Charles, started teaching jiu-jitsu classes as a purple belt and kept pushing Michael toward it as a second sport. At first, Michael had no interest in trying out something else. He was happy enough doing Capoeira. However, curiosity eventually got the better of him.

Michael admitted he is competitive by nature, so he especially liked the tournaments and competitions associated with BJJ. "There was just more adrenaline," he told me, grinning ear to ear.

By the time he was eighteen years old, Michael had earned his blue belt in jiu-jitsu and knew he wanted to spend the rest of his life dedicated to the sport; he wanted to teach, train, and live the true jiu-jitsu lifestyle. What he didn't know was how he would break the news to his father. He was almost 100 percent sure that his father wouldn't approve of his career choice. When Michael finally told his dad, Mr. Langhi said, "All right, I will support you, but you need to be the best."

Michael was grateful for the support, and he interpreted his dad's request of being the best to mean earning jiu-jitsu titles. So, Michael competed at lower-belt levels almost every weekend and captured one title after another.

Michael managed to go undefeated for three years. When he finally lost to Leandro Lo in 2011, he immediately felt that he was failing on his promise to be the best and had let his father down. He went home and said, "Hey, Dad. I'm sorry. I just lost."

His dad looked at him for a moment and replied, "Michael, I think there's a misunderstanding. When I said you have to be the best, I didn't mean you had to be the best *fighter* in the world. I meant be the best *person* you can be. You have to be better today than you were yesterday, and *you have to be a better person tomorrow than you are today.*"

To this day, Michael's dad is his biggest fan.

ON PRESSURE AND ANXIETY
BUREAUCRACY AND 24/7 COMMITMENT

Michael has faced his fair share of adversity, and he is intimately familiar with combatting feelings of hopelessness. Most of the obstacles in his path arrived in the form of injuries, but there was one challenge of another variety: bureaucracy.

In 2011, Michael was preparing to move from Brazil to the United States, where he was to become the head instructor at a new Alliance school in Orlando, Florida, but he ran into problems with his US visa. After being told that he would not be able to obtain an entry permit for the next *five years*, he almost abandoned hope.

"I was really depressed," he admitted, looking down at his sandals. "Because at the time, jiu-jitsu wasn't really popular in Brazil. If you wanted to make money, the United States was the best place to be."

Thankfully, his projected five-year wait was much shorter than expected. He received his visa after only one year and promptly moved to Orlando in 2012. Still, that year of uncertainty was agonizing, and he felt awful. Michael threw his arms up in the air as we sat there overlooking the city, and explained, "I thought, *What am I going to do now? I cannot compete in the United States. I cannot move to the United States. I'll have to stop jiu-jitsu. I'm going to give up.*"

Needless to say, it's a good thing he didn't.

Looking back, Michael said he owes most of his extraordinary success to Cobrinha, an athlete known for being exceptionally disciplined. Cobrinha taught Michael that being an athlete is a 24/7 commitment. Michael repeated Cobrinha's words for me: "You have to train hard. You have to be careful with your food and your sleep. You cannot spend your energy doing the wrong stuff."

Michael's lips tightened as he admitted Cobrinha was extremely hard on him. There were many times after training sessions where Michael was left in tears, thinking, *I have to kill this guy.* Although Cobrinha was tough, Michael's admiration of Cobrinha was apparent in the way he spoke of his coach, and he almost seemed to *enjoy* being pushed so hard.

"He pushed me so hard," Michael told me, "and spanked me so much. But he is the reason I won my first world title at blue belt after two years of training. He is the reason I won again as a purple and a brown belt and then got promoted to black belt in a total of five years of training."

Going from white to black belt that fast is basically unheard of in BJJ, especially as a competitor. The speed at which Michael was promoted *and* won major titles at each belt level along the way is nothing short of monumental.

BECOMING A CHAMPION
PREPARATION BUILDS CONFIDENCE

Michael acknowledged that he has always been at least slightly nervous before competitions. That said, he also enjoys having the extra adrenaline in his system. His confidence comes from hard work and preparation. "If I train at a hundred percent—and by this I mean jiu-jitsu, weightlifting, and diet—if I feel comfortable during the training, then I'm ready for anything. So, that's where my confidence comes from."

He also told me that he knows he is *exactly* where he wants to be going into any competition. "I've always enjoyed the time," he explained, "because I wanted to test myself. And after every competition, I was a bit different as an athlete and as a person."

Michael's philosophy on preparation, confidence, and change for big tournaments certainly matches the experiences of many others, even outside of jiu-jitsu. Every personal retreat, big seminar, and annual company convention I've attended attempts to reduce down into a week what would've otherwise taken months to learn. The focus and atmosphere at events like this can really shorten your learning curve through exposure to so much information, as if through osmosis. This isn't to say you should drink water from a firehose, but sometimes moving at a slow pace *isn't* the best way to learn. You can jump in feet first; the water is just fine.

I think the primary message here from Professor Langhi is to test yourself and stretch your limits. Sign up for that seminar to learn something, maybe a speaking engagement that you've been avoiding, and any other opportunity that presents itself. Those who know me understand I have spent several years curating investment opportunities and spending money on various ways to improve myself. Because of this, I am often asked, "What is the best investment I can make right now?" My answer remains unchanged: invest in yourself. If you are truly serious about making progress, this always has been and always will be the best money, time, and energy you have ever spent.

Of course, when it comes to martial arts, lessons can also come in the form of injuries. Over the years, Michael has had countless injuries and five major surgeries. Three of his injuries occurred just one week after he competed in a major tournament. After hurting his shoulder and his knee only two months before the World Championship in 2014, he was given two options: have surgery right away and miss the tournament, or prepare as well as he could, compete, and then have the surgery.

It may not shock you to learn Michael opted to compete. He still followed specific orders from his doctors. "During your training, you have to be careful," Michael's doctor urged him. "But on the day of the competition, you can give 110 percent."

Preparing for that championship was challenging, to say the least. Michael spent one week of fight camp sidelined with an ice pack. When he did spar to prepare for the competition, it was with white and blue belts because going against high-level black belts would have been too hard on his knee.

"If I had trained with Cobrinha... The man is a monster—and I didn't have my knee function at all...," Michael recalled. "I could feel it moving," he said with a grimace. He showed me with his hands how, at the time, his knee could move sideways. Michael knew that taking it easy was his only option, but as he looked around during his training and saw other top fighters like Cobrinha and Lucas Lepri working their hardest, he sometimes felt jealous. The competitor in him was dying to be on the same training mat as his peers. He was like a high-performance vehicle sitting in the garage because of a flat tire. He wanted to be unleashed on the proverbial racetrack, competing at full speed.

During that week where he was unable to train, Michael spent two or three hours every day weight lifting and doing "crazy exercises" to keep his mind strong. "This was about training my mental skills," he explained as he grabbed his knee, now cold from our training session two hours before. "I couldn't train in jiu-jitsu, so I had to suffer another way," he laughed.

Michael's take on training the mind points to a commonality found in the best athletes, regardless of their chosen sport. By being a student of the game when they are off the mat or the field, athletes can—and *should*—improve their performance. It's like Gordon Ryan says in his chapter here in *Jiu-Jitsu Bravehearts*, you need to study off the mat just as much as you train on top of it. When injuries oh-so-conveniently present themselves, mental rehearsal becomes that much more important.

I also firmly believe that those who study, take notes, and mentally repeat the training in their minds will improve without ever setting foot on the mat. This is particularly true if you've been benched by an injury. In fact, this has been my personal experience. Like Navy SEAL Jocko Willink says, "Oh, you hurt your knee? Good. We can get better by studying. We can work on upper-body strength. Our legs needed rest anyway... *Good.*"

Preparing in this way helped Michael get through competitions despite his injuries. Michael already had an excuse built in if he wanted to exercise the obvious handicap: he could have simply quit. Instead, whenever Michael felt his knee sliding and shifting during one of the fights, he would tell himself, *I'm going to win this.* He didn't have the physical training he would've liked, but he knew he put in the mental work both by studying and by understanding he could push past the discomfort. He was willing to fight through the pain.

Ultimately, Michael earned two world titles and one bronze medal in Worlds while enduring severe injuries.

As a professor, he can now draw on his experience and speak from a place of moral authority when students feel like giving up because of an injury. If he tells them not to give up, it not only sounds real, it *is* real because he already limped, walked, and *ran* down that path himself. This champion has been there. Poor leaders issue orders with no real experience in the trenches. Great leaders fight their way out and come back to empower others to do the same. Michael is quick to point out, "What could I say to them if I had quit too?"

BEHIND THE SCENES

AFTER MANY YEARS, PRIORITIES SHIFT

Michael announced his retirement from competing in June of 2019, right after Worlds. At the time of our interview in 2018, he was still competing at the highest level but already thinking about withdrawing from the tournament circuit. I remember running into him at the local *padaria* (Brazilian café) right across the street from the Alliance HQ. He was wearing his gi, and he sat at the table next to me. This was before our interview so, of course, he didn't know who I was at the time.

Still, I said hello and struck up a conversation with him about training. Michael had just finished his competition class and was going to eat some breakfast before going back to teach. I could see on his face that he was thinking about something important. Michael opened up and told me training was becoming really hard. The reasons were many—and they are a good reminder of how people on the outside often don't see the blood, sweat, and problems that are part of every victory. They only see the champions elevated on the podium and the medals gleaming around their necks.

Michael confided that after one-and-a-half decades of tournaments, training and preparation were beginning to feel harder than they had before. His fingers and lower back were beginning to hurt more chronically, and he was facing surgeries on his wrist and shoulder. Plus, his priorities were shifting toward the academy, his students, and his family. Most importantly, he wanted to give back to his wife for all the sacrifices she had made for his dreams.

"My wife lived my life for a *long* time," he said softly. "Now I want to give her the chance to do whatever she wants to do."

During our interview, I asked Michael to look back on his life as a competitor. Did he have any regrets? Michael smiled, shook his head, and told me he did not. "Jiu-jitsu is my love, my passion. I cannot complain about my career, my choices, or my decisions. I tried my best. It is what Cobrinha taught me: *give your best!*"

When asked about lessons the sport taught him in terms of his personal life and business, Michael told me jiu-jitsu has made him more confident about everything. He learned how to deal with problems, how to make decisions, and how to come back after failure. "I apply jiu-jitsu in all areas of my life," he concluded.

One parallel Michael draws between the sport and life is based on knowing that only training will lead to progress in jiu-jitsu. In the same way, only tackling a problem will lead to a solution.

"If you have a problem, don't run from it. Fix it," he advised. "If you don't, you'll have another problem the next day and after that, another one. And then you'll realize that it is so big, you can't fix it anymore."

Another parallel relates to decision-making. On the mat, especially in top tournaments, the pressure is always on. Decisions need to happen in just five seconds or less.

"If I put this kind of pressure on myself off the mat, things become easy," he said. "Because in the outside world, I often have more than five seconds."

This made sense to me. Great leaders are decisive. They aren't always right, but they do *decide* quickly. Analysis paralysis is a real thing. Think back to a time you were about to do something important, and instead of simply doing it, you second-guessed yourself, either by looking at too many options or just being indecisive. Then, by the time you *did* make a decision, it was too late!

In a *rescuetime.com* blog, *How to Make Hard Decisions Quickly*, writer Amy Rigby explains, "Most people think that decision fatigue is caused by making lots of decisions, but that's not always the case... Dragging out a decision is the equivalent of mental multitasking. Your brain is constantly switching back and forth between choices, weighing its options, which leads to burnout and decreased focus."

BEST ADVICE

Asked about the best advice he received, Michael goes back to his father's wish: *be the best person you can be.*

WORST ADVICE

While Michael didn't specifically share the worst advice he's ever been given, he did describe how wallowing in pain and self-pity should never be an option.

Michael described the process of coming back from failure as the hardest part of being a pro. While he is one of the few fighters to have gone undefeated for years at a time, he does know how devastating a loss can feel. Every time somebody beat him in a competition, his mind told him, *I'm not good enough.* But he knew to catch his own negativity, take a deep breath, and intentionally shift his thinking. To that end, he would tell himself, *Bro, let's go!* and *I can do it.*

"When you lose and you wake up the day after the competition, you can just sit there, cry, and feel sorry for yourself, or you can get up, find out where you made a mistake, and train a little bit more," he said. "It's really hard, but the good thing about losing is you *always have another chance*. You just need to decide whether you will take it or give up. I prefer to try again."

Michael's statement reminds us that losses are part of the game, whether it's on the mat, in business, or in life. "Failure," he told me, "is a mandatory stop on the way to success." Or as Winston Churchill is believed to have said, "Success is not final; failure is not fatal: it is the courage to continue that counts."

FINAL THOUGHTS
BEING A ROLE MODEL

It was no surprise to hear that Michael—a wise, dedicated teacher—wants to be a role model for others. "I want my students to love jiu-jitsu the way I do and to apply it in all areas of their life," he said, beaming. "I want to show them that it's not just a martial art, but that it can help with any problem they have off the mat."

CHAPTER 12
Leticia Ribeiro

@lettyribeiro
facebook.com/leticiaribeirojj

Born in 1978 in Rio de Janeiro, Brazil, Leticia Ribeiro is a nine-time world champion. She earned every belt level at Gracie Tijuca in Rio, where she first trained with Arthur Carthiar and Marcelo Machado. The champion received her black belt from both Vinicius "Vini" Aieta and Royler Gracie. As of this writing, Leticia just received her fifth degree stripe on her black belt.

Leticia moved to the United States in 2007, and competed up until 2010. She has since focused on her academy in San Diego, Gracie Humaita South Bay, and on her role as a well-respected professor—especially for girls and young women—and business owner. She is not only a world champion, but also the only woman to also produce from a young age and coach other female black belt world champions, like Beatriz "Bia" Mesquita (also profiled in this book), Carolina Vidal, and Gabi McComb.

Leticia and I met in 2019 for a training session followed by an interview at her academy. Training with her was a lot of fun because she was willing to go over an incredible number of positions. The session reminded me that an athlete's size or height barely matters in jiu-jitsu. While I'm about a foot taller and ninety pounds heavier than Leticia, she didn't hesitate when we drilled positions that required me to use a lot of force, weight, and strength. There was one instance where I was hesitant to execute a knee-on-belly move, a technique that requires one of your knees to push into the belly of your opponent while your other leg is posted on the floor. It is extremely painful and is one of only seven positions that rewards points in competition. She laughed at me when I attempted to be light with my pressure and when I apologized for putting weight on her.

Leticia is an incredibly hard worker, and on the day we met she taught *no less than seven classes* by the time we were scheduled to meet at 6:00 p.m. For the interview portion of our time together, the champion was willing to be surprisingly vulnerable in sharing her story. When I asked her to describe a common misconception people have about her, Leticia told me that she is a friendly person, but others tend to misinterpret her character and believe she is mean. I can see how her demeanor could be intimidating. In spite of her petite stature,

Leticia does exude quite the presence. However, my own experience with her was professional, friendly, and enjoyable. In fact, she was open from the outset and only warmed up more as we talked. In the end, she gave me a hug and a cool hat of the Rio de Janeiro skyline as a parting gift.

- For a video of her story, go to YouTube and search "Leticia Ribeiro: New Beginnings."
- To visit and learn more about her academy, go to *Graciesouthbay.com*.
- The academy address is 340 W 26th St., Ste G/H, National City, CA 91950.
- Several of her matches can be found on YouTube by searching "Leticia Ribeiro."

EARLY LIFE
FROM BJJ SPECTATOR TO JIU-JITSU ADDICT

Leticia has always been an athlete. In her youth, she was involved in swimming, soccer, and volleyball. At the time, she felt like as long as she didn't have to work too hard, it was always fun.

Enter jiu-jitsu.

Leticia was introduced to the sport when she first watched a tournament in 1995. She immediately liked it. Reflecting on that time, she told me, "I thought it was so nice to watch the takedowns and everything, and I wanted to give it a try. And ultimately, it was the first sport I stuck with."

When Leticia was fourteen years old, she and a friend decided to take a jiu-jitsu class. Only a few months after this introduction to the sport, Leticia was already competing. "In the beginning, it was addictive," she recalled. "I just wanted to train and train and compete."

Like many white belts at tough academies in Brazil, Leticia and her friend were beaten up on a daily basis. Her friend quit, but not Leticia. She smiled fiercely as she told me she wouldn't be broken. That said, to make things even more challenging, the academy was a forty-five-minute bus ride away, and each trip meant taking two different buses. The reality of Leticia's teammates submitting her over and over, day after day, class after class, no doubt made her feel disappointed and often defeated. At the same time, those submissions fed her desire to improve. She spent her bus rides home thinking about jiu-jitsu, mentally going through the triangle and armbar submissions others had used to make her tap.

In the end, the challenges fed her resolve to return for another session the next day, and they made her a fast learner. "I think it made me stronger," she said.

ON PRESSURE AND ANXIETY
MEETING RESISTANCE WITH TENACITY

Leticia has always shown remarkable tenacity in pursuit of her passion. This goes for the way she used to compete, for how she teaches and conducts business, and for how she has dealt with challenges like gender bias, a lack of funding, and family resistance.

Sadly, Leticia's father died when she was very young. As a result, Leticia came from a single-parent home and learned the value of hard work by watching her mother lead by example. To give Leticia the best life she could, her mother often worked twelve hours a day in a hair salon at the mall. For about three years, Leticia worked at the same mall, selling bikinis so she could help her mom with the bills. After work, she headed straight to the bus for BJJ training.

"My mom raised me in this way," Leticia said proudly of her role model, as she sat up straighter in her office chair. Hard work and persistence was the only way she knew, and it served her well in every stage of her life. Her mother had the recipe, and Leticia feels she simply followed the instructions.

Though generally very supportive, Leticia's mom didn't initially appreciate her daughter's passion for jiu-jitsu. Understandably, her mom didn't particularly like it because it replaced any interest Leticia once had in school, and she wanted her daughter to earn a university degree. Of course, Leticia wanted her mother's approval, but she knew she had to stay focused and unbothered by resistance if she wanted to reach her goal. So, Leticia kept practicing jiu-jitsu.

When her success as a fighter earned her a full scholarship to college, her mom's point of view changed. "I got a scholarship at the university just because of jiu-jitsu, and my mom loved it," Leticia recalled, laughing. "I started hearing from her, 'Okay, you can train.'"

Even so, money was an issue almost from the day Leticia became interested in jiu-jitsu. While her mom could scrape together the sign-up fee for Leticia's instruction at the academy, there were no funds available for the monthly gym membership. Leticia, who spent every free minute at the academy, started helping out there to pay her dues with sweat equity and elbow grease.

Her deep commitment, along with her athleticism, soon impressed her professor. As soon as she was a blue belt, he recruited her to help teach the academy's kids classes. After receiving her brown belt, she began teaching the class alone. Finally, as a black belt, Leticia picked up students of her own for private training and set out to build and fortify the women's program at the academy.

Leticia surprised me when she announced teaching wasn't something that came to her naturally. In fact, in the beginning, she even hated the job. "As a blue belt, I didn't like it," she explained. "It was tiring to teach, and I still wanted to have energy to train. But after a certain point, when I had my own students, I enjoyed it. I started to think about my future and decided to make a living in jiu-jitsu."

As things turned out, her early teaching career helped prepare her for the program she would eventually start in San Diego. Today, Leticia is considered by many to be the most successful trainer of women's jiu-jitsu, and she is equally passionate about demonstrating leadership for all of her students.

BECOMING A CHAMPION
THINK AND TRAIN LIKE ONE

Leticia's regular training at Gracie Tijuca consisted of two hours of jiu-jitsu a day. There was hardly any cardio and no strength conditioning, but still, the academy was physically demanding. Before big tournaments, she saw top athletes like Royler Gracie, Saulo Ribeiro, and Wellington Leal "Megaton" Dias execute hard rolls. Often, they would do as many as twenty rounds in a row. "There were ten or fifteen guys in the gym at any given time from different cities in Brazil, like Manaus, all in one room, training really hard," she described. "They lived in the same house, and some of them didn't even have a dollar in their pocket. They trained hard without eating well. That's a real challenge. But they came to Rio with a dream: to be a world champion. And some of them made it." Leticia said their dedication and passion taught her that hard work and tough days could make a world champion.

Her routine before tournaments began to include cardio training and still consisted of two jiu-jitsu sessions a day. Then, she added in strength and conditioning two to three times a week. She also made sure to eat healthy food because she learned that nutrition fueled her energy, recovery, and fitness level. "Of course, I like pizza and hamburgers," she added with a laugh. "But if you don't eat well, you feel it right away in the training. With healthy food, you're going to train better and feel less tired."

Leticia said that as a competitor, being the best athlete always came with an added sense of responsibility, which motivated her to be even more disciplined. "Being the challenger is easier!" she exclaimed. "You don't have anything to lose." Champions of nearly every sport hold themselves to a higher standard because they know what it takes to get to the top. Leticia is no different. Heavy lies the crown, indeed.

Leticia's decision to pursue a career teaching jiu-jitsu as a young black belt came with a realization: to make it happen, she would eventually have to start a new life in the United States.

"Being a jiu-jitsu teacher in Brazil isn't easy," she told me. "There are a lot of less fortunate and poor people doing the sport, and when they become champions, they don't want to pay the academy anymore." It's true that high-level athletes can fall susceptible to a sense of entitlement, where they feel they have mastered the sport and therefore do not want to pay a struggling academy's fees. Among other reasons, this can make it hard to survive trying to make a living in jiu-jitsu.

Together with her partner, Fabricio "Morango" Camoes, whom she met at the academy in Rio, Leticia moved to San Diego in 2007. The timing had a lot to do with a big change in the tournament circuit: that year, the IBJJF Worlds moved from Brazil to the US. The prospect of having to spend more money and time traveling to the championship felt just as daunting as a move. The Ribeiro brothers, Xande and Saulo, had already made their move to the US well before Leticia, but after she came to the States, other top fighters—including Royler Gracie—immigrated to America for the same reasons.

Leticia didn't shy away from sharing that life in San Diego was hard in the beginning. She and Morango arrived in the United States with only $300 between them. They barely spoke English, and both lacked visas. But having each other and believing in the same dream helped them overcome these challenges. After working for a series of different gyms and academies, the pair eventually ventured out to start a gym of their own. It was a dream that seemed impossible, and was laced with fear and the unknown, but it was one Leticia knew needed to happen.

Looking back, Leticia explained she sees those initial hardships as *necessary* steps on the road to success. "We even had a hard time finding enough to eat in the beginning," she said, pouring out her heart to me in that moment. I thought it was incredibly vulnerable and admirable of her to share that they didn't have enough to eat. "But all the hard times and the ups and downs—it was necessary for learning how the process works."

Leticia admitted that in retrospect, the choice was obvious, but like any big decision, it wasn't as clear to her in the moment. Tough choices, easy life. Easy choices, hard life.

BEHIND THE SCENES
LEADING THE WAY FOR OTHER FEMALE FIGHTERS

When Leticia started training at Gracie Tijuca in 1995, there were about five other girls already at the gym—an exceptionally high number for the time. Back then, people erroneously believed jiu-jitsu would be really hard for a girl. "Girls weren't seen as fighters," Leticia said on the subject. "It took a long time for us to be respected as athletes and teachers."

While Leticia never faced discrimination at her gym, competing in tournaments was still an entirely different experience from that of her male counterparts. For example, the female athletes got all the bad slots on the competition schedule, and there was no support for them in terms of marketing. Leticia's energy perked up again as she told me, "Nobody interviewed us. Nobody put us in a magazine." Her frustration was clear as she swung her arm from right to left, remembering the dynamic. "The girls were just pushed aside."

But Leticia, who considers herself a first-generation female fighter in Brazil, was once again undeterred. "We didn't have any support in the beginning," she started. "But the girls who made it through, the survivors—we loved the sport, and we *really* fought for ourselves. We would not still be doing it otherwise."

Reflecting on the progress female jiu-jitsu fighters have made since 1995, Leticia told me she sees Kyra Gracie as a big catalyst. "When Kyra started to compete, she opened up a lot of doors by being part of the Gracie family. She helped a lot, especially with IBJJF. She was really good for the sport and continues to work hard today for women in jiu-jitsu."

When she came to the United States in 2007, Leticia saw an opportunity to work on behalf of female jiu-jitsu fighters herself. Her goal was to build a nationwide women's program, and she worked hard to attain it. Leticia traveled frequently for seminars, sharing her expertise, spreading the word about jiu-jitsu, and helping girls wherever she could. By serving as a role model—a highly esteemed teacher with a black belt and numerous world champion titles—she showed them that they too could one day compete in Worlds, find sponsors, and succeed.

"My main goal when I moved here was to make girls believe that it is possible to earn *everyone's* respect in this sport," she emphasized. "I think I have already achieved a lot. Today, the women's category in jiu-jitsu is huge."

She isn't wrong. These days, Leticia doesn't travel as much as she used to, and her focus has shifted from empowering girls as a group to making an impact on an individual level. The champion explained that she now wants to serve as a role model for young people looking to open their own school. "I tell young people at my academy all the time, 'What you are learning here is priceless. It is how to teach and how to run an academy. When you bring all this experience to your own school, you're going to know a lot already.'"

At the same time, Leticia is trying to build champions through the kids' program and really enjoys helping children progress. "The beauty of the kids' program is that I can start when they are really small, maybe five or even just three years old, and then I can help them through the levels. I can build someone up from when they are a beginner and take them all the way to a black belt and a world champion title. It's nice to be able to do this."

For older athletes, many see jiu-jitsu as a sport of self-discovery, and many also say the martial art has taught them valuable lessons for life and business. Leticia says she owes her confidence—and, ultimately, her independence as a person—to the sport. "The most important thing jiu-jitsu gave me is *confidence as a woman*," she said with pride. "I used to not believe that I would be able to do everything I have done. But I have won many world champion titles and trained students who became world champions. I moved to another country and have my own business. I am really happy with my achievements, and today I am independent."

Her story reminds me of writer C. JoyBell. C.'s words: "The strength of a woman is not measured by the impact that all her hardships in life have had on her; but the strength of a woman is measured by the extent of her refusal to allow those hardships to dictate her and who she becomes."

BEST ADVICE

When I asked Leticia about the best advice she's ever received, she beamed at me and said it was to "keep going."

"The most important thing with the ups and downs in life," she stressed, "is persistence and perseverance. *Even in hard times, you must keep going and believe in yourself.*"

WORST ADVICE

Though Leticia didn't have any specific worst advice to share, she did describe the value of honesty and realism. When people in Brazil tell her that they, too, would like to move to the

US, run an academy, and drive a nice car, Leticia can give them advice from a position of experience. Sometimes, that means she provides people with a crucial reality check. "First you work for others and learn how to teach. Then, you learn what it takes to have an academy. *You take it step by step.* It's a process."

She also warns people that they will have to work very hard in the US if they want to be successful. "People think, *Oh, the American Dream!*" she said. "People instantly assume just because you arrive in the US that means you made it. You go there, and then things just happen, and you're rich. But it's not like that. In America, you have to work hard to be successful. *If you don't like to work, forget it.*"

FINAL THOUGHTS

RISE TOGETHER

During our interview, Leticia told me her toughest opponent was Bianca Andrade Barreto. The two women have competed at every level since they were blue belts: blue belt, purple belt, brown belt, and of course, black belt.

"It was a lot of back and forth. She submitted me in the black belt finals of Worlds in 2001. Then, the year after, I submitted her in the first round of Worlds in 2002. In 2005, she won by points, and in 2006, I won by points," Leticia said. The memory seemed to bring her right back into the moment, and a sense of gratitude seemed to come over Leticia.

Leticia knows tough opponents make you raise your level. You know what you're in for when you go against an opponent who has beaten you in jiu-jitsu and in life. We can prepare when we know we're about to go up against something that has knocked us down before. So, strap up and go after it because there really is no hiding, and the only way around any obstacle is *through*!

CHAPTER 13

Alex Atala

@alexatala
facebook.com/alexatalareal

Alex Atala, born in 1968 in São Bernardo do Campo, São Paulo, Brazil, is one of the world's most renowned chefs. Of Irish and Palestinian ancestry, he runs the Michelin two-starred restaurant D.O.M. in São Paulo. Since 2006, *Restaurant Magazine* has consistently rated D.O.M. as the best restaurant in South America. In 2012, the magazine ranked it fourth among the World's 50 Best Restaurants. In 2014, Alex and D.O.M. were honored with the Chef's Choice Award.

Alex came to cooking in a roundabout way. Before attending culinary school, he worked as a house painter and washed dishes in a restaurant. After graduating, Alex traveled in Europe to work with top chefs like Bernard Loiseau. Since his return to Brazil in 1994, he has become a pioneer in haute cuisine, celebrated for his use of native ingredients. Thanks to him, Brazilian flavors and foods have become known around the world.

I interviewed Alex in the middle of 2019. Our conversation took place over a WhatsApp phone call, and we chatted like old friends as Alex shared some amazing stories. He was sitting in his car outside his restaurant in São Paulo while we spoke, and I was in my living room in San Diego. Not only was Alex kind enough to make time for me, but he even put up with a dose of discomfort by sitting in his car to minimize work distractions. The restaurant was still closed but the kitchen was in full prep mode for the evening. This got me thinking about how chefs, like jiu-jitsu athletes, spend multiple hours a day in preparation—and if the prep work is good, success can only follow.

Since the interview, Alex and I have met in person. I, along with Fábio Gurgel, had the pleasure of sharing a bottle of wine while Alex talked us through an incredible, sixteen-course meal at his restaurant in São Paulo. Professor Fábio covered the bill by hosting a private training session for the three of us the next morning. Needless to say, he made Alex and me pay in blood!

The next day we all attended a Cobrinha seminar at the Alliance HQ with over one hundred athletes. Afterward we grabbed several pizzas from a local place and had some laughs. Alex is a world-class chef, but he's also just like one of the guys and enjoys a bit of junk food too.

- Check out an episode dedicated to Alex on *Chef's Table* on Netflix—it truly is a must-see. (We had to plan our phone interview around one of his trips to the Amazon region. This documentary explains exactly why.)
- To see more about his restaurant D.O.M., go to *domrestaurante.com.br*.
- For more videos about Alex, search Alex Atala on YouTube.

EARLY LIFE
STARTING OVER AFTER TWENTY YEARS

Alex first started training BJJ as a teenager in Brazil with an infamous Rickson Gracie student, Marcelo Behring. However, he took a long break from the sport because of his successful career as a chef. When Alex promised his two sons jiu-jitsu lessons a few years ago, the last thing he expected was to return to the sport. All he wanted was for his boys to be more confident. He thought his children could test their new skills in the friendly wrestling matches they fought to determine who in the family would be boss for the day.

Today, the boys, who were nine and seventeen years old when they first hit the mat, still train on occasion. However, they aren't really stoked about jiu-jitsu. Alex, on the other hand, had progressed from white to brown belt by the time we talked. A few months later, he received his black belt from UFC vet Demian Maia.

He also self-identifies as a jiu-jitsu addict.

"I didn't expect that I would be training jiu-jitsu again when I brought my kids to the gym," he laughed. "It was more for us to be together and to have fun moments with them. But now I look in the mirror and I say to myself, *You're a good guy and a good dad, but you're addicted to jiu-jitsu.*"

When Alex is in São Paulo, he trains with Maia, one of Fábio Gurgel's black belts. He also travels a lot in the Amazon basin, Europe, and the United States. He always makes sure to pack his gi. "It doesn't matter where I go, I always look for a friend who might know someone I can train with. It used to not be like that, but people now are super open to having you on the mat. Jiu-jitsu has become one big community. It's a great way to make new friends."

Alex also competes in the sport. In 2018, he participated in the World Masters Tournament in Las Vegas, the most prestigious tournament for athletes ages thirty and above. There's a video of at least one of his matches on YouTube. Although he wasn't victorious in that specific match, it's great to see him out there competing when he is a professional in his own field. This is a tremendous achievement. The dedication required to physically prepare for a tournament is immense. Add to that putting yourself in front of your friends and family on a stage of combat, and you have a situation that can feel extremely daunting and intimidating. The fact that Alex has been able to make the time to be a dad, husband, and business owner *and* still train for something as grueling as a jiu-jitsu tournament definitely commands respect and admiration.

ON PRESSURE AND ANXIETY
COMFORTABLY UNCOMFORTABLE

Being a chef, especially one of Alex's caliber, comes with a lot of pressure. At D.O.M., the goal is to excel at everything. In the kitchen, three rules apply: don't run, don't stop, and don't talk.

"We like to be precise and perfect," he told me. "And if you're not concentrating 100 percent and working in silence, you cannot achieve top results."

When I asked Alex how jiu-jitsu has helped him with his profession, he echoed the philosophy of the Stoics. "There is a lesson I carry with me in all situations and in my everyday life," he explained. *"Jiu-jitsu is about being comfortable in an uncomfortable situation.* It is about staying calm when you're trying to find a more comfortable position. If you're not in a good position, you can always switch, swap, or change your move—if you stay calm."

Generally speaking, Alex told me he sees jiu-jitsu as an inspiration for all of life's situations. "It can inspire you or give you hope for finding the best way of solving any problem."

Becoming a Champion: Self-Discovery through Jiu-Jitsu

I asked Alex what he'd discovered about himself on the mat, and the chef had more than one insight to share. He described how, when he first started training, he learned that it is indeed possible for the smaller guy to beat the bigger guy in BJJ.

"People always talk about this," he told me. "But when I first realized that I am able to do it—that was my first true moment of self-discovery."

Upon his return to the sport years later, he realized that jiu-jitsu makes him feel younger. "When I went back with my kids, my body was different. My balance was different, and so was my velocity and agility. But I soon felt huge pleasure from doing the sport because I was challenging myself. The challenge helped me keep alive the flame of youth."

Like everyone, Alex has bad days and good days in the gym. He knows that each comes with a different lesson. "A good day on the mat can maybe teach you better jiu-jitsu," he mused, *"but a bad day on the mat can make you a better man.* It can teach you about yourself and what you're doing. You can learn what you felt, what you missed, and what you can do better—and not only on the mat but in life, too."

BEHIND THE SCENES
EAT REAL FOOD

Of course, I had to ask the celebrated chef about the best food to eat before or after training. Alex said he tries to get the best value from food by consuming the best quality ingredients he can find. He explained, "I buy the best gasoline for my car and the best olive oil for my customers. I also put the best quality of any ingredient inside of me."

Before training, Alex reaches for a piece of fruit or for a cup of coffee. Afterward, he looks for protein in its natural rather than powdered form. "People sometimes overvalue this kind of powdered protein and undervalue the real stuff," he said, shaking his head. "An egg is cheaper and better. It's healthy."

BEST ADVICE

When I asked Alex about any advice he would give to others, he got serious. "My first advice for young kids is to believe in yourself and your dreams and keep fighting." He paused, and then took it a step further, adding, "No matter *how* old you are, always keep challenging yourself."

WORST ADVICE

Alex's worst advice mirrors his best advice. "You are too old!" he laughed. "We are never too old to start and never too young to quit."

FINAL THOUGHTS
BE HUMAN FIRST

Thanks to his travels and celebrity status, Alex has had the opportunity to train with some of the top athletes in BJJ, including Michael Langhi, Lucas Lepri, and Cobrinha. He sees them as role models, not just for the sport but for life.

The gratitude was clear in Alex's voice when he talked about these athletes. "What I learned with those guys is, no matter how big they are, before being world champions or black belts, they are amazing human beings. They are respectful and just great men. So, this beautiful discipline doesn't *only* teach you how to fight or how to choke. *It teaches you how to be honest and brave.*"

When working with his sous-chefs in the kitchen, Alex tries to live up to the example of his idols. He likes to be honest with people and tells them if he disapproves of their work. At the same time, he also makes sure never to disrespect them.

"I'm allowed to say, 'What you're doing is a shame.' But I'm not allowed to say, 'You are a piece of shit as a chef.' And if they *are* bad chefs, *then it's actually my mistake* because I picked them for my restaurant."

I find this fascinating, yet predictable of any true leader who is at the top of their craft. Alex refuses to place blame on anyone else; in fact, he does the exact opposite, and places the responsibility on himself when something isn't working out. To lead in this way is a lost art. Finger-pointing doesn't inspire anyone to follow you. Conversely, telling your team, "This is not your fault, I failed to lead you properly," is an entirely different conversation. As Arnold H. Glasow, American businessman and humorist, put it, "A good leader takes a little more than his share of the blame, and a little less than his share of the credit."

CHAPTER 14

Marcus "Buchecha" Almeida

buchechabjj.com
 @marcusbuchecha
 facebook.com/MarcusBuchecha

---

Marcus Vinicius Oliveira de Almeida, also known as "Buchecha" (which translates to "big cheeks" in Portuguese—which Marcus had when he first started doing jiu-jitsu), is currently considered by many to be the greatest of all jiu-jitsu fighters. His warm nature and big smile have made him one of the most popular athletes in the sport. He is a thirteen-time world champion, a six-time World Professional Abu Dhabi Cup Champion, and a two-time ADCC Champion, medaling a total of six times.

Buchecha was born in 1990 in São Vicente, São Paulo, Brazil, where he received his black belt under Rodrigo Cavaca. Today, he competes for the Checkmat team. The list of top athletes he has defeated includes André Galvão, Rodolfo Vieira, Leandro Lo, Felipe Pena, and Murilo Santana. He has also submitted Kron Gracie, Antônio Braga Neto, and Bernardo Faria. Buchecha has trained a number of celebrities, including one of his surfing idols, Kelly Slater, arguably the best surfer of all time.

At six feet three and 260 pounds, Buchecha is a massive human being, but he still moves like an agile panther. I see him as the BJJ version of Muhammad Ali: explosive yet graceful. He's obviously a champion from a physical perspective, but he also acts like one. Buchecha knows he's a role model for others, and to that end, he is gracious even in defeat. After losing a referee decision to João Gabriel Rocha in São Paolo in 2019 (at a match I attended), Buchecha showed gratitude, even though he didn't agree with the result. This is uncommon behavior in most combat sports, including jiu-jitsu, where the losing athlete often contests, in dramatic fashion, decisions like this. This is refreshingly not the case with Buchecha.

Buchecha currently resides in Huntington Beach, California. We met for a training session, followed by a ninety-minute interview, at my academy, Alliance Jiu-Jitsu San Diego. Of course, he squashed me like a grape during training, but we had a great time getting to know each other and shared some great stories afterward.

- For videos on his best moments in competition, search YouTube for "Marcus Buchecha." One of my favorites to watch is his match against Victor Estima.
- For a comprehensive library of his training videos, visit BJJFanatics.com.

EARLY LIFE

FROM RESISTANCE TO PASSION

As we began discussing Buchecha's outstanding career as a jiu-jitsu athlete, he immediately quoted his older sister, Ana Kelly. His face broke into a huge grin as told me she likes to joke, "You owe it all to me!"

Buchecha was around twelve years old when his sister asked their dad, Clayton Almeida, if she could attend jiu-jitsu lessons at a small gym in their hometown of São Vicente. Feeling protective of her, Clayton hesitated. "What is this jiu-jitsu?" their concerned father asked. "Is it the crab fight where people hug each other?"

In an effort to keep an eye on his daughter, Clayton initially accompanied her to the gym. Not long after, Clayton decided to give the sport a try himself. The next thing Buchecha knew, his dad was prodding him to take lessons too.

Buchecha described "semi-caving" to his dad's badgering. He had a passion for surfing and was hitting the waves every day, but he decided to take jiu-jitsu lessons once a week to make his dad happy. He started at the local gym and then moved to Integração in Santos, where Teco Shinzato was the main instructor. It was there that the future champion met Cavaca. Cavaca was a purple belt at the time, and as fate would have it, he would one day become Buchecha's instructor.

Even though Buchecha wasn't quite sold on jiu-jitsu yet, he used that fact to his benefit to negotiate small gifts from his father. "He wasn't the kind of dad to spoil me," Buchecha explained. "But every time he said, 'Go, do jiu-jitsu,' I asked for cake or a Coke or cheese bread. I took advantage of the situation," he admitted, with a big belly laugh.

BJJ didn't click for Buchecha until he was fifteen years old. He happened to be at the gym on the day the Integração team returned from the 2005 World Championship in Rio de Janeiro. Master Teco lined everyone up in a large circle and asked the competitors to talk about their experience. Cavaca, who had placed second, said that he'd be willing to give up *all* of his medals if he had the opportunity to get that one elusive gold medal from Worlds instead.

For Buchecha, this was an *aha!* moment. The deep desire for success he detected in Cavaca's admission sparked his own motivation. "I thought, *This is interesting. I would love to feel what Cavaca is talking about*," Buchecha recalled. In that moment, he realized he wanted to compete. Everything changed after that day. Buchecha stopped surfing and started training jiu-jitsu every day instead.

As for his dad and sister? Buchecha's sister is still a white belt and only occasionally takes jiu-jitsu lessons, but his father kept training. Clayton Almeida received his black belt on the same day as Buchecha in 2010. In 2017, Clayton fought at

World Masters in Las Vegas and became a world champion in the master division at the young age of fifty-eight.

ON PRESSURE AND ANXIETY
NEGOTIATIONS AND PERSISTENCE

Buchecha's commitment to daily jiu-jitsu lessons came with a new challenge: while the Almeida family wasn't poor, they also didn't have money to spare. Even though Professor Teco offered Buchecha a discounted rate, the training was still expensive. At the time, Buchecha's sister was in college and he was attending a private high school. The question quickly became how the family would pay for his training.

Buchecha had an idea. A master negotiator, he proposed that his dad take him out of the private school. "Dad," Buchecha recalled saying, "you're already paying for college for my sister. If I go to a public school, it will save you money, and I can focus on jiu-jitsu." Much to Buchecha's surprise, his dad agreed.

Buchecha shot me a mischievous grin as he went on to admit that the truth was he had wanted out of the private school because it came with a lot of pressure. Public school was easier and just what the proverbial doctor ordered.

Some jiu-jitsu athletes walk onto their very first competition mat and immediately prove themselves as winners. Buchecha wasn't one of them. In fact, during the first ten tournaments the future champion fought in, Buchecha never even passed the first round; he lost each and every time. "I was a blue belt, and I fought hard. I always fought tough," he said. "But I still didn't know what it felt like to get your arm raised in victory."

The constant defeats got to him. After yet another loss at Copa Dragão in 2006, Buchecha was ready to stop practicing jiu-jitsu. He recalled sitting right next to his professor with his head down. He told Teco, "This is not for me. I can't win, so I'm just going to quit and do something else."

There were a bunch of other athletes nearby, all of whom were listening in on the conversation. Knowing this, Teco said, "You know what? You can be the weak one and give up, or you can show up at the gym on Monday and train harder."

Buchecha was still upset. He told me that he planned to return to the gym that Monday and quit right after. At the time, he believed doing so would help him to save face. He believed it would enable him to tell himself that he *had* come back and, therefore, others wouldn't see him as weak.

Of course, Monday came and went, and Buchecha stuck with jiu-jitsu. His perseverance was ultimately rewarded, and Buchecha won his next tournament. When his hand was raised in victory, the champion finally experienced the positive, addictive reward he had been seeking.

BECOMING A CHAMPION
A HARD-EARNED VICTORY

Around five years later, Buchecha was again on the verge of quitting. His confidence had been sliding downhill during the months leading up to Worlds 2011. He was living in Florida and teaching at a new gym Cavaca owned when he heard that one of his main potential opponents, Rodolfo Vieira, was focused solely on training. The news was enough to knock some sense into Buchecha. He realized that training for the tournament *and* working as a professor split his focus too much. He quit teaching jiu-jitsu and moved back to Brazil.

"I saw Rodolfo crushing everyone, and I thought, *He is living with his parents in Brazil and training full time. I must do what he is doing. I'll move back to Brazil and do nothing but train jiu-jitsu.*" So, that's what he did.

Now back in Santos, Buchecha focused entirely on preparing for Worlds 2011. All his effort would prove to be in vain. First, he lost in the Absolute semifinal. His opponent was, ironically, none other than Rodolfo Vieira. Then Leo Nogueira defeated him in the 100 kg final. While Buchecha could live with losing to Vieira—"He was much better than I," Buchecha admitted—his loss to Nogueira felt devastating.

Now Buchecha doubted that he could ever make a real living from the sport, and he started teaching jiu-jitsu again simply to pay the bills. Unfortunately, his passion for training was gone. When some of his friends at his current gym tried to open their own place, things turned sour. Buchecha decided he'd had enough. He planned to fight one last tournament and then start college.

Needless to say, that "one last" tournament wasn't Buchecha's last. He won, and the next thing he knew, his dad bought him a plane ticket to California with the instruction to "stay for six months and see what happens."

The rest, as they say, is history. In June 2012, Buchecha won two gold medals at the IBJJF Worlds, and a newly crowned champion was born.

When I asked Buchecha what he learned from the two times he almost quit the sport, he told me this: *"Every time you think about quitting—if you persist, something changes."* Like Buchecha, that "something" could change your life forever.

BEHIND THE SCENES

IT TAKES A VILLAGE

During my interview with Buchecha, it was clear how utterly grateful he was for the support he has received throughout the years.

First, there were his parents and his sister. "Without them, I wouldn't be here today," he said seriously. "Being surrounded by the right people helped a lot."

He recalled how his mother sometimes suggested that he should have a Plan B, like attending a traditional university, but his father would quickly object: "The boy's going to be fine!" At times, his dad's faith in him was so strong that Buchecha worried whether it was even justified.

"I was enjoying the training, but I didn't really know what I would do and where jiu-jitsu would take me." At this point in our conversation, Buchecha looked up at the large gym ceiling fan, clearly reminiscing. "He believed in me so much that I sometimes thought to myself, *He's going crazy. He's getting old.*" As he spoke, the deep appreciation in his voice was abundantly apparent.

Today, his dad sometimes looks at his son knowingly when they pass one another in the house and says with a proud, fatherly smirk, "I told you so."

Belief in one's self is a huge factor on the road to success, but there's also something to be said for the force of love that is *other people willing us into greatness.* Many of us don't have the credentials or pedigree we think we need and may not believe in ourselves, but when others do, it can make all the difference in the world. Buchecha and his father are a classic example of exactly that, and we can all learn from them.

Be positive and uplift others and *believe* other people when they tell you that you *are* capable. Feeling the freedom to embody what we're capable of has tremendous power. Sometimes, all we need to access that freedom is a loved one's *permission* to be great.

Buchecha shared that he also feels indebted to a number of people outside his family, like Teco, his physical therapist Bruno, and his friend Bernardo, as well as Raphael Chaves and Lucas Leite.

When Buchecha moved to Florida at age twenty, a friend from Integração in Santos took him under his wing. His name was Raphael, and he invited Buchecha to live in his apartment, taught him English, helped him open his first bank account, and even advised him on how to talk with American girls.

"Raphael is like a brother to me," Buchecha said, leaning his head against the mat that bordered the wall of the gym. "I learned so much from him and still travel with him. I call him my godfather."

After moving back to the US with a mere $1,000 in his pocket in 2012, Buchecha found another supportive friend, Lucas Leite. Buchecha lived at Lucas's place and also substituted classes while Lucas went on vacation. Later, Lucas bought a new car for himself so that Buchecha could have his old one. After a while, Lucas even found Buchecha a job teaching jiu-jitsu at a school in Corona, California.

Buchecha described his first few months in Orange County as really difficult. He was living in the gym and never knew what the following day would bring. Commuting several hours a week to get from one school to the next took its toll on him. There were days when he was so exhausted from teaching class and commuting across Southern California's massive highways all day that he slept in the car for an hour upon arriving home before he could drag himself inside to go to bed. And also, he added, "This was the happiest time of my career. I never complained. I was happy. I started from zero in California and really had to fight for it. The struggle made me grow so much as a person. Without Lucas, I wouldn't be here today."

And of course, there is Leo Vieira. Leo was also a huge part of Buchecha's support system and, ultimately, became like family to him. To this day, the martial artists share a strong, brotherly bond that Buchecha is very grateful for.

Buchecha has dedicated the past fourteen years of his life to jiu-jitsu. He, like many of the other athletes I interviewed, said the sport helped shape his personality. Jiu-jitsu showed Buchecha his true self, and it changed him as a person, fighter, teammate, son, brother, and professor.

"It doesn't matter who you are; on the mat you can't fake it. At least not for long," he says, lifting his eyebrows a bit. "Sometimes you're tired, sometimes you're not having a good day, and because of the pressure, you pour it all out on the mat. You show your emotions." He paused for a moment, and then added, "The mat is the perfect way to see someone's personality."

Buchecha faced his biggest moment of truth when he was injured at Worlds in 2015. He faced Ricardo Evangelista in the Absolute quarterfinals and suffered a potentially career-ending injury, tearing three ligaments in his knee, all but destroying it. While the incident could have ended his career, Buchecha described it as starting a path to a rebirth of sorts, considering his accomplishments after the devastating injury. In fact, looking back, he told me, "The injury was the best thing that happened in my life."

Most people don't know this, but Buchecha intended for Worlds 2015 to be his last competition; after it, the champion planned to make the transition to MMA. So, the knee injury was something of a blessing. It kept him in jiu-jitsu, the game he loves the most, and as a result, his name was emblazoned on the pages of more and more record books.

Of course, none of that changed the facts of the injury itself. The moments right after the accident are forever seared in Buchecha's mind. He remembers screaming at the intense, excruciating pain. I winced as he described the agony for me. Buchecha explained the way he was laid on his back, looking at the roof of the infamous Walter Pyramid arena at Long Beach

State University, instantly understanding that he had blown out his knee.

"You know when you mess up in a fight and you start noticing the roof of the arena?" Buchecha asked me, pointing up to the ceiling. "Every time I've fought and lost, there was that moment where I started looking. This was the first time that I'd noticed the top of the pyramid. And when I looked up, I said, 'It's over.'"

Buchecha, who didn't have insurance, initially refused to be taken to the hospital, but the pain simply got too intense. In fact, it was bad enough that he required morphine. In the ambulance, he moped and told his friend Bernardo, "My career is done. I can't do this anymore. I blew up my knee. It's over."

"Okay," Bernardo said. "We better start looking at college or something. Imagine how cool it will be, you getting there at 8:00 a.m. and leaving at 5:00 p.m.! So good! Let's check tomorrow!"

The prospect of college was exactly the reality check that Buchecha needed in that moment. The champion looked at me and got into character for a moment, embodying himself that day in the ambulance. He told me he looked at Bernardo and announced, "Fuck you, dude!" Bernardo grinned at him. Buchecha wasn't done yet.

The doctors Buchecha saw in California believed his knee injury consisted of a single torn ligament. However, upon flying to Brazil for further treatment, Buchecha learned that he had torn his PCL, LCL, and MCL. It would be twelve months before he could train hard again. Uncertain about his future,

Buchecha fell into depression. He recalls, "I remember the first week I was just crying and crying."

Little by little and with support from his friends, he picked himself up, all while wondering whether he should get surgery for his knee or not. His physical therapist, Bruno, urged him to go on a long-planned vacation to Ibiza and Switzerland. Bruno told him to schedule the surgery upon his return. Buchecha was already considering canceling the trip and getting surgery right away instead. Why would he wait? Worlds was just eleven months away, and the recovery was supposed to take twelve months.

But Bruno insisted, *"Have a good time.* Party, drink, do whatever you want, because after the surgery, it will be tough."

Buchecha was finally convinced, and going on the vacation turned out to be a great decision. While he had been too afraid to do almost anything before the trip, in Europe he told himself, *I already don't have any ligaments,* and, *You only live once, go for it.* So, he threw caution to the wind and joined his friends Rodolfo and Leandro for bungee jumping on a bridge near Zurich. Not long after, he found himself rolling with Rodolfo in a gym.

"I did one roll," he told me, recalling the flood of inspiration he'd felt. "Just three minutes, but it was good. Because, in that moment, I knew I had to do the surgery so I could come back. I wanted to have that feeling of being on the mat again."

Buchecha scheduled his knee surgery in Brazil, where his lack of health insurance mattered less. In fact, he was so famous and revered in his home country that his doctors and hospital provided their services for free. He was charged only for the materials needed for the surgery.

Bruno's warning about the recovery process proved to be correct. After the operation came another round of intense pain and six weeks of not being able to so much as bend his leg. Buchecha initially resented the circumstances, but eventually he moved to acceptance. *Cavaca came back from so many knee surgeries*, he told himself. *I can do it too.*

The lesson here, as Buchecha put it, is this: "People deal with so many problems in life that are much worse than knee surgery. So, crying and saying, 'Why me?' isn't helping." After he accepted the reality of his circumstances, Buchecha got to work. He adopted a new mindset of controlling what he could: his effort.

His knee injury and the long recovery period that followed taught Buchecha a number of lessons about both himself and other people. On the day of the injury, he had a rude awakening when he checked his phone at the hospital: online, people were claiming he had *faked the injury* because he was losing the match.

Buchecha shook his head. "People are the worst," he said. "After that day, I decided I'll never again look at comments about me. It taught me not to give a damn about other people's opinions."

He went on to say that he has since lost his patience for what he calls "fake people in jiu-jitsu." He elaborated, "They slap your back. 'Hey, congrats, champ!' But they really want to see you lose. I used to be very political and diplomatic. Nowadays, if I don't like someone, I ignore them."

Thanks to the accident, the champion learned to identify his true friends: people who called to ask how he was doing. Others never reached out. "Those people didn't care," he said, in a somber tone. "They had been expecting something from me, and when I was out of competing, they disappeared. It was a hard punch to see stuff like that. But I never would have seen it without the injury."

As Buchecha spoke to me about his post-surgery recovery and the road back to Worlds, the word gratitude came up again and again. During his months of recovery, Buchecha lost some of his sponsors, so he struggled financially and had to move back to Brazil to make ends meet. Once he was in Rio, he found that he could depend on the support of two people in particular: his sister and his physical therapist.

"My sister stopped her life for me," he said, sounding emotional all these years later. "I couldn't drive, and she took me to physical therapy twice a day, *every day*. I had to sit in the back of the car like a taxi passenger because my leg had to be completely straight on top of the center console of the car and into the passenger seat in front. Forty-five days of this!" he said as he stretched his leg out on the mat to demonstrate for me. "When I had to return to the US to keep my green card status, Bruno came with me so we could continue with therapy. I became a better brother and a better friend because of them."

By the time Worlds 2016 came around, Buchecha had been training for almost three months. While he didn't feel ready for the tournament—"I was at 60 percent," he confessed— he was as hungry as ever to win. "In the one year after the injury, I had a lot of time to think. It was like a reset. I felt the same hunger that I had when I was twenty or twenty-one years old. When I got my black belt in 2010, I wanted to improve. I wanted to be a professional and fight. I wanted to be a world champion. I felt that same desire in 2016. It was like being born again."

His return to the World Championship was triumphant. "It was the best Worlds I ever fought," he said with pride. "I had seven fights and five submissions, and I made not a single mistake."

To this day, Buchecha believes his knee injury made all the difference. Afraid that opponents would get his leg, he improved his game in other areas, like pressure passes and armbars. "My fear of getting caught [by submission or injury] on my knee again made me better at jiu-jitsu," he concluded.

In my experience, this happens a lot in jiu-jitsu. Injuries teach us to improvise and adapt. Adaptation in circumstances that aren't favorable tends to make us more well-rounded. It forces us to focus on other parts of our game that might not receive attention if it weren't for the injury. Your arm is hurt, so you learn to be better at your guard using your legs and knees. Your stronger arm starts to give you pain, and you learn to rely less on that side of your body to save you every time you make big mistakes. This type of adaptation can create new neural pathways and can sometimes lead to even better results—at the very least, add multiple dimensions to your game.

In October 2012, Buchecha received an invitation he couldn't resist: Metamoris founder Ralek Gracie asked him to step on the mat and face off against his cousin, ten-time world champion Roger Gracie. At the time, Roger had already retired.

Buchecha immediately agreed. *They want me to fight him?* he thought. *Of course I'll do it. I know that they hope I'll lose. They want to say that even though Roger quit, if he fights, he still wins!*

Buchecha told me that his mindset in all aspects of life is, "Kill or die." People around him argued that the match was a bad idea because he had just won Worlds. They worried it might ruin his reputation if he lost, but Buchecha told them, "I'm never going to hide behind a medal or a title, and I don't care if I lose. So, let's fight!"

The match, of course, became a thing of legend. It took twenty minutes and ended in a draw.

Buchecha told me that he trained very hard for the fight. When it was over, he understood why he had been so motivated and why it went so well. He had accepted the invitation to go against Roger Gracie for a personal reason rather than for ulterior motives. Buchecha wanted to test himself by competing at the highest level.

He learned a lesson on that day. "I fought for the right reasons. It was very personal, but the times that I fought for the wrong reasons, either for somebody else or for a sponsor or even money, it didn't turn out well."

BEST ADVICE

When I asked about the best advice he's ever received, Buchecha told me he remembers learning from his dad that there's a right time for everything. When he first committed himself to training jiu-jitsu, Buchecha envied successful athletes at Integração for the fun they were having off the mat. Ten years his senior, they frequented the best nightclubs in the state and were his role models. When he complained about feeling left out, his dad would promise, "Just keep doing jiu-jitsu, and you'll be telling those stories too."

WORST ADVICE

Buchecha couldn't really pinpoint the worst advice he's ever received, but he did tell me a story that seems to apply here. He remembers that every time he won at Worlds, his friends back in Brazil asked how much money he'd made. When Buchecha explained that he didn't receive any money for the championship, they asked him what the point was.

This seemed to Buchecha like a way of insinuating he should do something that earned him money, as opposed to a "hobby" that didn't pay the bills. Bad advice indeed, particularly considering that Buchecha has now transitioned to an MMA fighter with ONE Championship, which is known to pay their fighters top dollar.

FINAL THOUGHTS
NO LIMITS

Buchecha told me he hopes his story will inspire others to believe in themselves. It was clear he is aware that many people dream of achieving what he has. "I didn't come from a rich family or from a traditional jiu-jitsu family, but I made it. You just have to want it more and try harder than everyone else."

That said, to this day, the champion keeps his medals in a shoebox. When people suggest he frame them and put them up for display, he says, "No. Imagine if I put my thirteen gold medals in one place, and I can't fit any new ones. I'm not going to limit myself in this way. When I quit, *then* I'll do it."

Buchecha concluded that he never knew how far he would be able to take his jiu-jitsu. In fact, he still doesn't know, and so he keeps fighting. "I'm still learning," he explained. "I try not to limit myself."

CHAPTER 15

Aubrey Marcus

aubreymarcus.com
 @aubreymarcus
 facebook.com/aubreymarcus

Aubrey Marcus is the founder and former CEO of Onnit, the lifestyle and fitness optimization brand. Onnit sponsors a number of professional jiu-jitsu athletes, including none other than Bellator MMA Champion Rafael Lovato Jr. (also featured in this book).

Aubrey hosts the *Total Human Optimization* podcast and the *Aubrey Marcus Podcast*, where he talks with top performers and celebrities in athletics, business, science, and spirituality. He gives seminars about mastering relationships, holds speaking engagements, and frequently makes guest appearances on podcasts and shows, including *The Joe Rogan Experience*, *The Jason Ellis Show*, and *Dr. Oz*.

His book *Own the Day, Own Your Life: Optimized Practices for Waking, Working, Learning, Eating, Training, Playing, Sleeping, and Sex* was published in 2018 and became a *New York Times* bestseller. Full of life-hacking tips, nutritional expertise, brain upgrades, and fitness regimens, it guides readers to live more happily and perform more efficiently.

Born in 1981 in Santa Monica, California, Aubrey studied philosophy and classical civilization at the University of Richmond. Today, he is based in Austin, Texas.

He and I spoke for this book via Skype in the autumn of 2019.

- For a list of supplements, apparel, and fitness equipment offered by Onnit, go to *onnit.com*.
- Listen to the *Aubrey Marcus Podcast* on iTunes (one of my favorite episodes is #198, on which he interviews Humble the Poet).
- Check out his book *Own the Day, Own Your Life*, available on both Audible and Amazon.
- To learn more about all the amazing ways to stay connected to Aubrey, check out *AubreyMarcus.com*.

EARLY LIFE

IT STARTED WITH A KICKBOXING COACH

Aubrey first heard about jiu-jitsu more than twenty years ago, from his kickboxing coach, Garth Johnson. Aubrey really appreciated Garth's teaching style. Back then, BJJ wasn't nearly as popular as it is today. Nevertheless, jiu-jitsu moves and principles were already a part of Garth's training repertoire. (As a side note, Garth's dad, Pat, played the tournament referee in the classic 1984 film *The Karate Kid*. He was also the fight choreographer for the movie.)

Garth joined the military after the 9/11 attacks, and Aubrey lost touch with him. Still, to this day he has the greatest respect for his former coach and remembers him fondly. As Aubrey told me, "Your early martial arts coaches—you'll always hold them in a special place in your heart and mind."

Aubrey learned positions like guard, half guard, side control, and full mount from Garth before he even knew which submissions were associated with them. The concept "position before submission" was drilled into Aubrey's mind. He said, "We would spar, we would roll, and it was just a lot of fun. I had a great time exploring something that was brand new, that not a lot of people were aware of, and I just really appreciated all the time I spent with him. He was a great guy."

I found it fascinating to learn Aubrey's coach was teaching him this methodology more than twenty years ago. I would've guessed the opposite and that jiu-jitsu would've been more aggressively taught to go straight for the submission back then. Yet, this is some fundamental teaching that I think has been lost in some of today's instruction. Sometimes, I find new students are enamored with learning a fancy submission or some YouTube trick, but "position before submission" is such a critical element of actually *getting* to the submission. Controlling your opponent and forcing them into bad positions is what I would consider to be true dominance. It isn't wise to rely on lucky, surprise tactics that may only work once.

ON PRESSURE AND ANXIETY
STRUGGLE AND SELF-DISCOVERY

A post on Aubrey's Instagram discusses how we, in general, want things yet don't want to pay the price. I call this the "microwave orientation" in society today. Everyone wants to be an expert overnight, create a successful business in two months, or get fitness results the easy way. The magic pill, the life hack, the get-rich-quick ideas—each of these creates a false narrative, and they're easy to buy into. However, as we all know, the secret is: *there is no secret*. Hard work *works*! Can you shorten the learning curve? Absolutely! Find someone who has done the work and follow that blueprint. The thing is, you cannot *inherit* the hard work. There is just no substitute for getting your hands dirty.

Applied to jiu-jitsu, this means that gold medals and titles can only come from hard work, study, focus, and training. There simply are no shortcuts.

"It's a level playing field," Aubrey told me. "There are no trust fund jiu-jitsu babies. You don't get good because your dad left you with his jiu-jitsu skills. Yeah, maybe you've had private lessons, but you still have to go out there and *work* on your physical fitness, strength, flexibility, and skill game on the mat. It's your sacrifice that determines how good you are."

Recently, jiu-jitsu has been gaining popularity with forward thinkers and self-development gurus similar to Aubrey.

For example, Ryan Holiday and Tim Ferriss both reference jiu-jitsu in their writing and in their various podcasts and blogs. It begs the question: why does something so complex, so physically and mentally demanding, appeal to him and his kind?

"I think we have a certain warrior ethos," Aubrey responded. "We're drawn to struggle because we understand that it creates adaptation and growth." Jiu-jitsu provides a safe outlet for the warriors and for anyone seeking to grow through struggle. We all want to be warriors. How awesome is it to be able to test your physical skills on another human being and try to impose your will without the risk of losing your life like you would on the street? Jiu-jitsu provides that atmosphere, allowing the ego some measure of security.

You can always tap and start over.

Speaking of safety, Aubrey admitted that, in a way, he regrets BJJ's recent shift toward the leg game. While highly effective, it has also "increased the danger threshold for competing." He went on to explain, "I think for somebody who's looking to just have fun safely, those old rules about 'nothing below the knee until you're a blue belt' are great. Being able to go full-out, but not get hurt—there's still a place for that."

BECOMING A CHAMPION
THE AUBREY MARCUS CHALLENGE

Aubrey has respect and admiration for jiu-jitsu, and even sponsors some fighters. That said, he never competed in tournaments himself. It wasn't due to a lack of confidence. As a student at the University of Richmond, Aubrey issued an open challenge: anybody at the university could submission-wrestle him in the study hall at any point. Just name the time and Aubrey would answer the call.

Aubrey's model for his idea was the Gracie Challenge. In the 1920s, the famous family used the same idea to promote their form of jiu-jitsu. Their goal was to prove that BJJ was superior to other martial arts. In one of these challenges, twenty-six-year-old Waldemar Santana famously defeated his former mentor, Helio Gracie, who was forty-two. The fight lasted almost three hours and ended with a soccer kick to Helio's head.

Even in the 2000s, when Aubrey issued his own challenge, people with BJJ experience were still few and far between. Back then, it was a great way to challenge himself. Today, he admitted with a laugh, it would be "the stupidest idea in the world because so many people train jiu-jitsu. It'd be people just wrecking me. But back then, I was super athletic and training off and on for about three years from when I was seventeen or eighteen. So, it wasn't a whole lot, but it was enough."

Interestingly, retired US Navy SEAL Jocko Willink, who is also in this book, told me the same thing in different words: "If I know how to play soccer, and you don't, I'm going to beat you in soccer. And if I know jiu-jitsu, and you don't, I'm going to choke you."

Aubrey remembers his challenge matches taking place *Fight Club* style. The study hall had indoor-outdoor carpeting, and fellow students lined up against the cinder block walls to prevent fighters from crashing head-first into the cement. The way Aubrey described it, most challenges felt easy. "Usually, I was playing around with people and just tapping them," he said.

Aubrey's last challenge match was the toughest one, and it was a spectacle. The audience was so large that the fight had to be moved to a bigger hall. Audrey's opponent outweighed him by thirty or forty pounds, and wasn't trained in jiu-jitsu. He had, however, done some pro wrestling.

"He knew some uncomfortable things he could do," Aubrey said, laughing.

His opponent showed up an hour late, carrying a boombox blasting music, just like in music videos from the 80s. Aubrey said, "He pulled a Miyamoto Musashi move where he made me wait. There were all these people talking shit on his side, his entourage, et cetera, and I was getting amped up."

"By that time, I'm already warmed up and cooled down, and I'm fucking pissed," Aubrey recalled. The adrenaline rush—and then down—was a clear advantage for the other guy, as adrenaline dumps are a real thing. It was an intense match, and overall, things seemed almost even for a long time. During the thirty-five minutes of back and forth, Aubrey's opponent almost had him a few times, but Aubrey wouldn't give in. There was literally too much ego and pride on the line. Finally, Aubrey got his larger opponent in a mounted guillotine and submitted him.

For anyone trained in jiu-jitsu or any grappling sport, a two-minute match can feel long enough. Thirty-five minutes in front of an audience would feel endless to most athletes. Despite this, Aubrey was determined to win.

"Everybody I knew was there," he said slowly, his eyes widening at the memory. "All the girls, all the guys. It was like a big fucking deal. I was just not going to lose, unless—he would have had to actually hurt me."

After that match, the challenges stopped. People obviously knew what they'd be signing up for. For Aubrey, it marked the only time he ever competed in front of a sizable audience; he never fought in any tournaments. He told me the way he sees it, the informal university match was enough of an experience for him.

BEHIND THE SCENES
A PASSION FOR THE STRIKING ARTS

Fast-forward almost two decades, and Aubrey occasionally still rolls with athletes like Kyle Kingsbury. Still, for the most part, he is no longer an active MMA hobbyist. Even when he was training, his focus and passion were more with the striking arts than with BJJ.

Aubrey told me for him, the difference boils down to adrenaline. "Jiu-jitsu feels more meditative. Whenever I roll with anybody, it's rare that I'll even have butterflies." In the striking arts, he could feel the excitement build even before the fight, in the moments, he said, "when you're putting on headgear and you're strapping it up and you're biting down on your mouthpiece."

The challenge with striking, he said, is, "You're reliably taking trauma to your head. It does rearrange the way your face looks." With this, he pointed to his nose, showing me that it's crooked from sparring. Still, he didn't really mind the actual pain of getting hit in the face that came with practicing strikes. What made him want to stop were the inevitable concussions. They really bothered him, and eventually he walked away from the striking arts. "It was never the pain. It was the concussive trauma. That's just not good," he says.

Aubrey stopped training MMA after a fight against UFC heavyweight Paul "The Headhunter" Buentello left him with a head injury.

"He was in Austin and needed sparring partners, and my fucking trainer decided I was a good partner to throw in with him. He just kicked my ass. He didn't put me unconscious. But he stunned me enough that I went out to the parking lot and was like, *What am I doing? Where am I? What's going on?* I obviously had a concussion. Two days later, I quit. I was just tired of getting hit in the head."

To this day, Aubrey misses one specific aspect of doing MMA: the strategy of the game, where you can, as he puts it, "set something up four moves down." He likens all MMA sports to "chess with the body." Aubrey always loved the idea of being able to strategically mislead the opponent and successfully set physical traps—cat and mouse at its finest.

BEST ADVICE

Aubrey shared two lessons from jiu-jitsu. First, he explained that if something fails or doesn't turn out right, it's okay to tap out. Real strength is the ability to acknowledge when you're wrong and keep coming back to something that's better. The bigger message he had to share, though, is one of anti-fragility. "Confidence comes from not being perfect," Aubrey said. "Confidence comes from not being fragile. And humility makes you not fragile."

WORST ADVICE

Aubrey says the worst advice he ever got was: "Don't talk about psychedelics." Aubrey freely talks about mushrooms and ayahuasca on his podcast and how they have changed his life and others' lives dramatically. He was told not to mention this by a lot of people back in 2010 when he was starting Onnit. But ultimately, he reflects, "they were absolutely wrong. The amount of gratitude I have received for sharing my stories honestly has been overwhelming, and it never hurt my business at all."

FINAL THOUGHTS
HUMILITY BUILDS CONFIDENCE

Aubrey believes that practicing jiu-jitsu can teach us about the need for humility in a way that extends off the mat.

"There's something very humbling about admitting defeat, about admitting that you've been bested," he said. He described how it is "good for the human psyche" to see its own vulnerability. Aubrey knows that opponents who are more athletic than him, like Kyle, will eventually tap him. The question is:

how long can Aubrey last without actually being tapped? "Is it two-minute intervals? Is it five-minute intervals? Can I last seven, eight minutes? And what are the strategies I can employ to hold off the advance?"

With a sparring partner like Kyle, there's also never really a "safe" moment on the mat. You can't just sit there and rest in a position because even when a half guard or a lockdown feels safe, a seasoned opponent will find a way to maneuver through the safe zone and submit you. Aubrey said the thing to do, then, is admit defeat and go again. "Now we go again. Now we go *again*." Of the tradition of bumping an opponent's fist and restarting, Aubrey says, "I think that is one of the magical elements of jiu-jitsu. You practice those things on the mat, and you apply them in life."

CHAPTER 16

Felipe Pena

@felipepenabjj, @fpteambjj
facebook.com/felipepenabjj

Born in 1991 in Belo Horizonte, Minas Gerais, Brazil, Felipe "Preguiça" Pena is one of the top BJJ fighters of his generation. He is also the only athlete to have submitted Gordon Ryan in competition. He won two gold medals at ADCC in 2017 (including the prestigious Absolute ADCC Champion), and secured gold medals at the Brazilian Nationals, the Europeans, the Abu Dhabi Pro Championship, and IBJJF World Titles.

"Preguiça" is Portuguese for *sloth*, or lazy. It may not seem a fitting nickname today, but Master Vinícius "Draculino" Magalhães came up with it when Felipe first started practicing jiu-jitsu because in his teens, Felipe was admittedly lazy, overweight, and slow.

He received his black belt from Marcelo Azevedo and Draculino in 2012. Before major tournaments, he trains at Romulo Barral's gym in Northridge, California, but otherwise he represents the Gracie Barra academy in Belo Horizonte. His older brother, Augusto "Tio Chico" Carsalade, is also a well-known grappler.

Felipe owns an academy in Belo Horizonte, Felipe Pena Jiu-Jitsu, a Gracie Barra Affiliate, located at 430—Vila Castela, Nova Lima, MG, Brazil, where he and I met for a training session and our initial interview. It was only a partial interview because we spent so much time training that we ran out of time to complete the interview before I had to Uber back to the airport. Months later, we finished our conversation on Skype.

Felipe was very approachable and kind. After a seminar he taught at our academy in San Diego, some high-level black belts told me it was the best seminar they've ever attended—high praise, indeed, coming from long-tenured black belts.

- For videos of Felipe competing, go to YouTube and search "Felipe Pena."
- To watch Felipe Pena vs. Gordan Ryan, search YouTube.
- One of my favorite matches from Felipe is against Erberth Santos in 2016 at the European Championship. Somehow, Felipe doesn't tap to an extremely deep armbar attack, and he comes back to submit Santos. A must-watch match!

EARLY LIFE
FROM RESISTANCE TO PASSION

In the early 2000s, fifteen-year-old Felipe seemed an unlikely candidate for a successful career in jiu-jitsu. Unlike his older brother, who was already a black belt at that time, Felipe had no interest in BJJ.

"I admired Tio Chico," he told me. "He was staying in shape, traveling the world, and finding friends because of jiu-jitsu. But I had no confidence. I was a chubby kid. And I didn't do sports."

When Tio Chico finally dragged him to the gym, Felipe remained outside of the "cool" circle for months, earning his "Preguiça" nickname. "I just wanted to stand near the wall, talking and joking," he admitted. "I was lazy. But I didn't like the nickname, and my brother kept pushing me, 'You're going to go to class today! You're going to go to class today!'"

Finally, Felipe stopped resisting. As he did, his life began to change. He was making friends; his body felt and looked different; his mental state shifted; his confidence improved. "I started proving to myself and everyone else that I really can do this," he said. "And after a while, I was saying, 'Oh, I can be good at this.'"

Felipe eventually found himself on the mat for hours and hours at a time. As he improved, he was learning more techniques and becoming increasingly competitive. About eighteen months after his first lesson as a blue belt, Felipe realized that he had fallen in love with the sport.

"It was a big gift for my life because it changed me," he said seriously, as we both dripped sweat after our training session. "It changed the way I think, and it gave me many benefits, not just on the mat but in all areas of my life."

ON PRESSURE AND ANXIETY
WORK HARDER

Once he had found his passion for jiu-jitsu, Felipe set an ambitious goal for himself: he wanted to be the best. "I always believed I could do it," he explained. "I was very confident and always saying, 'I'm going to be the best. You'll see!'"

Convinced that he could reach the top, he also made sure not to rush things, instead taking it one step at a time. "You need to put a goal in your mind that you really can achieve," he explained. "And with every goal you reach, you will build confidence for the next step. Winning the World Champion title is not something that happens overnight. It's a really, really long way."

When I asked him whether he ever thought about quitting, he admitted that defeats used to frustrate him. But he also described how they would drive him to apply himself even more. When he was training every day and still not winning, he decided to make the physical training more intense. When he was training harder but still losing, he decided to eat better. When he was eating better and still not winning, he found something else to change. "When I lost, I never came back and said, 'Oh, I don't want to train. I'm too sad.' I always returned more motivated than before, and with one thing more in my routine. After a while, I started to win."

While he didn't necessarily see himself as the most talented fighter, he told me that he was sure he could work harder than anyone else; he believed he would be the best because he was going to put all his energy into succeeding. In times of doubt, he remembered something he had learned early on in life: "There will be storms along the way."

BECOMING A CHAMPION
TRAIN LIKE ONE

When Felipe isn't preparing for a competition, he teaches until late at night and therefore likes to sleep in until about 9:00 a.m. Before tournaments, he trains three times a day and eats healthy food every three or four hours. His program includes jiu-jitsu, wrestling, and strength and conditioning training.

As a purple and brown belt living in California, he used to drive two hours a day to get to his preferred gym. Once there, he trained four times. Many times, he didn't feel like training, or he was sick, but he still kept going.

"Everyone has a way," he said, sitting up straight. "My way was really hard work. I trained more than anyone back in the day. Now, with the experience, I don't need to kill myself anymore."

Looking back, he told me, the journey to the top has been long and hard. "Everyone wants to win," he explained, "but no one wants to pay the price. People don't see the sacrifice.

If I could tell them what the real price is, 99 percent of them would say, 'Oh, that's what I need to do? Then I don't want that anymore.'"

Most jiu-jitsu athletes agree that BJJ is a sport of self-discovery; to this point, Felipe told me the sport changed his mentality. He went from being a shy, insecure kid to a mentally strong, confident fighter. The way he put it, "Even in the beginning, even when I was white belt, *I started discovering how tough I can be mentally.* Because this is not about physical strength. It is all about the mentality. If I'm in an armlock and I'm mentally weak, I will lose the fight."

One way to train the mind, Felipe said, is to keep pushing. "If your coach tells you to do twelve rounds of ten minutes, after the third round, you could say, 'I can't do this,' or you can keep pushing until you finish the training."

When I asked him whether the continued practice of dealing with obstacles makes it easier over time, he said, "One hundred percent! There will be many times in your journey where you can either give up or keep pushing. And the more you push, the stronger you get." He went on to explain that he has gotten used to overcoming obstacles. He no longer finds himself thinking, *I can't do this.*

I think many people believe obstacles disappear once you reach a certain level, but as Felipe described, the obstacles don't *ever* go away. They become a natural part of the journey. Instead of wishing that obstacles never rear their ugly heads, we should welcome them. *That* is where we will see our growth.

BEHIND THE SCENES
ROLE MODELS AND IMPACT

Felipe told me his dad is the most important role model and mentor in his life. As far as role models from the sport itself, he named none other than his professor, Romulo Barral.

"When I was just a blue belt," he explained, "he was already a world champion many times over. So, he's the guy I look to for showing me how I can accomplish my goals in jiu-jitsu."

He mentioned that, so far, Marcus "Buchecha" Almeida, Rodolfo Vieira, and Leandro Lo have been his toughest opponents. Buchecha beat him most recently in the Worlds 2019 quarterfinal, Rodolfo won against him in the ADCC 2015 final, and Leandro won in the Rio Open semifinal in 2013.

Felipe and I also talked about his ambitions for the sport. He has set them high. "I want to be the best of my generation," he said with passion. "I want to win Worlds at least four times and surpass André Galvão's record for superfight wins, which is also four. I can still do that because I'm young."

He also expressed a desire to be a role model for other BJJ athletes. He told me there's a growing interest in jiu-jitsu in both the public and the media, and he wants to set a good example to help the sport grow.

In February 2019, after the BJJ Stars final in São Paulo, Felipe had an experience contrary to what he would like to see in BJJ. There was a huge buildup to the heated rivalry main event: Felipe Pena versus Erberth Santos. I was in the arena in São Paulo that day, and the energy was palpable. The match started with ferocity, and in moments, Erberth seemed to injure his knee. As he was being attended on the mat by a medic for the injury, he heard people in the audience screaming that he was faking. In a split second, Santos jumped up and charged into the crowd, aiming for Felipe's team.

Unfortunately, this quickly deteriorated into a gigantic brawl involving what seemed like all the crowd. It took officials several minutes to break up the chaos, and the fight ended with Felipe winning by the disqualification of his opponent. He commented afterward on Instagram: "It's a shame what happened; despite the victory I'm sad today. I got ready and I dedicated a lot to give a show for you and unfortunately, it ended unexpectedly! Sad, [THIS] SPORT IS NOT THAT," followed by a thumbs-down emoji.

This moment was a black eye for jiu-jitsu, no doubt. The sport has a long way to go to truly step out of the shadows and into the mainstream. There is still work to be done to overcome some of the assumptions that the martial art is just for tough "thugs." Felipe's Instagram post showed the world that the future of jiu-jitsu is in good hands with athletes like him.

BEST ADVICE

Without hesitating, Felipe said the best advice he ever received was his brother's insistence that he start doing jiu-jitsu. He believes BJJ can be beneficial not just for the person practicing it, but also for their family, friends, and other people in their life. "It can happen in many ways," he said. "Everyone has their own story about why jiu-jitsu is good for them."

WORST ADVICE

Felipe remembers accepting a tournament invite even though he wasn't able to put his full effort into the camp. People around him encouraged him to take the match even though they knew he couldn't train for it the way he normally would.

He ultimately lost, and feels he shouldn't have listened to those who gave him this advice, because he knew he should always give a full effort. "Never do something if you can't do it 100 percent. Sometimes we think we can do a lot of things, but it's not worth it unless you can give your best effort. It's better to do less on your list and do it 100 percent."

FINAL THOUGHTS
DON'T GIVE UP

"Don't give up!" he exclaimed near the end of our interview. Whether in jiu-jitsu or in business, Felipe stressed that *not giving up* will make us stronger. "Nothing in life is easy," he added, "and if you want something, you have to go for it."

CHAPTER 17

Alexandre "Xande" Ribeiro

⦿ @xanderibeirojj, @sixbladesjiujitsu
🐦 @xanderibeirojj
ⓕ facebook.com/xanderibeirojj

Born in Manaus, Amazonas, Brazil, in 1981, Xande Ribeiro is a seven-time black belt World Champion, a two-time ADCC Champion, and one of only six men to have won two black belt IBJJF Absolute World titles. He is also an IBJJF Hall of Fame athlete.

A successful competitor from a young age, Xande received his black belt from his older brother, Saulo Ribeiro, in 2001. After moving to the United States in 2002, the two brothers founded the Ribeiro Jiu-Jitsu Association in Toledo, Ohio.

Five years later, they started the University of Jiu-Jitsu in San Diego, California. In 2020, Xande moved to Austin, Texas, opened an academy, and formed his new association, Six Blades Jiu-Jitsu.

Among other things, Xande is renowned for never having his guard passed in competition. In fact, in a 2012 interview with *GracieMag*, Dean Lister said, "Xande is very experienced and very calm... He's like a snake that hides without moving, very patient and smart. He doesn't look very strong, but he is, and when the time is right, he can hit you with a deadly move!"

Xande and I met for our interview at a café by the beach in San Diego for breakfast and coffee. A passionate storyteller, he came across as sensitive, calm, and cerebral. His academy is located at 13642 US 183 Ste. 300, Austin, TX 78750.

- Search YouTube for many of Xande's greatest fights.
- To see a list of his accomplishments, go to *bjjheroes.com* and *wikipedia.com*.
- Visit *BJJFanatics.com* for a Diamond Concept tutorial.
- Go to *BJJLibrary.com* for a comprehensive library of Xande's techniques.
- Xande was featured in his brother's book, Jiu-Jitsu University, which is available on Amazon. (This also happens to be the first book I read about jiu-jitsu—I highly recommend it).

EARLY LIFE
FROM GRASS FIGHTS TO JIU-JITSU SCHOOL

I asked about his introduction to BJJ, and Xande explained to me that rolling around and wrestling has always been in his blood. Growing up in Manaus, he and his group of friends settled disagreements with physical fights. "Let's go to the grass!" one of them would say, and the boys proceeded with a grappling match on the nearest patch of green. Xande had previously taken judo lessons because his mom hoped the martial art would teach him discipline. So unlike his friends, he was familiar with moves like headlocks, armlocks, and over-the-shoulder bridges.

But one day, at age ten, he came home from a fight on the grass angry and hurting. One of the smaller kids had managed to get inside Xande's guard and squeezed his neck until Xande tapped. Not only did it hurt, but it also really pissed him off. When Xande complained to his brother about the pain and the humiliation, Saulo said, "Maybe it's time for you to get a little stronger. I'm doing jiu-jitsu. Let's go!"

His decision was made. Xande immediately called his mom and said, "Mom, I'm going with Saulo to do jiu-jitsu. I don't know what it is, but I want to try." She subsequently bought him a gi, and he was off to the mats.

Xande joined Saulo for instruction at the Associação Monteiro academy, which was run by the Monteiro brothers. They were four lawyers with a passion for jiu-jitsu, passing on what they had learned from the Gracies. Xande described the Monteiro teaching style as unstructured, intuitive, and situational.

"Everybody talks about drilling now," Xande said. "But at the time, we just trained. In the first two hours of my first class, I learned hook sweeps and hip escapes. We also learned how to armlock from guarding. And then, once we drilled that portion of the class, it pretty much went like this: the guy is on top of you, now try to escape."

But he wasn't truly *sold* on jiu-jitsu until an early training session where he was learning to scissor sweep and mount. Xande got stuck underneath another kid and vowed to never let it happen again.

"The kid was smaller than me, and I couldn't get away from him," Xande said emphatically about the memory. "It was pretty nerve-wracking. I told myself, *I don't want to be smothered ever in my life. I don't want any human being near my face.*"

As his jiu-jitsu skills improved, Xande occasionally still grappled on the grass with his friends. Some of them were doing karate and taekwondo, but he would regularly take them down because his grappling skills were superior. Eventually, the other boys' interests turned entirely to girls, and their fights stopped.

ON PRESSURE AND ANXIETY
A GRACIE MOMENT

Xande and Saulo practiced jiu-jitsu side by side in Manaus for about a year before Saulo left for college in Rio to train at

Gracie Humaita. When Saulo came home to visit, he shared with Xande all the new secrets and techniques he was learning. Unlike the Monteiro brothers, the Gracies had a very structured approach focused on self-defense that was tailored to their clients—mostly executives. The Gracie approach cautions that to turn pupils loose to spar without structure is too dangerous.

This approach, by the way, seems to have formed the foundation for how jiu-jitsu classes are taught today. I believe this has also aided in jiu-jitsu's growth over the last few decades, because it has a much broader appeal since it allows students to practice and learn in a safe way.

As Xande grew older, Saulo showed him there was more to jiu-jitsu than "Let's go, guys!" He learned the real, gentle art. Xande also started competing, though not in a serious way. His plan wasn't to win Worlds; his plan was simply to have fun. Nevertheless, he kept winning and became state champion multiple times.

"In my first seven years of jiu-jitsu, I maybe lost two or three times," he recalled. "I just liked jiu-jitsu, and because I didn't approach it with so much pressure, I was able to be very free."

As an orange belt, Xande participated in a national tournament in Rio in 1993. It was his first time, and since there were no other athletes in his division—ninety-two pounds (forty-two kilo)—he had to fight in the heavyweight class, which represented a difference of twenty-six pounds. Xande couldn't help but notice how much bigger the other kid was. Clearly, the size difference made a big impression on him because, in the course of our conversation, he explained details as minute as his opponent's facial expression and hands when describing seeing him before the final. Xande was waiting at the gate, ready to be called for that final match, when he suddenly had a Gracie moment. The story, as he told it, goes like this: "Everybody was in the gymnasium. Carlos Gracie was there, talking about the Gracies. I was listening to him. Next thing, he was walking right toward my gate. I was looking at him. He looked at me. He touched my shoulder, smiled at me, and said, 'You're going to be good, kid.' I thought, *Wow, he touched my shoulder. Okay, I'm fighting next!* I was twelve, and I won the championship."

BECOMING A CHAMPION
ATTITUDE MATTERS

When Xande was fifteen years old, his mom grounded him from jiu-jitsu for an entire year because of his poor academic performance in school. This so drastically removed Xande from the world of BJJ that he even missed his brother's huge and victorious milestone: Saulo won the first-ever inaugural Worlds. Xande was only aware of it after the fact. "Jiu-jitsu didn't really happen or exist that year for me," he said. Xande resumed training in late 1996, and coming back felt like returning to family.

When a friend, first-ever World Champion William Couto, kept bragging about his Worlds title in the rooster-weight blue belt division, Xande wasn't impressed. William, obviously proud and confident, told Xande he was in trouble and he was going to get smashed. However, what happened next surprised William. "I trained, and nobody could do much to me," Xande explained. "Nobody passed my guard. *Nobody submitted me.* William got the best of me and swept me a few times, but I thought, *This is interesting. How could I be gone for a whole year, come back, and actually survive? Maybe I should try this Worlds stuff.*"

The following year, after training for only six months, Xande competed in a World Championship for the first time. Worlds was quite different back then, and it required that competitors win a state championship first in order to qualify—which Xande did. However, he and his training partner were actually juveniles (in jiu-jitsu, this means age sixteen and under). Therefore, Worlds had no specific category for them to fight in. Undeterred, the teens instead signed up in the adult lightweight division.

Incredibly, Xande won third place. He lost to Rodrigo Pinheiro, who went on to fight none other than Fernando "Tererê" Augusto himself. So, the podium consisted of Xande Ribeiro, Rodrigo Pinheiro, and Tererê. This was obviously quite the accomplishment for young Xande, and it was a sign of many big things to come.

As the younger sibling of a star, trying to make your own name in any sport or profession can be hard. During our interview, Xande humbly admitted to his own struggles with this very issue.

"I had this whole thing about being Saulo's younger brother," he said. Some people treated him with genuine respect for who he was, but others saw him only as Saulo's little brother. In one anecdote, Xande shared that he was competing in the Brazilian nationals in 1998 as a purple belt. He overheard a conversation between his next opponent and that opponent's friend.

"Hey, you're fighting Saulo's brother, Xande?" the friend said.

"Yeah, he can't be as good as his brother."

Then and there, Xande thought, *Okay! I'll beat the crap out of him*—which he proceeded to do. Xande won, twelve points to zero.

Of course, being related to Saulo also had its advantages. His brother taught him moves and techniques one-on-one. He introduced Xande to the Gracies at a very young age. Moreover, Saulo sponsored his younger brother. In 1998, during Xande's last year of high school, Saulo bought him a ticket to the Pan-Ams in Hawaii. There, Xande competed and won.

Still, Xande told me his brother's most substantial boon had nothing to do with money, connections, or BJJ technique.

It was about *attitude*.

The year was 1999. Xande, a purple belt, had made it to the finals of Worlds that year, where he eventually fought Ricardo Bastos. Before reaching the finals, Xande recalled for me his first opponent. Even then, he noticed how respectful the other man was.

"He was older than me, probably twenty-one, and I was eighteen, but he was very respectful. He looked me in the eye like a man and told me, 'It's an honor for me to fight you.'"

Xande won that first match and each fight after, which led to the finals against Ricardo Bastos. During that match, there was a moment when Xande mounted Ricardo. Once he secured the position, Xande allowed a big grin to spread across his face. At the time, he relished the victorious moment, and even showed off a bit.

He won the fight, but once it was over, Xande's brother set him straight right away. Frowning, he told Xande, "You looked like a clown smiling like that."

That marked a turning point in Xande's life and the humbling beginning of a new journey. Instead of celebrating being a World Champion at purple belt, instead of thinking, *I'm the best; I am the World Champion,* his thoughts became more reflective and mindful. *How could I let my attitude turn me into a disrespectful showoff—in the finals, no less—after someone just told me it's an honor to fight me in my first match?* He resolved to immediately change his attitude and always be the best version of himself.

"Yeah, I won," he said seriously. "But you're only a champion if you carry yourself as a champion."

BEHIND THE SCENES
INJURIES AND SETBACKS AND A LESSON LEARNED

Xande told me he never intended to make a living from jiu-jitsu. In his family, education was considered more important than sports, and after high school, he studied to become a lawyer while training jiu-jitsu on the side. Thanks to a series of challenges, he realized jiu-jitsu was his calling, and he was on a path that extended beyond the mat.

In my conversation with the champion, I learned that he approaches setbacks with a spiritual mindset—he takes them as a sign that there's learning to do. If the same challenges continue presenting themselves to us, in Xande's view, it's because we have failed to master the lesson. If we persevere, we will eventually succeed.

"At some point," he said, speaking to life and its iterations, "you will get what you deserve. It can be the World Championship, a big academy, or the love of your life."

The lessons aren't always easy to learn. In the year 2000, Xande hurt his knee in a fight against Bruno Bastos. Still, he insisted on participating in Worlds just two weeks after the injury, and he won the title in his division. However, as he was leaving the mat after his third fight, one he'd won by twenty-six points, his teammates seemed distressed. They were all looking into the distance with stunned, somber faces.

The unthinkable had happened: an athlete one mat over from Xande's match had died of a heart attack during Xande's fight. The incident rattled Xande. *What if I die?* he thought. The finality of death haunted him for years to come. This was only exacerbated as the champion grew older and more experienced.

The year 2002 marked the worst moment of Xande's life. He was competing in Worlds as a black belt and reinjured his knee in a match against Jefferson Moura. Xande collapsed on the mat in agonizing pain, and all he could think was, *This isn't fair. I was in such good shape. I don't deserve this. God, what the fuck?*

Xande left the mat in tears, but his big brother Saulo dragged him up the stairs. "Let's go," he told Xande. "You're not going to cry in front of these people." In that moment, the champion had forgotten to be the best version of himself. He forgot life happens *for* you and not *to* you.

As they were exiting the arena, the brothers came across a man sitting in their way, inadvertently blocking the aisle of the steps toward the upper exit.

"The guy looked at me with pity," Xande recalled, shaking his head slowly from side to side. "Like he was saying, 'Aww, poor Xande! He's crying. Let me make room for him.'"

As the man tried to move, Xande noticed the man *had no legs*. He was using his hands to lift his body to scoot over and give way to Xande. It was a seminal moment.

The guy has no legs! Xande thought, *And I'm complaining about a hurt knee?* After they passed the man, Xande stopped, turned to Saulo, and said, "You go ahead. I can walk." He wiped the tears off his face and told himself, *My mental therapy starts now.*

The encounter with the man on the stairs is seared in Xande's memory. "It was the moment of my life when I felt the most crappy," he admitted. "I felt crappy many times afterward, but that instance was the *pinnacle* of crappy." It was a reminder for Xande, as he put it, "Lessons are just lessons if your attitude doesn't change. It must become a habit. My new attitude hadn't become a habit yet."

His positive attitude was often tested. In 2003, Xande experienced his biggest challenge yet. By this time, he and Saulo had already moved to Toledo, Ohio, and started the Ribeiro Jiu-Jitsu Association. The future was looking bright. When Xande traveled to Rio to prepare for ADCC in March, he contracted a bacterial skin infection, cellulitis, on his shin. It became so severe, it could have very well resulted in the amputation of his lower leg.

The physician who attempted to drain the swelling failed to administer enough local anesthesia. After several unsuccessful numbing attempts, the doctor eventually just cut into Xande's leg to remove the puss. It poured out by the cupful. The drainage was horrific and agonizing for Xande. Unable to use his leg, he had to lie down for more than ten days, all while taking strong antibiotics. He hired a nurse to help him drain the wound every three hours, and his only way of getting to the bathroom was by crab-walking to it.

It was a bad situation. The ADCC competition only comes around every two years, and Xande really wanted to be there. The doctor's advice was, "If you can walk, maybe you can fight." Xande made it happen. After two weeks of zero training, he found a way to wrap his leg for the trip to ADCC and got on a flight.

But the nightmare wasn't over yet. On the plane to São Paulo, Xande sat next to another athlete, Alexandre Cacareco, whom he considered a friend. The two men agreed to share the prize money equally if they both made it to the final.

"Let's be honest with each other," they agreed. "And let's make the final." However, when the two men met in the semifinal, Xande was in for a surprise. Alexandre went straight for his injured leg and footlocked him right after Xande pulled guard. Xande was deeply disappointed. He felt betrayed by his friend, and questioned the concept of honor in jiu-jitsu. He was so unhappy that he was ready to quit the whole sport. *These dirty people! What does honor even mean?*

He moved back to Manaus, Brazil, and soon fell into a downward spiral. "I was living in my aunt's house with maids and cooks," he told me. "I got fat, my belly was big, and I smoked a pack of cigarettes a day. I was going out, drinking a bottle of whiskey every time I did. I had money from my sponsors coming in, and I spent it all."

About four months into Xande's depression, Saulo called him. His brother reminded Xande of the shared academy in Toledo and said, "We have a mission, bro. Don't lose your respect just to accept family money!"

That intervention marked another turning point in Xande's life. His leg still pained him, but Xande put down the phone, grabbed a pair of running shoes, and ran ten miles.

"I needed to lose this!" he exclaimed in our interview, pointing at his stomach. However, the pain in his leg was still troubling. He consulted with physicians and shamans and even tried spiritual surgery for healing. He moved to Rio, where he continued drinking alcohol, but also heard the pleas of his peers and friends in the BJJ community: "Jiu-jitsu needs people like you!"

By the end of summer 2003, Xande was ready for a comeback. He couldn't return to the United States immediately because his visa had expired, but he sobered up, began training incessantly at Gracie Humaita, and helped out at the academy as much as he could. His focus had returned.

By 2004, he was once again winning major BJJ titles. By 2006, Xande felt he had made it. First, he received a new US visa, and then he defeated Roger Gracie at Worlds.

"Finally, I was number one in my sport," he said, as he looked up toward the sky from our table at the café. "I remember thinking, *Look at everything I went through. I came back, and I learned to be humble.* The injuries broke me. But they also made me."

Listening to Xande, I was reminded of something inspirational author Eleanor Brownn once said: "A comeback is a setback that did its homework, learned the lesson, and then moved forward."

One of the secrets of Xande's success seems to be his demeanor; he is poised in any situation. I was curious to hear about his mental state before competitions. Does he go into a match thinking, *I've trained so hard for this, that's why I will succeed,* or does he tell himself, *I will give my best, and hopefully it works out?*

It turns out, it's neither.

"Everybody trains hard," he explained. "I try not to have *hopes and wishes.* What it comes down to is why am I here and what am I fighting for? It's about the intention: do I want to be here?"

To illustrate his point, he brought up Worlds 2008, where he spent the final two weeks before the tournament lying flat in bed because of a back injury. He knew he was otherwise in really good shape, and he didn't give up. Xande competed and won his second Absolute title by defeating Roger Gracie with a move he created, the "Xande Guruma."

"I beat the best in the world," he said with conviction, *"and it was because I freaking wanted to be there. I was happy to be there."*

His mindset was, *This is my moment. This is my place. There is no other place in the world I would rather be.* There was no posturing, no Instagram photos of hard training sessions, no chasing likes on social media. Being present in that moment at Worlds was all that mattered. As for the times when Xande lost a match, the champion knew deep down he really *didn't* want to be there. Yes, maybe he trained hard, and he was ready, but his intention had failed him, or maybe better put, he failed his true intention.

When I asked him how he deals with mental and physical pain, Xande told me he uses training sessions to find and extend the limits of his endurance. He deliberately pushes himself to the point of agony until, as he described it, the pain becomes pleasure.

His explanation reminded me of Navy SEAL David Goggins, who wrote in his book *Can't Hurt Me: Master Your Mind and Defy the Odds*, "I brainwashed myself into craving discomfort. If it was raining, I would go run. Whenever it started snowing, my mind would say, *Get your fucking running shoes on*. Sometimes I wussed out and had to deal with it at the Accountability Mirror. But facing that mirror, facing myself, motivated me to fight through uncomfortable experiences, and, as a result, I became tougher. And being tough and resilient helped me meet my goals."

BEST ADVICE

When I asked Xande how he managed to muster up confidence when his injuries forced him to sit out for weeks at a time, his response helped me realize he doesn't live in the negative thoughts.

"I don't fight negativity," he admitted, shaking his head. "I learned really early on that if you fight those thoughts, they come back stronger and they keep haunting you." Instead, Xande looks at disadvantages as a way to tell his mind it is a positive thing. A classic example is the ten days when he was confined to his bed and couldn't train. He simply turned the potentially negative narrative into, *This rest is needed.* As Xande put it, "I say, you know what? Those ten days, they're good rest days. I don't call them days I'm lying down. I just call them days where my body is getting ready."

WORST ADVICE

"Be careful where you get your advice from," Xande cautions. "There are a lot of black belts who think they are life coaches. There is a big difference between being a coach and being a leader." Remember, just because a person is a black belt, it doesn't mean they are above anyone else. Be careful if a black belt acts as if you should listen to everything they say.

FINAL THOUGHTS
JIU-JITSU AS A SPIRITUAL PURSUIT

Xande made it clear throughout our conversation that, for him, jiu-jitsu is more than a profession: it is his calling. He told me BJJ helped him grow into the person he is today, and to that end, he wants to help others see it as a spiritual pursuit.

"Jiu-jitsu is beautiful," he said fondly. "We in the jiu-jitsu community should want old ladies to go, 'Oh, I want to learn jiu-jitsu! It's so cool!'"

Xande is right. Jiu-jitsu can truly be for people of all ages, genders, and abilities. You don't have to be a big tough guy with cauliflower ears to be good at jiu-jitsu. Most gyms are populated by an extremely diverse group of athletes and enthusiasts. Go into any BJJ gym today and you'll find a melting pot of religions, ages, and genders right before your eyes. As a true ambassador of the sport, Xande's purpose, it seems, is to champion that message and share it around the world.

Since founding the Ribeiro Academy with his brother, Xande has traveled extensively for seminars and spent a good deal of time in Asia and Europe. There, he tries to be as relatable as he is at home, in spite of his jiu-jitsu celebrity status. If Xande can better connect with a BJJ athlete by sleeping on their couch instead of staying alone in a five-star hotel, he'll do so. He lives a simple life without the need for glitz, glamor, or first-class plane tickets.

And beyond just making an impact on the sport, Xande wants to touch people's lives in general. "Looking a person in the eye and seeing how they feel is the best thing," he said. "I want to touch people because that's what jiu-jitsu is about."

UPDATE

In the time since we spoke, Xande lost at the 2022 Worlds, and retired on the mats. When someone retires from jiu-jitsu, they leave their belt on the mat, a tradition that Xande followed. In a moving moment, as Xande laid his belt down, folded in front of his body, he knelt down on his knees and sobbed to himself as the crowd cheered on.

CHAPTER 18

Rafael Lovato Jr.

lovatojr.com
 @lovatojrbjj
facebook.com/lovatojrbjj

Rafael Lovato Jr. was born in Cincinnati, Ohio, in 1983. His family moved to Oklahoma City, Oklahoma, when he was eight. The son of a Jeet Kune Do instructor, Rafael practiced martial arts even as a small child. He also trained and competed in boxing.

In 2004, Rafael received his black belt in jiu-jitsu from Carlos Machado, and then began training with the Ribeiro brothers. In 2007, Rafael became the first non-Brazilian to win the Brazilian nationals in his weight class, and also the first American to win the Europeans. In 2013, he became the first non-Brazilian athlete to win Brazilian Nationals in the Open Weight Absolute Division.

Perhaps most impressively of all, Professor Lovato is also the first American to ever secure an industry "Grand Slam." A Grand Slam consists of winning gold in the same year at the four largest IBJJF tournaments: Pan-Ams, Worlds, Brazilian Nationals, and Europeans.

Today, Rafael owns and manages Lovato's School of Brazilian Jiu-Jitsu and Mixed Martial Arts in Oklahoma City. This location has replaced his old headquarters and is a powerhouse of a gym. He has clearly put a lot of time, heart, money, and effort into making it the premier jiu-jitsu academy in Oklahoma, and quite possibly of the entire Midwest. It is definitely worth a visit!

Rafael is a busy man, and I was grateful for any time he could make for me. Much of our interview took place at a local barbershop while Rafael was receiving a haircut, and our time together was enjoyable and low-key. I loved listening back to the audio of this interview and hearing the buzz of hair trimmers and friendly, ambient shop sounds in the background.

- His academy is located at 10944 N. May Ave., Oklahoma City, OK 73120.
- Check out a documentary by Ryan Smith featuring Lovato called "True Martial Artist ft. Rafael Lovato" (which I highly recommend!) on YouTube.
- For a comprehensive library of his training videos, go to *BJJFanatics.com* (I'm currently studying his tutorial "Pressure Passing and Top Game Domination").
- Many of his best fights in jiu-jitsu can be found with a simple search of "Rafael Lovato" on YouTube.

EARLY LIFE
FROM JEET KUNE DO TO BJJ

As the son of a martial arts instructor, Rafael can't remember life without Jeet Kune Do, Eskrima, boxing, and Muay Thai boxing. An only child, he told me his early memories include sitting off to the side playing with G.I. Joes during his dad's lessons, and play-sparring with him at home. He looked up to his father and wanted to be like him.

"I just wanted to train," Rafael told me. "At home, my dad used to put on mitts and gloves, and I'd hit the mitts. He'd get on his knees and spar with me. It made me tough early on."

Rafael was ten years old when his father was formally introduced to jiu-jitsu. He was attending a Jeet Kune Do instructors conference where Rorion and Royce Gracie taught jiu-jitsu. Lovato Sr. then started taking trips to California to learn more from them and, later, from the Machado brothers.

After Carlos Machado moved to Texas in late 1995, Lovato Sr.'s trips to California turned into weekly drives to Texas, all because he wanted to learn from others and bring that knowledge back to Oklahoma. Every Thursday morning, he got in the car and traveled the three-and-a-half hours to Dallas. There, he had a private lesson, followed by that morning's class. From there, he drove straight back to teach Rafael's martial arts class.

Needless to say, Rafael's dad was fully committed to his son's success.

"He did that for about three years straight, every Thursday, never stopped," Rafael said with a look of pride. "It was immediately a huge game changer for us. And, it was heaven-sent for my father."

Rafael began seriously focusing on BJJ when he was thirteen. Just two years later, he was taking trips with his dad to Dallas to train with Carlos Machado. He also started to fly west for instruction and competitions in the Los Angeles area and to Florida for the coveted Pan-Ams tournament.

In 1999, Rafael traveled to Brazil for the first time. It was an unlikely destination for anyone from Oklahoma, let alone a teenager. This trip to Rio, where he participated in Worlds (Mundials), changed his life. It was Rafael's first exposure to poverty, an experience that mentally separated him from his peers in high school. "I was sixteen and going to a third-world country, seeing real poverty, all the homeless people... It made me understand how good we have it here," he told me. "I grew up really fast."

Being at Worlds also changed Rafael's perception of jiu-jitsu. He saw people fight in their scrubs. There was screaming, banging on drums, and lots of sweat. "It was raw," he recalled. "I saw everybody fighting for pure pride and passion and the love of jiu-jitsu, representing their team and their family. No one's getting famous. No one's making money. It was intense, and I fell in love with it."

When Rafael competed in Worlds 2000 as a juvenile blue belt one year later, he placed third in his weight class and second in the Absolute Division that crosses all weight classes.

The blue and black belt Absolutes were held concurrently, and the two divisions shared a warm-up area. Since Rafael kept winning, he found himself sitting next to top athletes like Saulo Ribeiro, Margarida, and Roberto "Roleta" Magalhães. It was an exhilarating moment for young Rafael. "I remember being around them and feeling the energy. It was just so cool," he told me, smiling at the memory.

Rafael fought eight matches in the tournament. His opponents included Tanquinho, Vinny Magalhães, Luiz "Big Mac" Theodoro, and Ricardo "Demente" Abreu.

"Me being an Oklahoma kid without a black belt instructor on a daily basis, no access to anybody as world champion teammates, and being able to beat these Brazilian kids—that was when I first felt *I can be good. I can do something with this.*"

Rafael had good reason to be excited. In 2000, there were only a handful of American athletes who could successfully compete on an international level, and most of them fought in the blue, purple, and brown belt divisions. "It was already a *big* deal to be American, competing in Brazilian jiu-jitsu," Lovato added.

Hawaii's B.J. Penn was one such fighter. After winning a silver at Worlds 1998 and a bronze in 1999, in 2000 B.J. became the first American to win the Worlds black belt title. When Rafael saw B.J. win the championship that year, his own goal crystallized. *I'm going to be the next American to win Worlds at black belt,* he told himself.

ON PRESSURE AND ANXIETY
A STUDENT OVERCOMING DOUBTS AND DEFEATS

As Rafael discussed his success in 2000, I found myself with more questions than answers. How did Rafael do it? How did he compensate for his lack of access to top-level instructors on a daily basis? How did he make up for not being able to train at the best academies?

Rafael grinned at me in response. The answer was that he and his dad didn't just train—they *studied* the sport.

Relentlessly.

When they rolled, trained together, and worked techniques and positions, the pair always came up with questions. When one of them found somebody who might be able to help, they weren't shy to seek that person's advice. Rafael told me he made sure to write their answers down. "We were very studious and would put our minds together all the time," he added.

He also never missed a training opportunity. "I always trained with everybody," he explained. "I wanted to get my fix of rounds. I wanted to roll with the best guys, as much as I could. And I would write down the games they would play, the moves they were good at."

Rafael filled stacks of notebooks, mapping possible solutions to the problems he consistently recognized. The champion even took notes at tournaments if he didn't understand what he was seeing, and then later asked various athletes at the tournament for an answer to his question.

That said, there was a problem with this approach. Rafael wasn't able to develop a system because he received a wide variety of answers from so many different people. "I was learning so much, but I didn't really have a specific game," he explained. "So, my own game would wander. It changed a lot. Many times, I couldn't decide what I wanted to do."

Sometimes, when confronted with athletes like Rafael whom we admire and maybe even envy for their success, we can forget that every journey to the top comes with major challenges.

"Just like in life, it's never a smooth, uphill experience. There's always the ups and downs," Lovato said. "It's a lot of hard work. It only gets harder as you go through the ranks."

As if to punctuate his point, Rafael then told me his biggest crisis presented itself as a series of defeats, doubts, and setbacks before and after his promotion to brown belt.

It began with his entry into college. A student at Oklahoma University and living at home, Rafael's attention was split between classes and martial arts. As a result, he wasn't doing well in either school or in jiu-jitsu.

At eighteen years old, Rafael was on his way back to the university's campus when his car was struck by another driver. Rafael's vehicle lost traction on the road, spun around, and crashed. His back was severely bruised, and his spine was out of whack. The resulting injuries, coupled with ongoing litigation, kept him off the mats for several months.

"Even if I wanted to get on the mats, I couldn't happen to be seen training or just be around the school," the champion told me. Any attempts he might have wanted to make to stretch and heal in the gym could have resulted in issues for his court case.

Shortly after recovering, Rafael was promoted from purple to brown belt. As a purple belt, he had grown used to being successful. He had beaten stars like Robert Drysdale, and he left many tournaments with more than one gold medal. He was undefeated in the United States, and he'd even secured a bronze at Worlds in Brazil.

As a brown belt, it was immediately clear that things were different, and Rafael grew worried his promotion had come too soon. While his opponents had each developed a sharp game and specific systems as they worked their way up through blue and purple, Rafael realized he *didn't know who he was in jiu-jitsu*. His unsystematic approach to implementation and lack of high-level training with a squad of black belts were finally catching up with him.

He started losing.

During Rafael's first year as a brown belt, he had a .500 record with twelve losses and twelve wins. His reputation for being "America's Best Teenager" was threatened when Ryron and Rener Gracie began competing. In 2002, both athletes submitted Rafael.

Unaccustomed to losing, the young champion felt devastated. "I didn't know how to handle it," he admitted. "I thought, *Maybe I'm not going to be the black belt I thought I would be.* I lost a little bit of hope."

BECOMING A CHAMPION
CATCHING SAULO RIBEIRO'S ATTENTION

Thankfully, 2003 marked a turning point for Rafael. That year, Rafael competed in the Arnold Pro NoGi Worlds. At the time, it was the biggest jiu-jitsu tournament outside of the Abu Dhabi Combat Club World Championship (ADCC).

There, he met Saulo Ribeiro. The two athletes fought in the middleweight class, a class that goes up to 195 pounds.

Rafael and Saulo were on opposite ends of the bracket.

"This was destiny," Rafael emphasized, though he was careful not to move while the barber kept trimming. Still, his eyes lit up at the memory as he continued. "Saulo was already a legend. I was just in awe of him. He was a mystical figure to me. He might as well have been Batman or something."

Rafael faced one of Saulo's students, Regis Lebre, in the semifinal. Aside from Saulo, Regis was the only Brazilian black belt in the division, and so he was expected to defeat Rafael and then go on to face Saulo in the finals.

But Rafael defeated Regis.

"Saulo and Regis were killing everybody," he said, recalling the fateful match. He'd submitted Regis and stunned everyone. "I was just a random kid. No one knew who I was. And then I won. I'm in the finals with Saulo." He grinned at me and added, "Regis was *pissed*. I walked over to Saulo and said, 'Good luck in the final.' I think he could see something in me right away. But I was scared, *so* scared. I just beat Regis, and now it's Saulo who I have to face. He is super intimidating, and I'm a little kid, especially back then. But it was a good match. I went almost the full ten minutes with him. It took him over seven minutes to pass my guard. Then he got to my half guard, smashed me, mounted me, and he got the arm triangle choke in the last thirty seconds. He submitted me. Afterward, I said, 'Thank you, Mr. Ribeiro. It was an honor to fight you.' I took a picture with him and a picture with his brother Xande. Saulo gave me his rash-guard that he wore that day and his business card. And that was the end of that."

Fast-forward a few months to right before Worlds 2003, and Rafael received an invitation to train with none other than Saulo himself. Rafael spent one week rolling with the Ribeiro brothers and the rest of their team, and his doubts about his future disappeared. Jiu-jitsu *was* what he wanted to do.

In spring of 2004, Rafael dropped out of college to train with Saulo and Xande's team in Brazil. He returned to the United States four months later and received his black belt from Carlos Machado.

Rafael switched professors soon after.

The champion opened up and shared that telling Carlos he was moving on was one of the hardest things he ever had to do for his career. He emphasized that he hasn't forgotten how supportive Carlos was of his decision to move and train with Saulo.

"He knew I wanted to be a world champion," Rafael said fondly. "He held no grudge and told me, 'This is what you should do because I can't give you what you need.'"

Rafael described the weeks he spent studying with the Ribeiro brothers as grueling. Training sessions were called at a moment's notice. Warm-ups lasted one hour, and they included squats, push-ups, pull-ups, and, as Rafael put it, "hundreds of takedowns." After warming up, Saulo, Xande, and Rafael trained for two hours. Since there were three of them, the odd guy out exhausted himself on an Airdyne bike while the other two hit the mat.

Often, Rafael couldn't sleep at night because he dreaded the next day's grind. He woke up on edge each morning because he knew he was going to get beaten up.

"There was no way around it," he said, laughing now, although it wasn't funny at the time. Additionally, training time came at the mercy of Saulo's last-minute orders, so their schedule varied from day to day. As a result, Rafael held off on eating, sometimes until well after noon, just so he would not get caught on the mat with a full stomach.

"It was just crazy," he recalled. "We were all scared of Saulo. Whatever he said, we did. He showed no mercy. He would throw me, smother me, try to make me tired, choke me. Every day was a test, because I had to earn my place. But it brought us together. Made us brothers."

Rafael revealed that when talking to Xande years later, he discovered the Ribeiro brothers often wondered whether they might have seen the last of him. Xande told Rafael that after training sessions he and his brother sometimes asked each other, "Do you think he's going to come back?"

But Rafael always returned.

BEHIND THE SCENES
AN ATTITUDE OF GRATITUDE

Working with Saulo also taught Rafael some perspective when it came to training for tournaments. For one, what happens in training isn't necessarily an indicator for what might go down on game day. "The point of training is to give everything," he explained. "You do everything you're supposed to, but it's not make or break. And just because you're having tough days in training, it doesn't mean you can't win a match in competition. A match is only a ten-minute moment in time. All that matters is what happens in those ten minutes, not what happens in the hours of training before."

The other thing Saulo helped teach Rafael was, as he put it, "You don't have to be trained with other world champion black belts, 24/7." While working with top athletes for two weeks before a tournament leads to sharpened skills, there's value in training with blue belts and purple belts precisely because of their limitations. "You don't always do your A-game; instead, you work around different points," he said. "You focus on other things. Do you let them start in good positions? Do you let them start with certain grips? And from there, you make it harder on yourself to adjust and learn."

As I spoke with Rafael, I came to understand a key thing about him: he is big on gratitude, especially for the people who helped him grow in jiu-jitsu. Aside from his father—who he credits a lot to—it is clear that Saulo and Xande made him who he is today. Going from being Saulo's *opponent* to being invited to train and learn from him is something unique and very special to Rafael.

Rafael also found the oldest Machado brother to be a passionate and caring teacher. While Carlos didn't accompany him to tournaments, he was a patient instructor and generously shared his apartment in Dallas when Rafael came for training.

"I might as well have been an adopted son," Lovato said fondly.

Saulo helped Rafael learn to ditch the negative mindset that had Rafael convinced his opponents in Brazil and California had all the advantages, while he suffered alone in Oklahoma. Hours of back-to-back rounds with the Ribeiro brothers taught him confidence. Rafael's thought process before tournaments changed. He learned to tell himself, *Nothing's worse than what I've already done and been through. I'm doing everything Saulo and Xande are doing. Yes, I'm from Oklahoma. Yes, that's where I live. But I've sacrificed so much. I deserve this.*

BEST ADVICE

When I asked Rafael about the impact he would like to have on the sport, he shared a few thoughts. He was inspired by other BJJ athletes and instructors, including Saulo, and so he tries to pay it forward.

"Saulo saw something in me and took me in. He gave me a chance. I want to keep passing this on, keep our jiu-jitsu alive, and help the next generation," he said.

But there's also a message he wants to share for others who may feel disadvantaged: *it doesn't matter where you're from.* "I want to be an inspiration for others. Of course, it's going to be a lot of sacrifice but just know it's *possible*, regardless of where you are from, to become one of the best."

Rafael was just a kid from Oklahoma but he made it. Still, when he was coming up in the sport, athletes from Brazil used to see him and other American jiu-jitsu fighters as "gringos" who weren't on the same level as Brazilians. As a result, they often treated Rafael poorly. "If you're hungry for jiu-jitsu and want to learn and chase competition goals, you can get good at it no matter where you're from," he explained. "You don't have to come up inside of an academy that has multiple champions."

Finally, he told me he wants to be a spokesman for the sport. He knows martial arts have the power to change lives, help people grow, and bring them together, and he would like to see as many people experience the mindset of the martial artist as possible. "When people put their gis on to train, there should be a transformation, mentally. You should feel a bit of the weight of the gi, of all the great warriors and samurais before us who paved the way. We're doing this special art that's constantly changing and evolving, and we're all a part of the process. We're all connected."

WORST ADVICE

When Rafael decided to dedicate his life to jiu-jitsu, he met with resistance. "You should finish college first," people told him.

Fifteen years later, Rafael revealed he has no patience for this kind of thinking. "The *worst* advice is that you have to go to college to be successful," he emphasized. "If I could go back, I wouldn't have done any college at all. I'm not using any of it."

FINAL THOUGHTS
A FAVORITE BOOK

Rafael told me he always keeps a copy of *Think and Grow Rich* by Napoleon Hill in his bag. The champion said reading passages from the motivational classic before a fight keeps him focused and makes him see everything clearly. "It has had a huge impact on my life, and I'm just super grateful," he said.

Rafael even has a favorite Napoleon Hill quote (though it isn't specifically from *Think and Grow Rich*): "Victory is always possible for the person who refuses to stop fighting." Rafael sees it as a good reflection of his own attitude. He told me, "As long as you keep going, you always have the chance to accomplish your dream, and everything is just a temporary failure up until then. *Nothing is the final failure until you actually quit.*"

UPDATE

In late January of 2020, just a few months after our interview, Rafael publicly revealed he was diagnosed with a potentially MMA career-ending brain condition, *cavernoma*. Cavernoma manifests as clusters of blood vessels in the brain or spine. If these malformations bleed, it can lead to seizures and sometimes death.

Rafael first became aware of the abnormality when he underwent a brain scan before his title-winning MMA fight against Gegard Mousasi in 2019. Rafael relinquished his Bellator title and was still consulting with doctors about his MMA future, as well as BJJ competitions.

He announced his condition on *The Joe Rogan Experience* podcast, and it shook the world of martial arts (you can find this conversation on YouTube). As I watched, I was again captivated by Rafael's humility. While he spoke candidly about the events surrounding his diagnosis and his inner journey from disbelief to acceptance, he didn't make things about himself. He displayed neither anger nor self-pity. Instead, he expressed concern for the health of other MMA athletes and gratitude for those who have supported him through this crisis.

It was uncertain at the time of his announcement whether he would continue to fight in jiu-jitsu tournaments or focus solely on teaching. He ended up fighting, and retiring as an adult competitor in the Gi at the 2022 Worlds (on the same day as Xande Ribeiro), although he has since competed in a big NoGi event and competed in three "super fights," looking as impressive as ever in the process. He also announced he will make another run at the 2022 ADCC grappling championships in Las Vegas.

CHAPTER 19

Kyra Gracie

graciekore.com.br
@graciekore
@kyragracie
facebook.com/kyragracieofficial

Born in Rio de Janeiro, Brazil, in 1985, Kyra Gracie Guimarães is one of the greatest female competitors in the history of jiu-jitsu. The great-granddaughter of Carlos Gracie on her mother's side, Kyra was the first woman in her family to compete in jiu-jitsu and one of only three female Gracies to receive a black belt.

Although Renzo Gracie was her main instructor, Kyra learned from many other Gracies, including Rilion, Roger, and Rickson. At that time, most of them were with the Gracie Barra association. So, Carlos Gracie Jr. tied Kyra's black belt around her waist, but she was graduated by Renzo.

Kyra holds three ADCC titles in her division (2005, 2007, 2011) and won Worlds in 2006, 2008, and 2010.

A tireless champion of gender equality in the sport, Kyra Gracie has arguably done more for female jiu-jitsu athletes than any other woman. In Brazil, she frequently appears on popular TV shows and works as a commentator for UFC Brazil. In 2018, she opened her own academy in Rio, Gracie Kore, located at Avenida das Américas, 8585, 22793-081, Rio de Janeiro, Brazil.

After living in the US from 2004 to 2009, Kyra now splits her time between the US and Brazil. She, her husband, their two daughters, and baby boy live in Rio. Kyra's daughters, though still very young, are already receiving BJJ belt promotions.

This interview was particularly special for me because it took place during the Gracie Camp in Miami, Florida. It was a last-minute trip for me, and I wasn't sure that Kyra and I would even have the time to talk since the champion was very busy, due to the nature of the event. The camp was filled with people and it seemed the timing might not work out.

Thankfully, we ended up doing the interview on the last day of the camp—in the lobby hallway, on a side sofa. I couldn't be more happy. Of all the interviews in this book, this was one of the most impactful conversations I had.

Throughout our interview, Kyra struck me as someone who cares deeply about jiu-jitsu and about the treatment of female athletes.

- Check out *Kyra Grace Uncovered*, an in-depth interview and short film, on YouTube.

- To see her spar her cousin Roger Gracie at the Gracie Camp in 2020, go to YouTube and search "Roger Gracie vs. Kyra Gracie."
- Visit Kyra's YouTube Channel, Kyra Gracie, to learn more about the social project I highlight in the pages that follow, as well as to see videos of her podcast.

EARLY LIFE

"WHETHER YOU LIKE IT OR NOT"—DEFYING FAMILY

When someone's last name is "Gracie," it's easy to make assumptions about how they started out in jiu-jitsu. But the road to success is often different than we might expect, and Kyra's experience is no exception. Believe it or not, the trailblazing Kyra Gracie had to fight tooth and nail for her right to learn and practice jiu-jitsu.

Growing up in Rio de Janeiro, Kyra lived in the same house as her uncles Renzo, Ralph, and Ryan Gracie. There was a mat in the house, and the three men fought all the time. Kyra, who owned a gi, picked up a few tips and tricks for self-defense, but really, her gi was just for show.

To illustrate this, Kyra shared with me one of her earliest memories. As a three-year-old, she donned her gi for a family photo. Once the picture was taken, she took the gi off and returned to playing.

Despite her gi, whenever she expressed a desire to train jiu-jitsu, the answer was always the same: "No. It's not for girls."

Kyra's world began to change when she was eight or nine. Her mother, a third generation Gracie, began practicing jiu-jitsu. *That's nice,* Kyra thought, impressed by her mother's example. *I can do this!*

As a result, the men in her family surrendered—at least for a while.

"She's just a kid," they said. "Let her do it!"

Little did they know, Kyra wasn't experiencing a childish flight of fancy. With support from her mom, the future champion trained at her family's academy in Rio two or three times a week. She fell in love with competing and decided to dedicate herself to the sport. As a teenager, she got up extra early every day to get her cardio in before school started. Most often, Kyra revealed, this was a 6:00 a.m. swim session at the rec center's Olympic pool.

When she told me this, I was actually shocked. Her dedication from such an early age was impressive. Of course, lots of the male athletes profiled in this book had similar regimens, but the difference is Kyra did this on her own, without being propelled forward by an instructor or having a training schedule set for her to follow. What teenager in today's world does this? What *adult* does this?

The girls in Kyra's school couldn't believe she would pick jiu-jitsu and healthy food over parties, makeup, and clothes.

"Why are you doing this?" they demanded. "It's not a sport for girls! You should do dancing!"

Kyra told me this attitude toward women training jiu-jitsu was common in Brazil. This patriarchal worldview was widespread.

Men were supposed to take care of women and protect them, and women were to be homemakers who raised families. "The mentality was, *Why do you do jiu-jitsu? You can't make money with this. It's just for the boys. Let us take care of you,*" she said, seemingly still irritated by the comments that came her way.

I want to be clear that Kyra wasn't saying that the Gracies didn't like women. It was simply a different time. Women weren't as accepted in sports of any kind across Brazil in general. In fact, women in Brazil weren't even allowed to compete in *any* sport until the 1970s.

So, as Kyra began traveling to big tournaments like the Pan-Ams, the resistance she felt from her uncles intensified. They warned her, "As a woman you won't make money doing this. Nobody wants to take classes with a woman instructor. You must stop."

Kyra remembers how family pressure caused her mom to quit training after receiving her blue belt, but Kyra could not be stopped. After she received her own blue belt, she kept going. In fact, opposition only strengthened her resolve.

She was going to prove her naysayers wrong.

"I'm not stopping," she told her uncles, "whether you like it or not."

ON PRESSURE AND ANXIETY

SILENCING HER INNER CRITIC

One of Kyra's biggest battles wasn't with outside forces but with her own inner critic. As a competitor, she often doubted herself. Even when she was in top shape and succeeding, negative thoughts persisted. She found herself thinking, *I don't think I'm going to win this time; I'm not that good at this.*

But she learned to accept her inner critic as an inevitable part of life. Competing taught her not to doubt herself and to counter internal negativity with a firm, *Shut up! Don't say that!*

On the topic, Kyra added, "In the beginning, I would be stressed and paralyzed because of the negative voice. But as I kept winning tournaments, I could silence it. I said, 'Hey, you're telling me this but it's not true. I'm winning.' And *because I was winning, my self-esteem got much better for everything in my life.*"

These days, Kyra rarely doubts her abilities. When she decided to start her own jiu-jitsu school, some members of her family told her she would need a male business partner simply because she is a woman. But by this time in life, she had the confidence to follow her own instincts.

Kyra told me she doesn't worry about the possibility of failure anymore. "Now I just think, *I will do it, and it's going to be awesome.*"

BECOMING A CHAMPION

DEALING WITH SYSTEMIC DISCRIMINATION

It can be hard enough to hear from family and friends that you *can't* pursue a passion. As a woman in Brazil, Kyra faced resistance on a more systemic level—and she has shown remarkable resilience. People's actions and words have often insulted, hurt, or angered her or made her feel uncomfortable. But she didn't give up. Her mantra is simple—"I'll show them!"—and her victorious record speaks for itself.

When Kyra started competing, the sport was lagging far behind in its attitude toward women, and media coverage of female competitors was almost nonexistent. Magazines ran a three- or four-page spread for every male champion, but for the women? Those athletes were bunched up together, their names presented as a short, single-page list. Therefore, women had even less access to sponsors than men.

"If you don't have visibility, how are we going to sponsor you?" companies asked Kyra.

The gender gap for prize money at major events was also huge. When Kyra competed as a brown belt in Abu Dhabi, she defeated the best girls in the sport, yet earned little recognition. Reflecting on that time, she told me, "My cousin got $50,000, and I got $2,000. Come *on!*"

When Kyra was younger, women didn't have as many divisions to compete in as men. As a yellow belt, she had to go up two or three age groups just to get a match. For a long time, *all* women's belt categories—from white to black—were scheduled to take place in a single day. As she grew older, there were still only three weight divisions—compared to the *nine* divisions for men—so almost every fight felt like competing in an Absolute. Because there are no weight or size limits in that style match, "David versus Goliath" is a common theme.

The difference here is not *only* did Kyra fight in a quasi-Absolute Division, but she was forced to compete against athletes who were higher belt levels as well. In one tournament, just after Kyra had received her purple belt, she found herself in the same bracket as the brown and black belts.

Using her hands to signal a small, slim person, she says, "I was seventeen and a skinny girl, and I was getting matched up against a lot of big girls."

As I sat with Kyra in that hallway and listened to her story, I wondered how many athletes today, if faced with the same challenges, would compete like she did. Kyra didn't just fight despite discrimination, she actually fought to *change* things. And things needed to change. For example, after Kyra's first big international win as a black belt in 2004, the champion advised the IBJJF (International Brazilian Jiu-Jitsu Federation) that she would no longer compete on the same day as the male blue belts. The next year, the Federation scheduled all the women's finals for the same day as the male black belts, but *still* refused to host female athletes on the main event mats. It was a step in the right direction, but Kyra wanted all women's black belt finals to be main events, just like they were for the men.

For the uninitiated, let's just say *the mat matters*. The main event mat is quite different not only in its size, but also in presentation. It is simply more visually and physically appropriate for a finals fight. To have the women's finals take place on the much smaller side mats was an insult.

When Kyra was nineteen and ready for a career, the discrimination she faced in Brazil made it clear there was no way for her to make a living in the sport without making a huge change. She soon moved to New York, where she could teach at her uncle Renzo Gracie's academy. The job also allowed her to earn enough money for the training camps she needed to participate in as a competitor. However, being an instructor meant dealing with another stereotype: higher-ups claimed they couldn't bring her to teach seminars because, as they told Kyra, "Students don't want to learn from a girl." This meant she was limited to occasionally teaching only private sessions with a single student.

This was an issue. Seminars provide a way for athletes to travel to other schools. The instructors earn a seminar fee for teaching for a few hours. Generally, these seminar fees can provide competitors with substantial income compared to one-on-one fees collected from a private session with a single student. When schools are willing to pay hundreds or even thousands of dollars for a few hours of an athlete's time teaching a seminar, it can represent a huge increase in overall income. In many cases, this is one metric that lets you know you've "made it" in jiu-jitsu.

Kyra remembers well how hurtful such comments felt. *I'm working hard,* she thought. *I win all the tournaments. I train more than a lot of men. And just by being men, they do the seminars?*

One time, the champion flew to Mexico to teach a seminar, and only three people showed up. When she asked the hosting instructor about the lack of interest, he told her his students didn't want a female teacher.

As Kyra shared these stories, I could feel her emotion and passion, which gave me a small sense of how horrible she must have often felt. Imagine flying all the way to Mexico, taking time off of training, and arriving at an academy only to see just three faces waiting for you instead of a room full of eager students. Gut-wrenching. And yet, Kyra put on her gi, and taught her seminar with an inspirational fierceness.

Two years after that disappointing trip to Mexico, Kyra returned to teach again.

This time, the room was packed.

The three athletes who attended Kyra's first seminar two years prior had shown the other students—the same ones who had stuck their noses in the air and refused to attend a seminar taught by a woman—their new moves. Kyra's instruction and mentoring was so excellent that all but the three students who attended the initial seminar felt sorry they had missed it.

Kyra did what all great professionals do. She let nothing stop her, and she went above and beyond, regardless of the circumstances.

To put this in context, just imagine how different that first teaching trip would have been if Kyra was male, like one of her Gracie cousins. If any of them had shown up to teach a seminar in Mexico for the first time, it probably would have sold out. In spite of her famous name, because she was a woman, Kyra had to prove her worth.

And prove her worth, she did.

"Now, black belt women fight on the same days as the men with black belts—and on the main event mats. But in many places, the environment is still geared toward men because instructors grew up not caring about women in the sport. It's a process," she added.

Things have changed a lot in the decades since Kyra first began competing. Thanks in no small part to Kyra's professionalism, talent, and advocacy, there are now many different belt, weight, and age divisions for female competitors.

BEHIND THE SCENES
WHY AN ACADEMY ENVIRONMENT MATTERS

When people ask her how they can encourage female participation in BJJ, Kyra tells them that offering classes for women isn't enough. They must show respect to women. This means sparring with women outside of class and encouraging them with the same type of genuine comments they already share with male athletes, like, "You're doing well!"

Kyra also mentioned that the "locker-room" atmosphere must change so women feel comfortable enough to hang out at a gym after class. Harassment, like catcalling, and loud stories about sexual conquests have to come to an end. As martial artists, we need to come together to pave the way toward professional, inclusive environments where the talk is about actual jiu-jitsu; *everyone* deserves to feel comfortable in a jiu-jitsu academy.

"In an academy, jiu-jitsu must be the *main thing*," Kyra stressed. "Playing around and putting nicknames on everyone—that's crazy." It's also not an ideal way to build a culture that is accepting of all people.

She admitted that discrimination and sexism often drove her toward possibly quitting. While Kyra was training hard and fighting six or seven matches to win a tournament, her male counterparts still chose to denigrate her achievements rather than celebrate them. Their comments ranged from, "The girls' divisions don't have as many fighters as we do," to, "Kyra's competition just isn't strong."

Kyra took a moment, shook her head, and then looked at me. "I felt uncomfortable and thought, *This isn't for me*, many times."

Kyra has owned her own gym, Gracie Kore, since 2018. She tries to create a culture of caring and respect. She doesn't buy into the misconception, popular in some BJJ circles, that leaders can only earn respect if they are able to beat *everyone* else. That type of thinking, she warned, can backfire. "You're not going to smash your students for their whole life. And once they smash you, what will happen? What will happen when you're old? Because that time will come, and it *will* happen. And then what? Will your students no longer respect you? *Respect should come from gratitude, not from fear.* Fear is like the mafia: you fear, you respect, you're loyal. But once they can kill you, they will. They don't love you. They're not grateful; they *fear* you. And it's the same in jiu-jitsu if you treat your students that way."

Thanks in part to her tireless efforts, much has changed since Kyra first started teaching jiu-jitsu seventeen years ago. Yet even so, when she told family members she was planning to open a BJJ school of her own just a few years ago, there was more opposition.

"Are you crazy? You're going by yourself?"

"Yes," Kyra insisted. "Why not?"

"Okay, you're a champion. But you're a girl! You should have a partner."

Kyra's face twisted in irritation as she recalled asking why that should be. When she shared her answer, I felt my face move the same way.

"Because people don't respect women that much."

As undeterred as ever, Kyra opened her school as a solo entrepreneur. She is proud of the atmosphere of respect she has created, and half the instructors at her academy are female.

"The good thing is that people now respect me even more because I proved them wrong," she said. "It's nice. And it opens people's minds to have even more girls involved."

Kyra has every reason to be proud. Because of her tireless efforts and contribution to gender equality, women now have a better chance of making it in jiu-jitsu.

"I love what I do," she concluded. "I have a successful academy. I have my titles. Sometimes, I think I was born to change things for girls in my sport. It is my mission and I'll keep going."

Before our interview, I assumed every successful jiu-jitsu athlete with the Gracie name faced the same type of criticism from people who don't know better. "It's easy for you to succeed," critics say. "It's because you're a Gracie."

When I addressed this stereotype with her, Kyra responded with a one-liner. "Come on," she said. "Do you think my last name ever won me anything?"

That said, while Kyra may have occasionally felt that being a member of the Gracie clan was as much of a hindrance as it was helpful, she still sees herself in the context of her family and their legacy. At her academy, she often runs into elderly clients who trained with the Gracies before she was even born. One example she mentioned to me was when an older gentleman walked in and kindly said, "I had a class with Master Helio in the 1950s, and now I want my grandson to learn."

She cherishes those moments. "That's the best thing for me," she said with enthusiasm. "When you have generations of people who admired my family, and now they want to put their grandson into a class because jiu-jitsu changed their life—it's humbling."

BEST ADVICE

Kyra wanted to share two important concepts. First, she said there must be *focus*. "If you have a dream in your life or a goal, a lot of people will tell you, 'You can't do it. It's impossible.' But you have to focus and go on this path. And if your friends are saying, 'Hey, let's go out tonight! Let's do this! Let's do that!' you must still keep your focus and say, 'No.' You have to be really aware of where you want to go in life."

Next, she emphasized the value of taking risks. Looking back on her early career, Kyra said, "I didn't know if it would work or not. Maybe I would work and train and then lose the tournaments. But it's like everything in life: you go there, and you don't know if you will be a champion. *But you have to try.*"

WORST ADVICE

Kyra told me the worst advice she ever received was, "You're the best. You're going to beat up everyone." She explained that this attitude can make an athlete feel overly confident. This can lead to unhappy surprises on the mat, but it can also result in a lack of respect for one's opponent.

"I made this mistake sometimes," she admitted. From that place of experience, she added, "That's when life hit me, *boom!*"

Final Thoughts: Empowerment

Obviously, Kyra has made a huge impact on jiu-jitsu. Thanks to her persistence and her fight for the recognition of female athletes, women are becoming increasingly more present in BJJ. But Kyra hopes to do even more.

As an ambassador for jiu-jitsu, Kyra wants to get even more people involved to help change unfair, untrue stereotypes. Jiu-jitsu isn't just for "tough guys." To attract new audiences to jiu-jitsu, Kyra frequently appears on Brazilian television and teaches self-defense classes at companies and nonprofits.

She is already seeing results. "Women go from, *Oh, I don't want to see jiu-jitsu,* to, *Oh! Jiu-jitsu can be fun for a girl like me who never wanted to do any sport!* People look at jiu-jitsu with different eyes."

The champion also believes in the power of community outreach. She knows jiu-jitsu has the potential to change lives, and she also knows that many people can't afford to take lessons. One of her initiatives launched in Teresopolis, a city north of Rio. The project focuses on empowering children with Down syndrome, and over the past seven years, about fifty passionate kids have benefited from learning jiu-jitsu.

"It changes the way they interact with other people and how their families see them," Kyra said, beaming. "It's been awesome."

CHAPTER 20

Braulio Estima

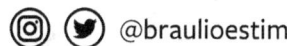

@braulioestima
facebook.com/braulioestima

B raulio "Carcará" Estima was born in Recife, Pernambuco, Brazil, in 1980. He started practicing jiu-jitsu at sixteen years old. Since moving to England in 2002, he has been one of Roger Gracie's main training partners and now owns and operates the Gracie Barra in Birmingham, UK.

In 2003, Braulio made headlines as a brown belt when he submitted seven opponents in under six minutes *combined*. I still have a hard time wrapping my head around this accomplishment. He received his black belt in January 2004 from Carlos Gracie Jr. and has won *every* major tournament, including the coveted ADCC Absolute Championship in 2009.

Miraculously, eight months after the champion broke his neck in an MMA training accident, Braulio also *defended* his

Superfight Championship ADCC belt in 2011. Since he received his black belt in 2004, Braulio has made it to every single final in every tournament he has *ever* competed in.

Wow.

Braulio and I met at his academy, Gracie Barra Birmingham, on a cold and rainy UK morning. Hands down, Braulio is one of my favorite athletes. Due to travel, he and I both had a long night prior to our interview. Though we were working with very little sleep, once we started chatting, it was like we had known each other our entire lives. I credit this to Braulio's openness about his life and his willingness to be truly vulnerable.

- Braulio's academy is located at 1 Stanhope Street, Birmingham, UK B12 0UZ.
- For an illuminating video of Braulio's thoughts on ego in BJJ, search YouTube for "Braulio Estima ego."
- To see his infamous submission in the ADCC final against André Galvão, search YouTube for "Braulio Estima vs. André Galvão."
- For a comprehensive library of Braulio's instructional videos, go to *BJJFanatics.com*.

EARLY LIFE

AN INSPIRING ENCOUNTER

As a child, Braulio was admittedly hyperactive. His dad put him in judo, and while Braulio liked it well enough at first, he turned away from the sport two years later when his professor tragically died in an accident. He then trained in soccer, only to realize after four years that team sports weren't for him. Braulio wanted to practice an individual sport where the responsibility for wins and defeats rested squarely on his shoulders.

When a surfer friend introduced him to BJJ at sixteen, Braulio thought, *Why not learn jiu-jitsu?* A skinny kid, Braulio realized the moves in BJJ would allow him to defend himself even against a stronger person; it would allow him to submit someone without hurting them. He loved that jiu-jitsu was the *only* martial art where you could fight from your back.

"Technique over power: this was something that fascinated me," he told me.

His early experience with jiu-jitsu was a series of ups and downs. In the beginning, smaller opponents smashed him, but after a few months, he started winning in local competitions.

Things took a turn for the worse when he began traveling to Rio de Janeiro for larger tournaments. Traveling took hours, and worse, Braulio was losing.

In fact, over the course of two years, Braulio participated in four IBJJF tournaments and was defeated in the first round, every single time. Somehow, he found the sheer will to continue training, despite the emotional devastation of his consecutive losses.

Fatefully, Braulio caught the attention of Carlos Gracie Jr. at one of those early, disappointing tournaments in Rio. After learning Braulio was from Recife, Carlos told him, "You have good potential, but when you go back home, avoid those little gangs—the little groups that smoke weed and party. *Focus!* Enjoy yourself around good people. Focus on what you want!"

This memorable encounter with a father-like figure stayed with the young athlete. And, though he could never have known it at the time, Braulio would become Carlos's right-hand man years later in London.

"There was a connection there," Braulio recalled with fondness. "Carlos's integrity and his values are very similar to the values that my dad had. We connected straightaway."

Braulio came from a family of academics. Though he always knew he wanted to be an athlete, in high school he decided he would study production engineering. Juggling college and jiu-jitsu took a lot of dedication. A BJJ-related scholarship paid for half of his tuition, but to afford the other half, he got up at 6:30 a.m. and spent his mornings working. The rest of the day was divided between studying engineering and jiu-jitsu training. These days ended very late, with a BJJ teaching session that stretched from 10:30 p.m. to midnight.

"By the time I was home, it was one o'clock in the morning," he told me. "Then the story repeated over and over again."

Even before he had finished college, Braulio realized he wouldn't be happy doing something he didn't love—and his passion wasn't for engineering. He loved jiu-jitsu. He was also getting good at it. By this time, Braulio had won the BJJ World Championship at the purple level, and already experienced some success as a brown belt.

Jiu-jitsu presented the athlete with a different career path. *You know what?* he thought as he reflected on his progress. *I'm going in the right direction with jiu-jitsu.*

Oftentimes, I see people looking for a quick and easy route to success as opposed to a path that gives them the most joy. They ask, "What product can I invent to make myself rich?" They forget that the product is not the key ingredient. The key ingredient is love for what you're doing so you don't feel like you're trading your time for dollars. If you've perfected a craft, people will actually *want* to pay you top dollar. Ultimately, this will help you reach the financial goal you were aiming for in the first place, to say nothing of the more enjoyable, enlightening journey you will take to get there.

Braulio's story is a great example of how things eventually work out if we focus on doing what we love. In his case, it was jiu-jitsu. When a former training partner invited him to spend the semester break training jiu-jitsu in London in 2002, Braulio jumped at the opportunity. Before leaving, he made sure to have an important conversation. Braulio's parents had always supported his pursuit of BJJ, but his dad wasn't shy about sharing his doubts about whether his son could make a decent living from practicing the sport. The trip to London and the two months that Braulio wanted to spend there would be a solid step toward turning his passion for jiu-jitsu into a career.

But how would his father take the news?

Naturally, Braulio's dad was concerned his son was abandoning a promising career path. "You went to a university for three-and-a-half years!" he protested. "What are you going to do?"

Braulio had already prepared his response. He told his dad that a career in production engineering would only leave him feeling frustrated because his heart wasn't in it. He promised his passion for jiu-jitsu would carry him through any of life's inevitable challenges.

"Dad," he said, "if you're good at what you do, it doesn't matter what you do, you will be fine. If someone wants to be the best wall painter in the world, he'll be fine. If he wants to be the best gardener in the world, he'll be fine. I want to be the best in jiu-jitsu, and I'll be fine."

Braulio wasn't only saying that a gardener or painter would be fine financially. Beyond that, he was trying to convey his belief that when we do the things we love and things are going well, it's easy to keep going. It's the passion for something you love that will help carry you through the *tough* times that matters. Even when pursuing our dreams, we encounter bumps in the road—and these "bumps" are sometimes *major* obstacles—but a love for what you want will always provide a guiding beacon of light to keep moving forward.

Braulio described how he saw his dad's eyes well up with tears as he was talking.

"You're ready," his father said.

Braulio felt his dad would never have given his approval if he hadn't believed in him. Braulio also knew he would have chosen jiu-jitsu either way, but his father's blessing still meant a great deal to him. "I was happy and proud he understood what I was telling him was from my heart."

On his way to London, Braulio made a powerful promise to himself: he would make his time in England worth the separation from his family. Being away from them would not be in vain.

ON PRESSURE AND ANXIETY
SELF-DOUBT AND SETBACKS

Like most athletes, Braulio faced setbacks and challenges almost from day one, but he persevered. Even in the beginning, when the most advanced training partners and instructors to be found at the academy in Recife were merely purple belts, he had a few things going for him: the curious mind of an engineer and an equally unbreakable spirit.

When Braulio first trained in jiu-jitsu, it was with an instructor who was much smaller than he was. Still, the professor insisted things be done *his* way. Braulio complied but he also pictured in his mind a style that might work better for his own body.

Later, as a purple belt, Braulio found himself on the verge of quitting. He'd lost a tournament in Rio after giving everything he had in training. He told me he was doing exactly what he was supposed to be doing and trained his ass off—but that was, in fact, the problem.

"The secret to jiu-jitsu is understanding yourself within," he told me. Braulio needed to find what worked for him, his body type, and his style of fighting.

As a teacher, he now tries to adapt to the needs of an individual athlete. He explained, "Everything I do is reverse engineering. It's about understanding that everyone is different. Maybe you like chocolate and I don't. Maybe you like steak and I don't. If something works for me, it doesn't mean it's the only way to do it. It just means it's the best way for *me*."

Throughout his career, Braulio has used losses as an opportunity to go back and analyze the fight. He asks himself, *What happened? Why was I defeated? Can I fix it?* instead of getting depressed or being unnecessarily hard on himself.

"Understanding the whys of everything is what makes you learn," he said. "I've always been very curious."

Never afraid to ask questions, Braulio also talked to training partners and other jiu-jitsu athletes whenever possible. "My friends, my training partners, that's where I learned jiu-jitsu the most," he said, nodding. "Not only from my instructors."

Curiosity has kept him coming back to the mat, trying things over and over. When he was still a blue belt, he rolled with a brown opponent who tapped him about half a dozen times. This was only possible because Braulio was willing to go back into the fire over and over so he could learn *precisely why* he was losing.

His curiosity also helped him figure out how he might get himself out of situations he hadn't been in before. Braulio sat up straight in his chair as he told me, "There are so many things in jiu-jitsu I started doing by myself that people didn't recognize. I realized there isn't just one way in jiu-jitsu... I can actually make my things up; I can do it my way."

The discovery that he could do things his own way, with his own input, gave him confidence. His no-surrender spirit, which he credits to his dad, kept him going no matter how often he was beaten.

"It doesn't matter how many times you fall, as long as you stand back up," he said. "My dad always used to tell me, 'Fall seven times, stand up eight. Stand up, and get ready to fall again—because you *will* fall.'"

Like every athlete—and every type of top performer, for that matter—Braulio has had to overcome self-doubt and nerves. For example, he revealed he "felt like hell" at ADCC 2009, where he had an almost perfect run. Before his Absolute Division semifinal fight against Vinny Magalhães, he was so nervous he had to go hide.

"I always doubted I would be a champion," he admitted. "I got smashed so many times, and I always felt nervous."

He controlled his nerves by reminding himself that his opponents were feeling the same way he was. Even the most confident-looking opponents sometimes crumbled as soon as he gripped them, and he used that experience to learn that the face doesn't always show what's inside the person. He also understood that a dose of anxiety could help him fight better. To that end, he told me, "I fought once without nerves and I lost because I thought I was much better than the other guy. That means your guard goes down. When you're not nervous, you don't have awareness."

BECOMING A CHAMPION
PUSHING THE LIMITS, BIT BY BIT

Full of energy, hungry for knowledge, and holding true to his ultimate vision, Braulio spent those two months in London training hard—and then he stayed four more months. *It doesn't matter how long it takes*, he told himself. *I will just keep doing it.*

I'll keep doing it, because I will regret it if I don't give it everything I have. If I do all I can, then I will be happy with myself.

After the 2003 Pan-Ams, Braulio knew he had made the right choice. Not only did he win in his weight class *and* in the Absolute Division as a brown belt, but he also set a record that still holds to this *day*: Braulio tapped seven opponents in a combined match total of five minutes and twenty-four seconds.

Ever humble, Braulio admitted his success surprised even him. Never one to set goals for himself that seemed out of reach, he developed confidence by pushing the boundaries a little bit at a time. As a white belt, he wanted to be the best white belt in his academy or category, then the best in his state. Next, he simply wanted to receive a blue belt. He recalls, "When I was a blue belt, I never aimed to be a black belt. I never felt it could even be possible."

Braulio stayed in London four months longer than he'd originally planned, and he was still a brown belt when he later made England his permanent home. He started training with Roger Gracie soon after. Looking back on how he left college and moved to London, and all the success that followed his decisions, Braulio described feeling immense gratitude.

"It all was only possible because I truly had good people around me," he said while raising his head high. *"But I had the discipline.* Motivation takes you out of bed, but discipline is what takes you through the darkest times."

Braulio had a few big lessons ahead of him about goal setting. For example, the first time he approached a potential sponsor, Braulio was competing in Worlds as a purple belt. As he'd won third place the year before, he asked a gi maker if they would support him.

"I'm Braulio. I'm from Recife," he told a company representative. "I got third place last year and was wondering whether you'd be interested in helping me. Maybe two gis a year?"

"Can you beat Fernando Pontes?"

"Margarida? No, man. I'm a purple belt."

"When you beat him, you can talk to me."

Braulio remembered feeling angry about the response; Fernando "Margarida" Pontes, after all, was already a Worlds Double Absolute Champion—as a black belt.

"They could have said, 'Sorry, no. We have so many people asking,'" Braulio told me. "But instead they say, 'When you beat Margarida'? That's not how you treat a kid with a dream!"

The same anger motivated him. *One day, I will beat Margarida, and these guys will want to sponsor me*, he thought.

And that is exactly what happened. After he tapped Margarida in 2005, the gi company offered to support him, but Braulio was no longer interested. "I didn't want someone with this kind of vibe sponsoring me," he said, as he shrugged his shoulders.

In 2009, Braulio learned yet another lesson about goal setting. His story started during ADCC in 2005, when Roger Gracie won gold in both his weight and Absolute divisions, and submitted all eight of his opponents. Braulio remembered feeling elated for Roger—so much so that he cried with happiness. The power of that experience left Braulio wondering if *he* would ever do anything similar; he wondered if he would ever feel what he had just felt, but in Roger's shoes as a winner.

He tried imagining what it would feel like to be victorious in this way. *It's perfect,* he thought. *It must feel so amazing! I wonder how he is feeling all by himself, taking a shower as the champion!*

Four years later, also at ADCC, Braulio almost matched Roger's accomplishment when he tapped six of his eight opponents, also for double gold, including Marcelo Garcia, Xande Ribeiro, Vinny Magalhães, and Rafael Lovato Jr. After the victory came the obligatory photos, interviews, and congratulations, but later that day, as Braulio turned on the shower and stood there with the water running down his head and pouring off his face, there was just silence. He was a champion, *the* champion, and yet all he felt was emptiness. He ruminated over this, thinking, *It cannot get much better than this, and I don't feel happy. What am I going to do now?*

The problem was that he had set an ultimate goal for himself: perfection. Reaching it inevitably meant there was no more room for improvement. "It was a weird feeling," he said. "On the flight home, I was afraid the plane might crash because I had fulfilled my purpose. I thought, *Maybe that's it. Maybe it's time for me to go.*"

At that very moment, Braulio experienced an epiphany. *Going forward, he would have to aim for goals that weren't fixed.* "My purpose changed," he said. "I started putting my family first. Then, I wanted to become a better instructor and monetize what I had achieved. Then, I started doing MMA."

By setting goals that were dynamic rather than finite, Braulio was able to maintain an ongoing sense of purpose and satisfaction. Goals that gave him meaning, fulfillment, and gratitude shaped his life in ways no finite goal ever could.

His new outlook would prove necessary later on. In June of 2010, Braulio injured his neck while training during his fledgling MMA career. After falling on his head, he lay paralyzed for a few minutes before the feeling in his lower extremities returned. "My body was dead," he recalled, with a dark tone in his voice. He reenacted the moment as he spoke, putting his arms to his side and remaining motionless. "I wanted to move my arm, but nothing. I waited for it and thought, *Where's my arm? Fuck, where's my arm?*" Finally, he was able to move his limbs just a little bit.

I could hear the emotion in his voice when he added, "For twenty-four hours, there was no feeling. It felt like I had lost my life."

His first worry was, *I won't hold my kids anymore.* The second worry was, *Jacaré!*

At the time, Ronaldo "Jacaré" Souza was his biggest rival. All four fights between the two men had ended in defeat for Braulio, who had been looking forward to their next match at ADCC 2011.

His doctor delivered a devastating diagnosis: two prolapsed (herniated) neck discs. The physician told him, "You're lucky to be alive. And now, forget about martial arts. If you want to be an athlete, throwing darts would be good because they're the only moves you can do."

But Braulio was unwilling to call it quits.

First, Braulio felt he still needed to settle the score with Jacaré. Second, the ADCC Superfight wasn't something he was willing to miss. This one-time event happened every two years on the biggest platform possible. For context, in the ADCC Superfight, the Absolute champion gets their shot at the Superfight champion from two years prior. Hence, to fight the Superfight champion, you have to wait for two years *after* you win the Absolute Division.

Eventually, Braulio found a surgeon who allowed him to keep the flexibility in his spine by substituting the injured discs with titanium. He was unable to train for four months following the surgery, but Braulio put everything he had into the *following* four months as they represented his last opportunity to train before ADCC 2011.

In what would seem like an insurmountable task or even a *miracle* after suffering such a devastating injury, Braulio faced and finally defeated Jacaré Souza. "It was my biggest achievement," he told me, smiling with well-deserved pride. "It's all about how much you really want something."

BEHIND THE SCENES

BECOMING A BETTER PERSON

Jiu-jitsu is often described as a sport of self-discovery. During our conversation, Braulio reminded me this learning comes in part through the observation of another person's behavior on the mat. "You can see what kind of a person someone is when they roll, and this makes you understand yourself," he said. "You start to think, *Maybe I shouldn't do this. Maybe I shouldn't use this person as a role model* (in my gym or life) *because of the way they show their character on the mat.*"

He added that understanding ourselves and watching other athletes model positivity can help us become better people. This will, in turn, inspire others to grow in the same way. People who don't *want* to grow with this positive vibe eventually fade away from the gym. It's as if they almost force themselves out through self-elimination.

I've sparred with guys who were much better than me and would hurt me or take advantage whenever they had the opportunity. I've experienced that negative use of power, and I've also rolled with people who were much better than me, people who did not take advantage.

To be clear, of course I understand the need for a winner and a loser; that is the point of submission grappling, after all. When people use their power to instill fear, though, it's like Kyra Gracie said: they don't *earn* any long-lasting respect. When the inferior practitioner gets as good as or better than the superior practitioner, then what will they do? How will they command your respect when the tables are turned and they cannot turn them back?

Braulio also sees parallels between jiu-jitsu and life. He told me that each taught him about the other. "Jiu-jitsu helped me a lot in life, and life taught me a lot for jiu-jitsu." An example he pointed to is the feeling of being stuck in a bad place and thinking there is no way out. In both BJJ and life, if we don't panic and instead try seeing things from a different perspective, we will always find a solution.

Jiu-jitsu also taught Braulio about trust. Martial artists are usually well aware that a partner or opponent *could* use the sport in a dangerous or even deadly way. So, trust is necessary, and athletes create connections with each other in the gym to foster it. For example, they accept that they're in a potentially fatal choke by tapping and ultimately being let go.

On the subject, Braulio elaborated, "Subconsciously, I know if I wanted to, I could kill you. And you, as my opponent, know that too. But you trust me, and I trust you to trust me. This bond is unique and different from any other martial art, any other sport I've ever seen. It's one of the things that made me enjoy being around people in jiu-jitsu. It is how they became my real family."

Like many top fighters, Braulio worries about the image of the sport. One thing he told me he wants people to understand is that being a champion doesn't mean you've developed a reason for not respecting others. "It doesn't mean you're a better person than anybody. It just means you're doing well at what you're doing. You might be a good brown belt, and another person might be a good doctor. Just because he's a doctor, he's not better than you either."

BEST ADVICE

Braulio stressed the importance of selecting and committing to your focus. "Anything is possible if you have a vision and put in time, effort, and focus. You need to pick your side. If you want to be the good guy, focus on the good. If you don't want to work, you can't expect anything. That's it."

WORST ADVICE

On the topic of bad advice, Braulio simply said, "I think there's no best or worst way of living. You just need to be true to yourself."

FINAL THOUGHTS
FADING OUT AND SHIFTING FOCUS

Braulio, who will always have to be careful with his neck, doubts he will compete in top-level tournaments again. Rather than announcing his retirement and then potentially retracting his words, he said he instead wants to "fade out." His focus is shifting toward inspiring others with his passion for jiu-jitsu. He is fully aware of what the sport has done for him, and wants to help pay it forward to the next generation of athletes through the Gracie Barra Ambassadors program, which sponsors young competitors.

"When you appreciate, you give back," he said. "And people who appreciate what you give will also give back. It's a positive cycle that creates strength and support."

CHAPTER 21

Russell Brand

russellbrand.com
 @russellbrand
 @rustyrockets
 facebook.com/russellbrand

B orn in Essex, England, in 1975, Russell Brand is a comedian, actor, and activist. Popular in Britain since 2004, he became internationally known in 2008, when he played a rockstar character named Aldous Snow in the romantic comedy *Forgetting Sarah Marshall*. As a campaigner and activist, he has addressed topics such as wealth inequality, addiction, and climate change.

Years ago, I was going down a YouTube rabbit hole when I came across some of Russell's videos. I recall thinking, *Man, this guy is extremely cerebral and well-spoken. I'm almost jealous of how well he can construct his thoughts and put them into words.*

Naturally, I wanted to interview Russell as soon as I learned that, in addition to his many talents, he also trains in jiu-jitsu. As a longtime fan of his community outreach projects, his social media posts, and his books (including his latest one, *Mentors: How to Help and Be Helped*), I knew he'd make for a great chapter in *Jiu-Jitsu Bravehearts*.

If you've followed him in any way, you already know that Russell seamlessly transitions between serious topics and humor, and expresses his thoughts as they occur to him in a free-flowing way. He uses his own experience to explore issues we all struggle with, including ego, fear, and pride, and he never shies away from being vulnerable. For him, the gym has become something like a school of life. "Jiu-jitsu echoes loudly with things that are real in life," as he puts it.

Russell trains at the Roger Gracie Academy Buckinghamshire. I've also known him to privately train with Xande Ribeiro in Los Angeles, California. He and I spoke on the phone in January of 2020. He had me laughing, and I was extremely grateful for both his candor and his time.

- For his podcast *Under the Skin*, go to Luminary or Apple Podcasts.
- Find his books, including *Mentors*, *Recovery*, and *Revolution*, on Amazon and Audible.
- Search "Russell Brand BJJ" on YouTube to find videos highlighting his thoughts on BJJ as it relates to life.

(NOT SO) EARLY LIFE
A LATE INTRODUCTION TO JIU-JITSU

Several years ago, Russell watched the 1999 documentary *Choke*, featuring Rickson Gracie as he prepared for an MMA competition in Vale Tudo Japan. The film made Russell realize that his thoughts about fighting, combat, and violence were fear-based. Russell had previously tried kickboxing and Krav Maga, but had never been good enough for serious sparring. Thanks to the documentary, he saw a new opportunity for learning. "Even when you have something that feels neurotic," he told me, "I feel like there might be information in it."

What finally pushed him to the gym was a conversation with comedian and podcaster Joe Rogan. Joe was positive and open about his experience with jiu-jitsu, and Russell was finally ready to give it a try.

In late 2017, Russell started training with a Roger Gracie black belt, Chris Cleere. Naturally, Russell felt intimidated when he walked into the gym for the first time. Being in this type of male-dominated environment brought out some of his worst psychological fears. "I didn't like having people physically close to me—men close to me," he explained. "I don't want to feel I'm physically being dominated or I'm not good enough."

Now, more than five years into his jiu-jitsu journey, Russell has felt an almost therapeutic effect. By forcing himself to inhabit the fears he used to avoid in the safe space of a gym, he has reduced their debilitating potential.

Still, he readily admits he isn't without anxiety on the mat. "When somebody's choking you out," he said, "that's an intense feeling of powerlessness and loss of control."

On the flip side, he now shies away from altercations. Knowing what people are capable of has made him "more chill."

"Funny enough, even though I've obviously learned a lot about self-defense, I would be much less inclined to mouth off or get in confrontations than at any time in my life because you don't know what you're dealing with. You don't know."

ON PRESSURE AND ANXIETY
EGO, PRIDE, AND GRATITUDE

In his social media posts, Russell often talks about the ego as one of our primary enemies. I was therefore curious to ask him how he practices humility while also enjoying the recognition he receives as a celebrity.

His answer surprised me. Russell uses a spiritual approach to think about achievement. In his view, we shouldn't take credit for our accomplishments; they became possible because we received a gift of some kind.

"Say you're a person who jiu-jitsu comes easy to and you pass through the belts at record speed. No one gives themselves that ability. Or even if you're a person who trains hard and a person who works really hard and commits to things and gets up early—you didn't give yourself that ability either. Everything we've got, somehow, we've just been given, whether it's jiu-jitsu itself, the language we're speaking, the phones we're talking on now, we are just floating around on the rest of this stuff, consciousness itself, our own biological systems, our heart beating, or our lungs breathing. So, to take seriously your own achievements on or off the mat is a kind of delusion," Russell paused, and then continued, "...and I like knowing that."

When I brought up his promotion to blue belt as a potential moment of pride, he said he felt pleased to receive it because it stands for something he had done and would not have done before. The achievement became possible only because his gym and the masters he trained with let him access their knowledge and expertise.

"My achievements, whether it's a blue belt or whatever else, are a result of luck and opportunity and aren't actually that big of a deal," he explained. Instead, Russell suggested we should respond to success with gratitude rather than pride. "A teaching I heard once is, 'Wherever you would be proud, be grateful.' Even if it's something like being proud of your kid for being good at baseball, what you're really saying is, 'That's *my* kid who's good at baseball, and he wouldn't be good at baseball if it weren't for me.' Instead, if you're grateful, it's like, 'Oh, wow, man, I got a kid who's good at baseball,' and even if you taught him baseball, be grateful you are able to and grateful you have the time to."

If this all sounds like Russell might be a living embodiment of humility—that's hardly the case. He says his natural tendency is actually quite different. He told me the reason he knows all this stuff is "because I've had to be taught it to not turn into an asshole." Feelings of ego and pride still surface. For example, he says he "felt really disappointed" when a white belt choked him out shortly after his promotion to blue belt. The event inspired reflection. *Do I really want to do this?* he wondered.

That brought me to my next topic. A question I asked almost every interviewee was, "Were there times you wanted to quit the sport, and if so, what kept you going?" Russell's answer was unique. While he pushes himself to continue training jiu-jitsu multiple times a week, before almost every training, he must overcome an inner voice that tries to keep him away from the gym. He told me he keeps going because he looks forward to the post-training session where he invariably feels good; he comes out of the gym feeling a closer bond with people, and he feels better about who he is. "I feel like I've done something kind for myself," he said.

Even sparring with athletes who are bigger, stronger, more experienced, or more effective than he is energizes him. Russell told me about a brown belt and former rugby player known as "Smasher" with whom he sometimes spars. Smasher goes easy on Russell, but he's so fluid that Russell can never find an opening for himself.

"He's like hard water," Russell said. "The way he moves, the way he establishes grips, is brilliant. But the fact is I get to feel what that energy feels like, and I never regret it."

Overall, he tries to remember something he heard Ryron and Rener Gracie say: "Everybody eventually gets a black belt, everybody. You just don't give up. And it doesn't matter if you tap out in an individual roll. Just don't tap out of jiu-jitsu forever."

BECOMING A CHAMPION
SELF-DISCOVERY ON THE MAT

Like many champions I spoke to, Russell sees jiu-jitsu as a sport of self-discovery. "I am learning a lot more than techniques," he said. "I am learning about myself." Being on the mat forces us to become honest about ourselves; it reveals things about us we'd rather not see and puts us in touch with feelings we'd rather not experience, including helplessness, inferiority, anger, and fear.

Russell used an image to describe our reluctance to know more about ourselves. "It's like there are all these rooms in the mansion of yourself that you are never allowing yourself to go into because you're too scared to touch the door handle."

Different from many other athletes, Russell practices jiu-jitsu with the explicit goal of learning about himself. "If you don't go to the mat," he explained, "you're never experiencing all those places where you are helpless like a baby. You're avoiding reality instead of accepting that reality."

Russell described jiu-jitsu as a humbling experience because it has not only shown him who he is, it has also, as he put it, rooted him in the reality of *where* he is. The question at the heart of his search for self-discovery and a deeper understanding of the self is this: "Are you going to go through life avoiding everything that makes you feel uncomfortable? What kind of a life are you going to have then?"

BEHIND THE SCENES
HUMILITY AND TRUST

As someone who was already in his forties when he started doing jiu-jitsu, Russell has had to accept that he must progress in the sport at his own pace. "It's different for me when there are obviously white belts who are in their twenties," he groaned, rolling his eyes. "And it's like, oh fucking hell, *these* guys? So I enjoy being continually confronted with humility *instead* of avoiding it. I enjoy it, and I embrace it now."

Training with people who are a lot stronger means that Russell is, as he puts it, "completely dependent on their kindness for my survival." This has taught him about trust.

"There's an amazing amount of trust that exists in those spaces," he told me. "People don't go, 'No, fuck you, you shouldn't have got into that situation!' And subsequently kill you. If you tap, they stop. And, that's sort of amazing."

BEST ADVICE

My own experience has been that jiu-jitsu forces me to be present in a way that other sports don't. Sparring—or rolling, in particular—feels like forced meditation; it refreshes my mind. When I mentioned this to Russell, he told me he sees an almost surprising crossover with yoga, which he also regularly practices.

"Combat sports seem so aggressive, and yoga feels social, flowing, feminine, and gentle," he described. "But the crossover is about *being present in your body* and recognizing the division between the mind and the body is an arbitrary one."

WORST ADVICE

Russell didn't explicitly share any bad advice, but he did explain that jiu-jitsu not only forces and encourages us to be present and in our bodies, it rewards us for it. "You don't want to spend all your time in the intellectualizing, reflective mind," he warned.

To be *really good* at something, we must go beyond what Russell called the "plodding understanding of things" and get to the point where certain moves become embodied, when we no longer think about the process and achieve a flow state. "I can see, from my teachers and from people who are further down the path than me, that to have such a sense of harmony with physical movement is fantastic," he said.

FINAL THOUGHTS
RITUALS, HIERARCHIES, AND EQUALITY

Russell, who described himself as a slow learner with regard to physical challenges, told me it took a while before he understood even the basics of jiu-jitsu. While elements like the warm-up rituals used to baffle him, he now embraces them and sees them as something "we should be mimicking more widely."

In the summer of 2019, Russell had an epiphany of sorts when he was at a grading ceremony. He was to receive his blue belt that day, and he became aware of jiu-jitsu's powerfully equalizing effect, as well as its inherently hierarchical structure. Three or four gyms from the area had come together at Roger Gracie's academy in London to grade their students, all of whom came from very diverse backgrounds.

"There were a lot of Muslim guys taking belts, a lot of Eastern European men and women, working class, white people, a variety of backgrounds," he said of the other students and their promotions. "But every single person who stood up received the same round of applause and the same, 'Well done, mate! Well done!'" He said the experience made him see that where you're from, what you do, and how much money you have doesn't matter in jiu-jitsu.

All that matters is the jiu-jitsu.

On the flip side, he recognized for the first time the value of hierarchies and how they can be "a fantastic thing" if they are based on fairness and respect and the rules are the same for everyone.

"Everyone knows that if this person's a purple belt, they earned it, or if they're a brown belt, they earned it. No one cares about anything else. It makes you realize all the other stuff in life is just made up."

CHAPTER 22

Jocko Willink

◎ @jockowillink, @victorymmasd
🐦 @jockowillink
ⓕ facebook.com/jkowillink

Jocko Willink is a retired US Navy SEAL officer and the bestselling author of *Extreme Ownership: How U.S. Navy SEALs Lead and Win*, *Discipline Equals Freedom*, *The Dichotomy of Leadership*, *Leadership Strategy and Tactics*, and an entire series of children's books, *Way of the Warrior Kid*. As the co-founder and CEO of a leadership consulting company, Echelon Front, he teaches individuals, teams, and companies to apply the leadership principles he learned on the battlefield to everyday life. He also created and hosts his top-rated podcast, *Jocko Podcast*.

Born in Torrington, Connecticut, in 1971, Jocko spent twenty years with the US Navy SEALs. His military awards include the Silver Star and the Bronze Star. During the Iraq War, he commanded what would become the most highly decorated Special Operations Unit of the conflict, SEAL Team Three's Task Unit Bruiser. After returning from the Middle East, he became the Officer-in-Charge of training for all West Coast SEAL teams. He retired from the Navy in 2010.

I've been a big fan of his ever since I heard him on another podcast, *The Tim Ferriss Show*. Jocko's central message, "Discipline Equals Freedom," is embroidered on my belt. He and I spoke via Skype in the spring of 2020, during the height of the COVID-19 outbreak. I would've much preferred to chat in person, but in Jocko fashion, we got it done in the midst of a pandemic, no excuses!

- All of Jocko's podcasts feature BJJ-related interviews; his new podcast, *Grounded*, is dedicated to the sport.
- Check out his MMA/martial arts/jiu-jitsu academy, Victory MMA, IG: *@victorymmasd*, located at 3666 Midway Dr., San Diego, CA 92110.
- He has written several children's books, including *Way of the Warrior Kid*.

EARLY LIFE
BJJ IN THE US NAVY SEALS

Jocko's introduction to BJJ goes back to the early 1990s. He had completed his basic SEAL training and was on deployment with a SEAL platoon in Guam when a SEAL Master Chief by the name of Steve Bailey asked the guys in Jocko's platoon, "Hey, who here wants to learn how to fight?"

Jocko piped up right away, "Yup!"

Back then—and this was before the first Ultimate Fighting Championship (UFC) in 1993—most people in the United States had never heard of jiu-jitsu. But Steve Bailey, who was a Muay Thai practitioner, had studied with the Gracies in their garage in Torrance, California. When Jocko and a few other men from his platoon showed up for their first fight with the SEAL Master Chief in a Quonset hut, they were in for a major surprise.

Jocko watched Steve lie down on some judo mats, and then the Master Chief instructed them to attack him one at a time.

The young men took turns mounting Bailey. He immediately reversed positions and choked or armlocked them.

"There were probably four or five of us, and we were all young, and this guy was like one of the oldest people I had ever seen at that time—probably thirty-eight or forty—ten years younger than I am right now," Jocko added with a laugh. "But despite the fact that he seemed old to me, he just crushed us all."

Jocko stuck with the training, and after three months of learning new moves, he was winning friendly tussles against SEALs who weren't practicing with Steve.

"I'd be able to get their back and choke them, just through knowing a little bit and being in good shape, and them not knowing anything," he told me. "So, I realized that jiu-jitsu is very powerful."

In October of 1993, the first UFC championship was fought in Denver. That first UFC tournament was nearly a no-holds-barred event. It was not like today, where the UFC has many weight classes, strict rules about gloves and other apparel, and very specific rules about types of legal strikes and submissions. In 1993, there were no weight classes, almost all strikes were legal, and it was presumed that the biggest, strongest guy was going to win.

Jocko and a friend, Jeff Higgs, who was from a sister SEAL platoon, already knew enough about jiu-jitsu to predict who would win the title. "This guy Royce Gracie is going to win," they said as they watched. "*Guarantee* he's going to win."

They were right.

Royce Gracie wore his gi into the octagon, kept it on for his fight, and won it all. Jocko and Jeff made a bold prediction that Royce was going to win, but in retrospect, they had been learning firsthand the power of jiu-jitsu. Of course, for the masses, Royce's victory was anything but a sure thing.

ON PRESSURE AND ANXIETY
HOW TO LEAD

Obviously, Jocko knows a thing or two about leadership. So, I asked him what jiu-jitsu has taught him as it relates to leadership that he *didn't* learn in the SEAL teams.

He told me when he first became a Navy SEAL, there was no formal leadership training or "a doctrinal course they would put you through to teach you how to lead." He learned to lead as a SEAL by "paying attention to good and bad leaders, emulating the good ones, and avoiding the pitfalls of the bad ones. That meant figuring out how leadership worked."

Practicing jiu-jitsu helped him with this task.

"There were a million lessons I learned from jiu-jitsu," he added. One such lesson had to do with overcoming resistance in others as a leader. "When people are resistant," he told me, "don't go head-to-head against their resistance."

He told me that imposing one's will on a team based on rank never works because team members will stop complying as soon as that leader is no longer present. Jocko explained the solution to resistance, like in jiu-jitsu, is to "allow them to move into areas where they want to move to, and then you come in from other angles where they can support your plan."

BECOMING A CHAMPION
A TRAINING TITAN

In his podcast-based book *Tools of Titans*, Tim Ferriss says that Jocko "used to tap out twenty Navy SEALs per workout." He goes on to label Jocko "one of the scariest human beings imaginable."

I've always wanted to hear this story for myself. How did Jocko do it? Did he line up twenty guys and say, "You're up next!"?

Here's what he told me: By the time Jocko was a blue belt, he was very dedicated to jiu-jitsu and wanted to get better. This required continuous training, even on deployment where there were no other jiu-jitsu practitioners to be found. His solution was to teach others.

"Believe me," he said, "if someone wanted to learn jiu-jitsu, I would teach them everything I could. I would try and get them to train. But a lot of guys didn't feel like it or they didn't like it."

To better meet his training needs, Jocko started scheduling his platoon mates in fifteen-minute intervals. He told the first person to be there at 6:00, the next at 6:15, and so on. "I would just train for a couple of hours with guys for like ten or fifteen minutes at a pop," he said. He tried to teach them during these brief sessions, but he would also train with them. However, because he knew more jiu-jitsu than they did, Jocko always won.

"If I know how to play basketball and you don't, I'm going to beat you in basketball," he said. "If I know how to play soccer and you don't, I'm going to beat you in soccer. And if I know jiu-jitsu and you don't, I'm going to choke you."

When I talk with people, they come up with all kinds of reasons for why they can't start doing jiu-jitsu. I've heard everything from, "I'm going to wait until I lose weight" to "I'm too old."

After almost thirty years of practicing the sport, Jocko still trains as often as he can. If he's not on the road, he's on the mat seven days a week. Plus, he makes a case for jiu-jitsu whenever he can to anyone who will listen.

"Every time I go on someone's podcast and get interviewed, we end up talking about jiu-jitsu. *Train jiu-jitsu!* That's my message. Maybe I haven't said that loud enough." To emphasize his point, he repeated himself a little louder while staring into the computer camera: *"Train jiu-jitsu!"*

He said the number of people who *really* shouldn't train because of medical issues is very small, and his message for everyone who thinks they have an excuse is, "Whether you're overweight, too old, or too young, there's almost no excuse to not start training today. For 99 percent of the population, you should just start training jiu-jitsu immediately."

Jocko said jiu-jitsu helped him understand many things in life, including tactical decision-making on the battlefield and how to interact with people.

"Then, of course, I understood fighting itself," he added. "And when you overlay that with your own life, you realize you take away a lot from jiu-jitsu."

In our conversation, Jocko described some parallels among specific BJJ maneuvers, situations on the battlefield, and leadership. For instance, in a jiu-jitsu maneuver, if you want to get someone's arm, you don't attack it directly. Instead, you go for your opponent's neck. In trying to defend their neck, they will expose their arm, and at that point you can take their arm.

"You have to set them up," Jocko explained. "You have to flank them; you have to come at them from a different direction."

He told me the same principle applies to taking down a target on the battlefield. "You have to set up a base element to distract and engage the enemy so another, smaller element can come around from the flank and actually destroy them."

He uses the same strategy in personal interactions. "If I'm dealing with someone who's got a big ego and I attack that ego, they're just going to go into a hardcore defensive mode," he explained. "Whereas if I talk to them, open up, maybe massage their ego a little bit, then I can sneak in from the flank and influence them to move voluntarily."

BEHIND THE SCENES
WHY JIU-JITSU IS JUST WARMING UP

The sport has been attracting more and more practitioners for a while now, and Jocko thinks it will spread even more. "It's just getting warmed up," he said, sounding pleased. He added that people will turn to jiu-jitsu because they perceive combat sports like boxing and Muay Thai to be too risky in terms of concussions and brain trauma.

"I think people right now are a lot less apt to put their kid in a boxing ring or in a Muay Thai ring than they are to put them on the jiu-jitsu mat or on a wrestling mat. Especially for kids—you don't want to have people getting punched in the head when they're young. Their brain is not even developed yet. Jiu-jitsu is the answer."

Many people would agree with him that one of the big advantages of BJJ over boxing and MMA is its relative safety when it comes to blows to the head. It's why people quit boxing and instead dedicate themselves to other sports, like jiu-jitsu; they simply don't want to get punched in the face anymore.

Jocko explained, "With jiu-jitsu, you and I can go at each other as hard as possible, and neither one of us is going to get hurt. That's the amazing thing about it. And if you've ever sparred stand-up or MMA—you know it's much harder to do that. And you definitely can't do it every single day, and you can't do it for two hours at a time. So that's a huge advantage."

BEST ADVICE

Jocko said he would agree jiu-jitsu is addictive, at least for people with an addictive personality type, because there is always something new to learn. "When you do jiu-jitsu, the more you learn, the more you realize you don't know."

WORST ADVICE

Jocko didn't specifically share the worst advice he'd ever received, but we did have an interesting conversation about humility, a human quality that is diametrically opposed to what we call "a big ego." There's no question that anyone who trains jiu-jitsu will go through the same experience of having their expectations about their own strength smashed when they get tapped or choked out, and this is humbling.

Jocko shared that this is one place where he sees a difference between BJJ and traditional martial arts.

"In old school, traditional martial arts, they would say, 'Oh, we're going to teach you humility,' and then they would maybe talk about it or tell you to be humble. But in jiu-jitsu, you are going to *get* humbled. There's no escaping it."

Catching himself, he then said, "Actually, there *is* a way to escape it. The way you escape becoming humbled by jiu-jitsu is by quitting and never doing it. Even then, you know in your heart you're weak. So jiu-jitsu is one of the best teachers of humility in the world."

Since he mentioned quitting, I had to ask him, of course, whether he had ever thought of giving up. Jocko answered in the most concise possible way: "No."

FINAL THOUGHTS

DISCIPLINE, FREEDOM, AND THE BEST GIFT

In podcasts and interviews, Jocko frequently talks about the connection between mental and physical discipline and freedom in all aspects of life. His mantra, *Discipline Equals Freedom*, is the title of a bestselling book he wrote, and he applies the same philosophy to jiu-jitsu.

"If you want to have the freedom to escape, to set things up, to defend yourself in situations, to be able to walk around with confidence, you have to have the discipline with jiu-jitsu," he concluded. "I tell parents jiu-jitsu is absolutely one of the best gifts they can give to their kids."

CHAPTER 23

Rubens "Cobrinha" Charles Maciel

@cobrinhacharles
facebook.com/cobrinhacharles

Rubens Charles Maciel, a.k.a. "Cobrinha," is the best featherweight competitor in the history of jiu-jitsu. Born in 1979 in Londrina, Paraná, Brazil, he is the *only* black belt worldwide to have completed the "Super Grand Slam." This requires *winning all five major BJJ tournaments in one year*—ADCC, World Championship, Pan Championship, European Championship, and Brazilian Nationals—an extraordinary accomplishment that Cobrinha secured for himself in 2017.

Cobrinha, who is a member of Alliance Jiu-Jitsu, received his black belt in 2005 from Fernando "Tererê" Augusto. Since then, he has won thirteen World Jiu-Jitsu Championships—almost every world tournament in which he has competed. Renowned for his attacking style and his guard, at black belt, he is a five-time World Champion, five-time Pan-American Champion, four-time World NoGi Champion, and three-time ADCC Champion.

Before doing jiu-jitsu full time, Cobrinha worked as a baker. For a while, he actually had his own bakery. Old YouTube videos show that he still enjoys creating cakes and pies. His son, Kennedy Maciel, is a rising BJJ star. In 2019, Kennedy won the silver medal at ADCC in Anaheim, California.

I first met Cobrinha in person by chance at an annual Alliance Association meeting in São Paulo, Brazil. Cobrinha taught a seminar for all the students at the Alliance São Paulo Jiu-Jitsu Academy HQ for more than two hours.

At one point, I was lucky enough to go out and get some pizza and drinks with Alex Atala, Fábio Gurgel, Michael Langhi, and about fifteen others. Cobrinha showed up a few minutes later (obligatory photos and conversations after his seminar surely held him back) and sat at the large rectangular table with us. The restaurant was crowded, and though the staff did their best to accommodate us by pushing together several tables, it still seemed as if we took over the whole place.

As the pizzas came out one by one, we all grabbed multiple slices and chaos ensued—except for Cobrinha. I didn't know at the time, but he had ordered separately: steamed veggies and tea. I remember thinking, *So it's true, he really is a samurai.*

Our interview took place months later at Cobrinha's academy in Los Angeles, where he is also the head instructor. On the day of our get-together—scheduled for 8:00 a.m. on a Saturday—I left San Diego early to account for traffic. Generally speaking, for most of the interviews, both the athlete and I showed up on time, traded *how-are-yous*, changed into gis, and started a training session.

Meeting the legendary Cobrinha, however, was quite different.

I arrived at 8:00 a.m. sharp, winning a moral victory of sorts for punctuality, but as soon as I walked onto the mat, I immediately felt like I had failed. Cobrinha was already dressed and on the mat, in the corner with his headphones on, getting warmed up like he was preparing to compete.

Samurai.

His academy, Cobrinha Brazilian Jiu-Jitsu & Fitness, is located at 4929 Wilshire Blvd., #104, Los Angeles, CA 90010.

- Check out his documentary *Cobrinha's Recipe for Success* on YouTube.
- Go to *cobrinhaonline.com* to see his collection of his teachings on jiu-jitsu and movement training.
- Check out YouTube for a comprehensive library of his fights; type in "Cobrinha vs."

EARLY LIFE

FROM CAPOEIRA TO BJJ

Cobrinha remembers his introduction to jiu-jitsu as a humbling experience. It was the year 2000, and having practiced Capoeira for fourteen years, he thought he'd already found his niche when a taekwondo black belt friend told him he'd been smashed by a BJJ purple belt. Intrigued and confident in his own grappling skills, Cobrinha agreed to show up for a BJJ lesson.

He was crushed just like his friend, but he told himself he was simply having a bad day. *It will be better tomorrow if I go home and rest,* he thought. He came back to the gym to try again, only this time, it was actually much worse.

"The guy just *smashed* me," he recalled. "He didn't hurt me, but I couldn't do anything."

Impressed and hungry for more, Cobrinha asked his friend immediately afterward, "What is *that*?"

"That's jiu-jitsu," the friend responded.

"Okay, *that's* jiu-jitsu," Cobrinha echoed, nodding. "Then that's my sport from now on."

ON PRESSURE AND ANXIETY
SUCCESS COMES FROM STRUGGLE

From the outside, Cobrinha's many titles may seem like a given. People say, "Cobrinha? Of course, he wins! He's *supposed* to win." What they don't see is the struggle behind the success and the mindset the champion had to adopt to make it possible.

Cobrinha approaches challenges with a bring-it-on mentality and embraces adversity because he understands it will help him change and grow. When people complain to him they have a problem, he'll say, "Give your problem to me! I like it. Because every problem is an opportunity."

He told me he sees struggle not only as inevitable, but also as proof that something is important to us, that it matters enough for us to put work into it. "If you really need something, you will make things happen and this means you will struggle," he explained. "If you're struggling, it is because something is important to you."

As Cobrinha and I were talking about struggles, we briefly hit on a Ryan Holiday book that we have both read, *The Obstacle Is the Way*. The philosophy behind the book, Stoicism, is two thousand years old, but Holiday presents it in a way that we modern-day readers can understand.

Cobrinha smiled when talking about the book and Ryan Holiday. "He's telling my story. It's crazy."

BECOMING A CHAMPION

QUITTING, STARTING OVER, AND DEFYING NAYSAYERS

Cobrinha's jiu-jitsu career was anything but a smooth ride to the top. His journey included doubts, setbacks, and resistance. Feeling torn between the bakery he owned and training jiu-jitsu, when Cobrinha was a brown belt he quit the sport for a while to focus on his business. Before long, however, he realized he missed the mat. So, when legendary Professor Tererê invited Cobrinha to join his team, Cobrinha decided to sell the bakery and start training in São Paolo full time.

Money problems ensued. Cobrinha recalls falling behind on his bills. He was barely able to afford child support for his son,

Kennedy, and he was about to quit for good until he reached a turning point in 2005: Cobrinha received his black belt and won his first World Champion title at CBJJO. The win came with 5,000 Brazilian Reais in prize money, making him feel like the richest man in the world.

From then on, the champion won title after title. "I started from humble beginnings," Cobrinha acknowledged. "I had nothing. But then, I started winning."

There was, however, one area in which victory eluded him for the longest time: ADCC. Twice—in 2009 in Barcelona and in 2011 in London—Cobrinha lost in the final and took second place. After his second defeat, people suggested he stop trying.

"Look at your age," people said. "You're getting old."

I can only imagine how grueling all of this must have felt to him. ADCC happens only every two years, which meant Cobrinha had to wait two years to even have the opportunity to try again. Then he had to wait another two years for London, and again he lost in the final. He was thirty-one years old at the time, and at this point, I think, most people would just write off ADCC.

Cobrinha admitted the naysayers almost convinced him to quit. He was close to them, so he trusted their opinions. But ADCC was his dream. He slept on the problem for one night, and then the day after his defeat in London, he told himself, *I can't let other people direct my life. I have to be the director of my life.*

His resolve served him well. In 2013, Cobrinha traveled to Beijing and won the tournament. Then he repeated history in 2015 at ADCC in Brazil.

Two years later, in 2017, he became the only person to complete the Super Grand Slam. This means he won all gold medals in IBJJF Worlds, IBJJF Europeans, IBJJF Brazilian Nationals, IBJJF Pan-Ams, and the 2017 ADCC *once more*. What's even more impressive, not a single point was scored on him in that three-time ADCC run.

Cobrinha accomplished all this when he was thirty-seven years old.

If there is a secret to why Cobrinha was able to keep improving his game, it might be this: he learned to leave his ego aside. At some point, he realized he was getting physically hurt on the mat as well as mentally stuck in the same positions. Once he understood that he needed to open up his game more, things changed for him.

"The reason we don't get better," he explained, "is because of our egos. Because we don't want to learn and try something new."

Hearing this from Cobrinha made me think of a quote from Ryan Holiday. In Holiday's *Ego Is the Enemy*, published in 2016, he says, "The world can show you the truth, but no one can force you to accept it."

If we want to make room for learning, we must be willing to see reality for what it is and then get out of our own way.

BEHIND THE SCENES

JIU-JITSU AS A LIFESTYLE

Like many athletes, Cobrinha started practicing martial arts to learn self-defense, but he has since learned to appreciate jiu-jitsu as something much bigger. For him, like for many others, it is a lifestyle.

"I went to Capoeira for self-defense, and then I went to jiu-jitsu for self-defense," he said. "Later, I discovered that it's more. It's a lifestyle. Whatever we do on the mat is applicable to life."

One of the concepts Cobrinha likes to apply in jiu-jitsu and all other areas of life is to *drill*. In other words, repeat the same movements or series of movements over and over. As a baker's apprentice, Cobrinha used to stay in the kitchen after hours to practice decorating cakes with leftover cream and sponge cake. "It's unbelievable how much you have to drill in pastry!" he exclaimed. "Because customers are very particular about the design of their cake."

He says he learned the value of drilling even before becoming a baker, and actually credits learning it first from practicing sports other than jiu-jitsu. As a soccer player in Brazil, he learned that certain moves became a habit when he practiced them over and over. Doing Capoeira taught him that drilling breeds confidence. He also learned to drill both sides of his body for attacks and defense, and not just his strong side, as is often recommended in BJJ.

He told me he knows drilling can be an unpopular strategy, and some people see it as a waste of time. However, Cobrinha even uses it to improve his English-speaking skills. If he can't pronounce a word properly because he's a non-native speaker—an example he gave me is the word *peripheral*—he'll practice saying it at home over and over to ensure his students will understand him when he uses the word in class.

Cobrinha says, "I drilled in soccer, in Capoeira, and in a bakery. And then I went to jiu-jitsu and drilled, drilled, drilled. Then I realized, *everything* you want to do in life—if you want to get better—you must drill."

Another concept he takes from jiu-jitsu into life is problem-solving. Getting stuck in bad positions on the mat taught Cobrinha to think things through and find a workable solution before reacting. "If I have a problem on the mat while training, I stop. I don't move like crazy. If I do, I'm going to get caught or hurt. In life, it's the same thing. Wait a second! Don't move, don't react! First, let's find what caused this problem."

Or, in the words of Albert Einstein, "You can never solve a problem on the level on which it was created."

The parallels one might find between the practice of jiu-jitsu and the task of life are obviously limitless. In our conversation, Cobrinha added "competitiveness" to the list. When I asked him whether he would still compete, he said he doesn't like the word "retire" because it reminds him of the word "tired"—that, and the fact he would never actually say "I'm done."

Still, his focus is currently on his family and his business. He wants to expand his academy and then open another one.

"I'm very competitive," he said as he lifted his chin with pride. "I will take the competitiveness I have in jiu-jitsu and put it into the business."

What's his approach for taking the business to the next level?

"I'll do what I did my whole life competing in jiu-jitsu. It's the same system: consistency, drill, study."

His work ethic and dedication are incredibly admirable. Growing up, Cobrinha didn't have a mentor. Since then, one man in particular has played an important role in his life: Fábio Gurgel. Fábio guided him, and as a result, Cobrinha learned that mentors can always take us one step further. Thanks to their experience, they can keep us from going in the wrong direction and show us how to do things right. "They can take your life to the next level because they have already lived that part of their lives," Cobrinha explained. "And then, if you listen to them, that's it. You're going to take your game to the next level."

Cobrinha told me it took him a while to realize it's okay to ask for help. "If you need help, ask for it," he said. "Don't keep trying to figure out things on your own."

It's important to note that asking for help is not a sign of weakness. Rather, it is a sign of strength. Shedding the stigma of asking for help should be a focus for many of us, especially at this point in human history. Studies show that others actually *want* to help because providing someone with assistance can give people a sense of purpose. So the person receiving help wins by learning, and the one giving help feels better because they see value in themselves through others.

While some people have dismissed private lessons or business coaching as too expensive or without any value, many people see it as an investment. You may not see the results immediately, but like any investment, it takes time to grow, and the compound effect of time gives you something much larger than you would've had without starting early.

BEST ADVICE

When I asked Cobrinha about the best advice he ever received, the champion said, "Study! Be a student of life. That's it. That's what I have been doing."

WORST ADVICE

Toward the end of our interview, I asked Cobrinha about the worst advice he ever received. He immediately said, "It's when you tell someone about your dream and what you want to accomplish, and they say, 'It's impossible. It's not going to happen.'"

Hearing somebody say you should give up on your dream hurts, but what I've learned is that people often bring others down because they simply don't believe in themselves. Therefore, they are afraid of being left behind by those they love and care for. We must try to make sure someone else's insecure projection doesn't result in holding us back from our own goals. It can be hard, but Cobrinha kills that negativity with kindness.

Cobrinha's answer to naysayers is, "I come from humble beginnings. If I could do it, anyone can."

FINAL THOUGHTS
ADVICE FROM A LIVING LEGEND

1. Stick with the Winners

"Eagles don't fly with pigeons," he told me. "I never see champions surround themselves with losers. If you want to be a champion, surround yourself with champions." More specifically, he added, "If you want to be a positive person, walk with positive people. If you want to be good in business, walk with successful businessmen."

2. Create Opportunities for Yourself

"If an opportunity presents itself, take advantage of it," Cobrinha advised. "If it doesn't, *present yourself to the opportunity.*" He wants us to create opportunities for ourselves rather than waiting for them to appear, because sometimes they don't. This could mean helping in a business if we want to learn more about it or spending extra time in class at an academy if we want to improve our jiu-jitsu.

When Cobrinha was a baker's apprentice, he volunteered his time to the boss.

"You'll have to wash the dishes and clean the floors," the guy told him. "Are you willing to do that?"

Cobrinha was. He wanted to learn baking, even if the price was performing free grunt work. But he was willing to pay that price with his time.

3. Find a Mentor

Finally, we talked about the best piece of advice he wants to give others.

"Find a good mentor. That first," he said, nodding. "Why? Because sometimes you're lost. And if you don't have a mentor, you're going to be lost for the rest of your life. But if you have a good mentor, that person will guide you."

A REFLECTION

What Jiu-Jitsu Means to Me

When I first discovered jiu-jitsu, I was a typical male in my early thirties. I wanted to work out, but I hated running. The cardio machines at the gym made me want to exit stage left as soon as I saw them in my periphery. When I was introduced to a boxing class, I immediately realized it was a quick way to get in a good workout and have some fun, without having to focus on a treadmill screen. Watching the mile counter creep up each hundredth of a mile is mind-numbing for me, and truthfully, I would rather watch paint dry.

As it turned out, boxing had a way of humbling me. Yes, it was easy to throw punches to the top-forty music hit list and do some push-ups or squats between hitting the stationary heavy bag that, of course, didn't hit back. But one day, I had the courage to get into the ring and do some "light" sparring. I was rewarded for my courage with many blows to the head, early and often, and saw stars twirling before my eyes like I was in an old Looney Tunes cartoon. Getting hit in the face was a whole new concept, and I didn't like it.

Even if I got the best of my opponent for that round or exchange, I remember how much my head hurt on the days when I sparred—and in some cases, it hurt for the next *several* days after sparring. The bruises on my face were clear signs of a fight, and the large, physical bumps on the back and side of my head felt tender to the touch long after I'd gone home for the day. I didn't have a clear mind, but rather, a foggy one. It was like being in a mini war whenever I did the sparring class, and now I wonder how many times I might have had a concussion.

Ironically, for all the pain I endured from the punches to the face, nothing ever hurt as badly as the body shot near my liver, delivered by my coach. Coach Calvin Jones was six feet three and rangy, with a background in boxing that included well over seventy fights for the US Navy Boxing Team. In one of our training sessions, I ducked to avoid one of his head punches and thought I was in the clear. But instead of me being elusive, I now realize that Calvin had thrown a left hook right after I ducked, and I caught it under my ribs, near my liver. After what felt like a slow-motion, painful fall to one knee, I finally had the energy to spit out my mouthpiece as I hit the deck. My body shut down and I couldn't breathe, let alone move. I could barely muster up some painful, steady groaning, as saliva simultaneously dripped off my bottom lip.

Calvin took a step back and said, "Pick up your mouthpiece. The round isn't over yet!" He made me pick myself up off the canvas and finish the round. To this day, that is the only time

I have ever been knocked down by a punch, and I can still feel it if I think about it hard enough. I suppose I should be grateful to Coach Calvin. He inspired me to try jiu-jitsu because I didn't like getting punched!

Fortunately, the gym offered multiple fighting arts aside from boxing: Muay Thai, jiu-jitsu, and MMA. One of the other boxing coaches, who was also a jiu-jitsu blue belt at the time, said something to me that clicked, "You can't train boxing forever, but in jiu-jitsu, you can train until you're old because in jiu-jitsu you don't get hit in the head." That planted the seed in my brain. Here was an opportunity to try something new that allowed me to avoid the treadmill, and I wouldn't have to get punched in the head to prove how tough I was. Jiu-jitsu also seemed to engage my brain without shaking it against my skull like a marble in a large box. Sign me up!

Of course, nothing is as easy as it seems, and jiu-jitsu was no different. In fact, it may just be the most complex, ever-evolving martial art out there. Because the other competitor is usually in such close proximity so often throughout the match, any inch given is an opportunity for them to capitalize and send you on a very fast downhill spiral. Unlike typical striking sports, where you can disengage and dance around, there is no downtime in jiu-jitsu. You can't disengage and "walk backward." You literally have to learn to relax, breathe, and find a way out when you are in a bad position. Alternatively, if you are in a good position, your opponent will naturally try to escape, which will require you to try to maintain control in turn.

Jiu-jitsu is as much a mind game as it is a physical one. It is problem-solving at the highest level, which is why I say that practicing jiu-jitsu has allowed me to compete again. I don't mean "compete" as in compete at a tournament, but rather to compete with my brain. It tests me in ways I've never been tested before.

I would be remiss if I didn't mention a few other things the sport has done for me and explain why I think every single person reading this book needs to schedule a one-week trial at their local jiu-jitsu academy now. This isn't an advertisement to get more students for academies around the world, but it is a calling for all of us to take a look in the accountability mirror and ask ourselves in daily life, "What am I really afraid of?"

FEAR OF FAILURE

I know walking into a gym where you are the new face with zero knowledge of the rules is challenging, and frankly, even paralyzing for some. Also, many of us doubt we will withstand five minutes during warm-ups in jiu-jitsu. But if you can manage that first, most difficult step of *trying*, that is success in itself.

When it comes to jiu-jitsu, do some beginners perform better than others right off the bat? Absolutely. Factors like talent and athleticism will always exist. However, like anyone, even these practitioners will encounter failure, doubt, and anxiety along their path.

Failure will happen. In anything we do, failure is always imminent, but never permanent. In fact, we're supposed to suck at the beginning of anything. Babies try to take their first steps, yet they fall for days, weeks, and sometimes months. I suppose we could all look at these tiny humans as the greatest example of why failure is not only okay but necessary. Babies generally don't understand that failure is looked down upon by society. They only know they want to walk like their parents, and they innately understand they will suffer bumps, bruises, and falls in order to eventually succeed at walking.

Although the fear of failure has been ingrained in our collective psyche, I've never met—or even heard of—a single person who was always successful in a linear fashion. Failure is not only imminent, but it cannot be avoided. Improvement, of course, is up to us, but taking that first step when it comes to anything you want to try is absolutely necessary.

Otherwise, there would be a lot of crawling adults.

PREPARATION AND REPETITION

Among the many lessons I learned from practicing jiu-jitsu is that in business and in life, you must prepare. You must build repetition into your life for what I call the "live" moments. Repetition brings the most critical component to success: *being able to react appropriately without thinking.* If you need to stop and think once you're in a situation, you're already behind. Your reaction needs to be built into muscle memory. This applies to all things in life. Look at doctors, pilots, and any athlete. They prepare, practice, and repeat over and over for these live moments.

You are never too good for the fundamentals. In fact, you are not good at all unless you're good at the fundamentals. As Jocko and the Navy SEALs say, "Slow is smooth and smooth is fast."

Preparation is key, and drilling the same moves is paramount to retention and sharpness. The combination of preparation and drilling is a necessity if we are to succeed. Just showing up, as I've done throughout parts of my life, simply won't cut it. Talent, charm, personality, and athleticism are great attributes to possess, but those qualities alone will *not* suffice for greatness. It's the people who prepare relentlessly who excel at the highest levels.

COMMUNITY

In high school, I spent most of my time playing sports. Then, when college and adult responsibilities began to take over, it was easy to forget the camaraderie of the locker room. Over the years, I've watched many retired professional athletes inducted into the Hall of Fame give speeches, and they almost always say what they miss most is "playing with the guys." They never say, "I miss winning games," or, "I miss being rich and getting huge paychecks." What they miss is that true sense of belonging.

Practicing BJJ has allowed me to be part of a team again.

Famed and popular psychologist Abraham Maslow created Maslow's hierarchy of needs in 1943. His work made it clear that once our basic needs for food, shelter, and safety are met, we immediately look for love and belonging. Being alone can be refreshing and a required reset for many, but ultimately, humans want to be a part of something. Jiu-jitsu satisfies this need on all levels. It has given me—as it gives many others—the chance to experience that feeling of belonging. For those who have never been a part of any sports teams, this new experience is waiting for you.

THE GIFT OF NOW

Quite possibly the biggest and most surprising gift I received from practicing jiu-jitsu is the gift of now, the present moment. In today's world, we are continually bombarded by people, opinions, things, and advertisements vying for our attention. Our email inboxes fill up while we sleep at night. Our phones push notifications to us. (My advice is turn these off because they're a huge distraction.) Social media feeds draw us in, and ads that are specially targeted to appeal to us beg for our attention. The list doesn't end there. Kids need to be dressed, fed, and put to bed. Spouses and partners need and deserve attention. Bosses demand focus at work. It goes without saying that we can become slaves to our to-do lists.

Jiu-jitsu solves this problem—at least temporarily. Jiu-jitsu is a pure form of self-love. When I'm training, nothing else matters, or even exists. There are no outside issues or problems in those moments when my attention is locked into jiu-jitsu. I definitely can't bring my phone on the mat, so the temptation to grab my device and check a likely meaningless notification is simply removed.

Being on a jiu-jitsu mat is much different from any other workout I know. When we're waiting on the twenty-minute timer to tick seconds away on that treadmill, the mind can wander, but when someone is trying to choke us or break our arm, it's hard for the mind to focus on anything other than getting out of that situation.

There are dozens of apps out there that help us meditate, help us find that sense of now, help us be present in our breathing, and help alleviate anxiety about the future or sadness or anger about our past. But a jiu-jitsu session rivals any meditation I've ever personally tried, and it gives me a huge, refreshed reset feeling. Even on my worst days, in training, I'm filled with gratitude and mentally ready for what is still in front of me the rest of my day. Why? Jiu-jitsu *requires* us to be present.

Jiu-jitsu, for me, is a type of forced meditation. I need to be present. I must be present. Most importantly, I *want* to be present. Because of these critical components, the sport does for me what no treadmill, phone app, or weightlifting session will ever do: it gets me out of my own head and brings me to the now. It is, for sure, the most wonderful gift we can and should give to ourselves.

OSS!

—Bobby Armijo

Thank You, Thank You

First and foremost, I would like to thank my jiu-jitsu professor, and one of my best friends, João "Johnny" Faria. He has been there for me since the beginning of time and encouraged me on so many occasions to write the book and "just do it!"

Johnny was this book's biggest cheerleader and seemed to love every idea I ever had that related to the writing. Each time I would schedule a new interview or write another chapter, he appeared to be more excited for me than I was. Johnny also opened the door for many of these interviews, as he is one of the most well-liked people in the sport. There is one key reason for that: Johnny gives without expecting anything back. Thank you, Professor Johnny! *Tamo junto!*

I would also like to thank Christina Schweighofer and everyone who helped and advised me during the writing and editing process.

Of course, I would be remiss if I left out my friends and family. It's so nice to be encouraged to finish a seemingly long, daunting task like writing a book. A task I thought would be quickly done and damn near write itself. And as Ryan Holiday once told me at a conference, "You can't be the noun without being the verb." To be a writer, you need to write. And the support and positive feedback from all of you has really been the fuel to get me to hunker down and be the verb! (Three and a half years might be a stretch to be classified as *hunkering down!*)

Thank you to Alliance San Diego students, teammates, and professors. We beat each other up on the mats, but I can say without a doubt we have a fun, caring environment that builds each other up for each of us to see our dreams through.

Finally, I'd like to give a big thank you to each and every person profiled in *Jiu-Jitsu Bravehearts* for making room in their busy schedules for an interview. Every one of them made sure all my questions were answered, and many gave me much more of their time than I expected because they also believed in this project. For that, I am grateful.

Call to Action

To learn about the two amazing charities receiving 100% of the proceeds of the sales of this book, take a look at the links and the description of their good deeds below.

ROAD DOGS
www.roadogs.org

"We collect, care for, and protect the lemons of the dog world." In having two Frenchies of my own, I know how important an organization is like roadogs.org to help those bullies who have poor genetics and are cast to the side. This beautiful 501(c)(3) takes in all pups or adult bullies, no questions asked, and provides them an opportunity to be rehomed, regardless of medical condition.

AMERICA'S MIGHTY WARRIORS
americasmightywarriors.org

"America's Mighty Warriors mission is to honor the sacrifices of our troops, the fallen, and their families by providing programs that improve quality of life, resiliency, and recovery." Because this book was inspired and hatched at Jocko's Echelon Front "MUSTER," I thought it was a natural fit to benefit the nonprofit of a former and fallen soldier of Jocko', Marc Lee. Marc's mom, Debbie Lee, kept his legacy alive by creating this nonprofit to help the families of our military who have lost a loved one while serving our country.

For book resources and photos, visit *jiujitsubravehearts.com*.

Drop me a line. I'm curious how this book may have influenced your life or your jiu-jitsu journey: *bobby@jiutjitsubravehearts.com*.

Connect with me on Instagram: *@bbbyjjitsu*.

www.ingramcontent.com/pod-product-compliance
Lightning Source LLC
Chambersburg PA
CBHW070126080526
44586CB00015B/1579